A 2002 HOMETOWN COLLECTION

America's Best Recipes

Oxmoor House®

©2002 by Oxmoor House, Inc.
Book Division of Southern Progress Corporation
P.O. Box 2463, Birmingham, Alabama 35201

ISBN: 0-8487-2506-9
ISSN: 0898-9982

Printed in the United States of America
First Printing 2002

Editor-in-Chief: Nancy Fitzpatrick Wyatt
Executive Editor: Susan Carlisle Payne
Art Director: Cynthia R. Cooper
Copy Chief: Catherine Ritter Scholl

America's Best Recipes: A 2002 Hometown Collection

Editors: Allison Long Lowery, Leah Marlett, Kelly Hooper Troiano
Copy Editor: Donna Baldone
Editorial Assistant: Diane Rose
Director, Test Kitchens: Elizabeth Tyler Luckett
Assistant Director, Test Kitchens: Julie Christopher
Recipe Editor: Gayle Hays Sadler
Test Kitchens Staff: Jennifer A. Cofield; Gretchen Feldtman, R.D.;
   David C. Gallent; Ana Price Kelly; Kathleen Royal Phillips; Jan A. Smith
Senior Photographer: Jim Bathie
Photographer: Brit Huckabay
Senior Photo Stylist: Kay E. Clarke
Photo Stylist: Ashley Wyatt
Director, Production and Distribution: Phillip Lee
Books Production Manager: Larry Hunter
Production Assistant: Faye Porter Bonner
Publishing Systems Administrator: Rick Tucker

CONTRIBUTORS
Designer: Rita Yerby
Indexer: Mary Ann Laurens
Test Kitchens Intern: Tamra Brown
Project Consultant: Jean Wickstrom Liles
Editorial Consultant: Janice Krahn Hanby
Editorial Intern: McCharen Pratt

To order additional copies, call 1-800-633-4910.

For more books to enrich your life, visit **oxmoorhouse.com**

Cover: Berry Tart with Mascarpone Cream *(page 238)*

Contents

Introduction   4

Make-Ahead Recipes   5

Quick and Easy Recipes   35

Appetizers and Beverages   57

Breads   75

Cakes   95

Cookies and Candies   121

Desserts   137

Eggs and Cheese   153

Fish and Shellfish   169

Meats   191

Pasta, Rice, and Grains   211

Pies and Pastries   227

Poultry   243

Salads   263

Sauces and Condiments   281

Soups and Stews   291

Vegetables   307

Acknowledgments   320

Index   326

Introduction

Let us take you on a cook's tour across the country to discover favorite regional cuisine and treasured family recipes from fund-raising cookbooks written by America's best cooks. From these cookbooks, we've selected the best recipes, tested and tasted by our Test Kitchens, using their exacting standards, to bring you *America's Best Recipes–A 2002 Hometown Collection.* Here, you'll find favorite dishes from childhood as well as new recipes destined to become favorites among your family and friends. Any minor changes from the original recipes reflect new ingredient sizes, cooking techniques, or updated products.

This edition of *America's Best Recipes* will appeal to cooks of every skill level who enjoy making creative recipes from around the country. In this collection, you'll find:

- A special chapter that highlights do-ahead recipes, which includes casseroles, marinades, dressings, and desserts. The Make-Ahead Recipes chapter promises that less is more—that family meals will be on the table in less time and with more ease. You'll also find handy tips on freezing and storing—another timesaving bonus.
- Tantalizing ideas from beverages to desserts that can be cooked and prepared in 45 minutes or less from our Quick and Easy chapter. Once you try these, you'll use them again and again.
- A vast range of traditional and updated recipes guaranteed to entice and delight innovative cooks. From Chocolate Turtle Tart to Glazed Cornish Hens with Curried Rice, there's a recipe for every occasion and taste.
- Exciting twists on time-honored standbys that will streamline everyday fare.

We're honored to bring these wonderful recipes into your home and to introduce you to the charitable organizations across America that make this book possible. If a particular cookbook interests you and you'd like to buy a copy, you'll find the addresses beginning on page 320. When you buy these books, you're not only receiving outstanding recipes, you're lending a helping hand to the charitable organizations across the country. In turn, the communities of the sponsoring charitable organizations benefit from the proceeds of the sale of these cookbooks. What a great way to show your generosity and give back to America.

The Editors

Make-Ahead Recipes

Cherry Thing, page 29

Make-Ahead Recipes

This recipe collection provides insightful alternatives to the lure of ordering pizza, picking up fast food on the way home, and frozen dinners. Making meals ahead requires knowing which foods keep well, how to store and serve them, and the amount of time they will keep. You'll find all this information and more on the facing page. Make-ahead doesn't always mean freezing. You'll find recipes that simply require marinating and chilling. Take pride in knowing that the meals you put on the table are made from scratch and have your stamp of approval. Our goal is to provide you with the tools and recipes to make your life easier and the extra time to enjoy with loved ones. Make-ahead meals are the ultimate solution because ingredients or even whole dishes can be removed from the refrigerator or freezer and made into a meal—fast!

There are three key steps to successfully preparing make-ahead dishes.

1. Be organized. Decide on a game plan for meals a week at a time and plan accordingly, keeping in mind sale items and seasons. Make an effort to stick to your list, but be flexible for changes in your schedule and unexpected guests. It always helps to have a backup plan.

2. Find the time. This could be a few hours on the weekend or an hour before you go to bed. Break down cooking procedures into small tasks. For example, if you're making a soup, wash and chop the vegetables one day, and cook the soup the next.

3. Use helpful kitchen equipment to speed up your preparation time. This includes mini-choppers, handheld blenders, food processors, salad spinners, and the microwave. One of the best tools you can own is a sharp knife to ensure quick chopping and slicing.

To Freeze	OR	Not to Freeze
Crumb toppings		Cooked egg whites
Baked cake layers		Aspics and gelatins
Breads		Salad ingredients
Cookies		Cream pies
Shredded cheese		Potatoes and rice
Soups and stews		Canned foods

HELPFUL MAKE-AHEAD TIPS

- To store foods, use containers with tight-fitting lids, heavy-duty zip-top plastic bags, and aluminum foil.

- Look for reusable containers that go from freezer to microwave to dishwasher.

- Using a permanent marker, properly label everything that you store in the refrigerator or freezer so you can easily locate what you need. Include a description of the food, date, and the number of servings on the label.

- Convenience products such as chopped cooked chicken, precooked bacon, bagged salads and vegetables, canned fruits, and shredded cheeses make putting a meal together a breeze.

- Check the refrigerator and freezer weekly for food items that need to be discarded.

FREEZING 101

- Foods to be frozen should first be refrigerated to chill before freezing. The lower the temperature of the food, the faster it will freeze, and the fresher it will taste when reheated and served.

- Choose the proper size of storage container for the amount of food you're freezing, and make sure it's sealed tightly to prevent excess air from entering the container. The least amount of air in the container, the better, because that reduces the chance of freezer burn.

- When freezing liquids such as soup, don't fill container all the way to the top because liquid expands and can cause the container to crack or the top to loosen.

- Place individual foods such as cookies and hamburger patties between squares of wax paper to easily remove just the amount you need.

- Slightly undercook dishes that contain pasta so they won't dry out when reheated.

- Never let frozen foods thaw on the counter or by running under hot water; this could increase the chances of harmful bacteria. Remember to store frozen foods in the refrigerator the night before, or thaw partially in the microwave, and cook as directed.

- Do not refreeze cooked dishes that have been frozen and reheated because the flavor, nutrients, and taste will be affected.

Antipasto Kabobs

These diminutive kabobs feature bite-size morsels of cheese-filled tortellini, olives, salami, cheese, tomato, and artichoke marinated in a zesty Italian dressing for full-size flavor.

1 (9-ounce) package
   refrigerated cheese-filled
   tortellini
24 thin slices salami
1 pound provolone cheese, cut
   into 24 (1-inch) cubes
1 pint grape or cherry
   tomatoes

1 (14-ounce) can artichoke
   heart quarters, drained
1 cup pimiento-stuffed olives
1 (16-ounce) bottle Italian
   dressing

Cook tortellini according to package directions; rinse with cold water, and drain well.

Thread tortellini, salami, and next 4 ingredients evenly onto 24 (6-inch) wooden skewers. Place skewers into a 13- x 9-inch dish. Brush kabobs with dressing, turning to coat. Cover and chill 8 hours; drain well. Yield: 2 dozen.

Creating a Stir
The Fayette County Medical Auxiliary
Lexington, Kentucky

Spanakopita Rolls

4 (10-ounce) packages frozen
   chopped spinach, thawed
   and drained
3 bunches green onions,
   chopped (about 3¼ cups)
¼ cup olive oil
½ cup chopped fresh parsley
1 tablespoon chopped fresh
   dill
½ teaspoon salt
¼ teaspoon pepper
4 cups (16 ounces) crumbled
   feta cheese

1 (12-ounce) container cottage
   cheese
½ cup ricotta cheese
1 tablespoon grated Romano
   cheese
6 large eggs, lightly beaten
2 tablespoons butter, melted
1½ (16-ounce) packages frozen
   phyllo pastry, thawed in
   refrigerator
2 cups butter, melted

Press spinach between layers of paper towels to remove excess moisture; set aside.

Sauté green onions in hot oil in a large skillet over medium-high heat 5 minutes or until tender. Combine spinach, green onions, parsley, and next 3 ingredients in a large bowl; stir well, and set aside.

Combine feta cheese and next 3 ingredients in a bowl. Add cheese mixture to spinach mixture, stirring well. Stir in eggs and 2 tablespoons melted butter.

Working with 1 phyllo sheet at a time, place phyllo sheet on a large work surface (keeping remaining phyllo covered); lightly brush with melted butter. Brush 2 more phyllo sheets with butter, stacking the 2 sheets on top of the first. Place a sheet of plastic wrap over phyllo stack, pressing gently to seal sheets together; discard plastic wrap.

Spoon ¾ cup spinach mixture along 1 long edge of phyllo, leaving a 2-inch border. Fold over the short edges of phyllo to cover 2 inches of spinach mixture on each end.

Starting at long edge with 2-inch border, roll up phyllo sheet, jelly-roll fashion. Place seam side down in a 15- x 10-inch jellyroll pan coated with cooking spray. Lightly brush roll with butter. Repeat procedure with remaining phyllo sheets, spinach filling, and melted butter.

Bake at 350° for 35 minutes or until golden. Cut into 2-inch-thick slices. Yield: 12 appetizer servings.

Note: To freeze, wrap unbaked rolls in wax paper. Wrap in aluminum foil, and freeze. When ready to bake, let rolls stand at room temperature 2 hours. Bake according to directions.

Café Weller . . . Tastes to Remember
Apple Corps of the Weller Health Education Center
Easton, Pennsylvania

Palmetto Cheese

You won't want to miss this pimiento cheese with personality, thanks to plenty of pimiento-stuffed olives and ground red pepper. Bragging rights to this lively version of the Southern staple belong to the palmetto (fan-leaved palms) state of South Carolina.

2 (7-ounce) jars diced
  pimiento, drained
1 cup finely chopped
  pimiento-stuffed olives
¼ cup mayonnaise
1 tablespoon chopped fresh
  parsley

½ teaspoon freshly ground
  black pepper
⅛ teaspoon ground red pepper
5 cups (1¼ pounds) shredded
  sharp Cheddar cheese
¼ cup grated Parmesan cheese

Stir together first 6 ingredients in a large bowl. Combine cheeses, and add to pimiento mixture, stirring well. Cover and chill at least 8 hours. Serve with crackers. Yield: 5½ cups.   Lisa Brown Price

Angels in the Kitchen Cookbook
Community Presbyterian Church
Celebration, Florida

Two-Cheese Spread with Spinach

Mediterranean style shines throughout this marriage of goat and feta cheeses plus spinach, mint, and lemon rind. The spread can conveniently be made up to 2 days ahead.

1 (10-ounce) package frozen
  chopped spinach, thawed
1 garlic clove
8 ounces goat cheese, softened
½ cup crumbled feta cheese,
  softened

2 teaspoons chopped fresh
  mint
1 teaspoon grated lemon rind
¼ teaspoon salt
⅛ teaspoon pepper

Drain spinach in a colander, pressing with paper towels to remove excess moisture.

With food processor running, drop garlic through food chute; process until finely chopped, stopping to scrape down sides. Add spinach, goat cheese, and remaining ingredients; process 30 seconds, stopping to scrape down sides. Process 30 more seconds or until smooth. Transfer mixture to a bowl. Cover and chill at least 8 hours. Let stand 1 hour before serving. Serve with crackers or toasted pita bread wedges. Yield: 1⅔ cups.   Nan D'Ercoli

Taste Buds–A Collection of Treasured Recipes
Alliance of the Illinois State Dental Society
Springfield, Illinois

Cheese Balls with Sun-Dried Tomatoes

Chilling this dried tomato and cheese blend makes it spreadable, but if you're looking for a tempting party dip, simply serve it after blending.

3 (8-ounce) packages cream
   cheese, softened
1 (7-ounce) jar dried tomatoes
   in oil, drained
2 teaspoons dried basil

1 garlic clove, halved
¾ cup coarsely chopped sliced
   natural almonds or pine
   nuts, toasted

Process first 4 ingredients in food processor 2 minutes or until smooth, stopping to scrape down sides. Cover and chill 2 hours.

Divide mixture into 6 portions; shape each portion into a ball. Place almonds in a bowl; roll each ball in almonds, pressing gently with fingers. Wrap each ball in plastic wrap; chill up to 5 days. Serve with crackers. Yield: 12 appetizer servings.   James Taylor

Diamond Delights
Diamond Hill Elementary School
Abbeville, South Carolina

Marinated Shrimp and Artichoke Hearts

Pair this hearty appetizer with a loaf of crusty French bread to create a satisfying main dish. To save time and effort, buy steamed and peeled shrimp at your fish market instead of preparing them yourself.

6 cups water
2 pounds unpeeled, medium-size fresh shrimp
½ cup olive oil
⅓ cup balsamic vinegar
2 tablespoons sugar
1 teaspoon salt
½ teaspoon dry mustard
1 garlic clove, minced
1 bay leaf
2 (14-ounce) cans artichoke heart quarters, drained
1 onion, thinly sliced
⅔ cup pitted ripe olives
Garnish: lemon slices

Bring water to a boil; add shrimp, and cook 3 to 5 minutes or just until shrimp turn pink. Drain and rinse with cold water; chill. Peel shrimp, and devein, if desired.

Whisk together olive oil and next 5 ingredients in a large bowl; stir in bay leaf. Add shrimp, artichoke, onion, and olives; toss well. Cover and chill at least 8 hours. Discard bay leaf. Garnish, if desired. Serve with a slotted spoon. Yield: 6 to 8 appetizer servings.

Bay Tables
The Junior League of Mobile, Alabama

Chicken Pâté

2 (5-ounce) skinned and boned chicken breast halves, cut into ½-inch pieces
¼ teaspoon salt
¼ teaspoon pepper
3 tablespoons butter
1 tablespoon chopped garlic
¾ cup grated Asiago cheese
½ cup finely chopped onion
⅓ cup lightly salted roasted cashews
⅓ cup mayonnaise
½ teaspoon hot sauce
¼ cup chopped fresh basil

Line a 2-cup bowl with plastic wrap; set aside.

Sprinkle chicken with salt and pepper. Melt butter in a large non-stick skillet over medium-high heat. Add chicken and garlic; cook 5 minutes or until done, stirring often. Cool slightly.

Process chicken mixture, cheese, and next 4 ingredients in a food processor until smooth. Add basil, and process until smooth. Press mixture into prepared bowl. Cover and chill at least 2 hours or up to 2 days. Invert pâté onto a serving platter; remove plastic wrap. Serve with crackers. Yield: 2¼ cups.

More Enchanted Eating from the West Shore
Friends of the Symphony
Muskegon, Michigan

Seafood Wonder

Having a crowd over for supper? Try this awe-inspiring dish—it abounds with generous amounts of linguine, shrimp, and snow peas.

6 cups water
1½ tablespoons salt
1½ to 2 pounds unpeeled,
   medium-size fresh shrimp
16 ounces uncooked linguine
2 cups fresh snow pea pods
   (about 6 ounces), trimmed
6 green onions, chopped
4 medium tomatoes, peeled,
   seeded, and chopped (about
   1¼ pounds)

½ cup olive oil
⅓ cup white wine vinegar
¼ cup chopped fresh basil
¼ cup chopped fresh parsley
1 teaspoon garlic salt
¾ teaspoon coarsely ground
   pepper

Bring water and 1½ tablespoons salt to a boil; add shrimp, and cook 3 to 5 minutes or just until shrimp turn pink. Drain and rinse with cold water. Chill. Peel shrimp, and devein, if desired; set aside.

Cook linguine according to package directions, including salt; rinse with cold water and drain. Set aside.

Cook snow peas in a small amount of boiling water 2 to 3 minutes or until crisp-tender. Plunge into ice water to stop cooking process; drain.

Combine shrimp, linguine, snow peas, green onions, and remaining ingredients in a large bowl; toss well. Cover and chill at least 8 hours. Yield: 8 to 10 servings.   Pat Lake

Down Home Dining in Mississippi
Mississippi Homemaker Volunteers, Inc.
Water Valley, Mississippi

Green Turkey Enchiladas

6 fresh Anaheim chile
  peppers
2 pounds fresh tomatillos,
  husked
1 (14-ounce) can chicken broth
6 fresh serrano chile peppers,
  seeded
1 small onion, quartered
2 garlic cloves
½ cup firmly packed fresh
  cilantro leaves
1½ teaspoons chopped fresh
  thyme
½ teaspoon sugar
6 cups chopped cooked turkey
  breast
1 (16-ounce) container sour
  cream
2 teaspoons dried oregano
Vegetable oil
24 (6-inch) corn tortillas
6 cups (1½ pounds) shredded
  Monterey Jack cheese

Broil Anaheim chile peppers on an aluminum foil-lined baking sheet 3 inches from heat about 5 minutes on each side or until peppers look blistered. Place peppers in a heavy-duty zip-top plastic bag; seal and let stand 10 minutes to loosen skins. Peel peppers; discard seeds. Set peppers aside.

Combine tomatillos and chicken broth in a large saucepan. Bring to a boil; cover, reduce heat, and simmer 12 minutes or until tender. Pour tomatillo mixture through a wire-mesh strainer into a large deep skillet, reserving tomatillos. Set broth in skillet aside.

Process roasted Anaheim chile peppers, tomatillos, serrano chile peppers, and next 5 ingredients in a blender or food processor until smooth, stopping to scrape down sides. Stir tomatillo mixture into reserved broth in skillet. Bring tomatillo mixture to a simmer over medium heat. Spoon 1½ cups into each of 2 lightly greased 13- x 9-inch baking dishes.

Combine chopped turkey, sour cream, and oregano in a large bowl, stirring well.

Pour oil to a depth of ½ inch into a small skillet. Heat oil to 375°. Carefully holding 1 tortilla with tongs, quickly dip into hot oil, 1 second on each side, then into tomatillo mixture, 1 second on each side. Place in a baking dish. Spoon about ⅓ cup turkey mixture in center of tortilla. Roll up tortilla, and place seam side down in dish. Repeat procedure with remaining tortillas and turkey mixture, placing 12 enchiladas in each baking dish. Spoon half of remaining tomatillo mixture over enchiladas in each dish. Sprinkle enchiladas evenly with cheese.

Bake, uncovered, at 350° for 30 minutes or until thoroughly heated. Let stand 10 minutes before serving. Yield: 12 servings.

Note: To make ahead, cover and freeze up to a week after sprinkling with cheese. To serve, let stand at room temperature 1 hour, then bake, uncovered, at 350° for 1 hour.

Sounds Delicious: The Flavor of Atlanta in Food & Music
Atlanta Symphony Associates
Atlanta, Georgia

Barbara's Summer Refresher

Come in out of the sweltering summer sunshine and stir together this refreshing blend of lemonade, limeade, orange juice, lemon-lime soft drink, and vodka. If you don't have the soft drink on hand, relax and try club soda or sparkling water.

3½ cups water
2 cups vodka
1 (12-ounce) can frozen lemonade concentrate, thawed and undiluted
1 (12-ounce) can frozen limeade concentrate, thawed and undiluted
1 (6-ounce) can frozen orange juice concentrate, thawed and undiluted
½ cup sugar
1 (2-liter) bottle lemon-lime soft drink, chilled (we used 7UP)

Stir together first 6 ingredients in a large bowl. Pour into a large freezer container. Cover and freeze at least 8 hours.

Spoon slushy mixture into glasses, filling half full. Pour in enough soft drink to fill glasses. Serve immediately. Yield: 9 cups.

Savoring the Seasons: Riverside
The Craven Regional Medical Center Foundation
New Bern, North Carolina

Camper's Chocolate Mix

Here's a hot cocoa mix guaranteed to contribute to your daily calcium requirement. Most prepackaged mixes don't offer that advantage, as they aren't made with dry milk powder like this one.

1 (25.6-ounce) package instant nonfat dry milk powder
1 (16-ounce) package powdered sugar, sifted
1 (16-ounce) can cocoa
1 (6-ounce) jar powdered non-dairy coffee creamer
Marshmallows (optional)

Combine first 4 ingredients, stirring well. Store mixture in an airtight container. To serve, place ¼ cup chocolate mix in a mug; add boiling water, and stir to dissolve mix. Top with marshmallows, if desired. Yield: 15 cups mix.

Past and Present Meatless Treasures
Kaneohe Seventh-day Adventist Church
Kaneohe, Hawaii

Whiskey Snowballs

Mix up a batch of this slushy adult-only beverage, and it'll stand at the ready in your freezer up to a month.

1 cup sugar
1 cup water
1 (750-milliliter) bottle bourbon
1 (48-ounce) bottle lemon-lime soft drink (we used 7UP)
1 (46-ounce) can pineapple juice
1 (6-ounce) can frozen orange juice concentrate, thawed and undiluted
2 (10-ounce) jars maraschino cherries, undrained

Combine sugar and water in a large container, stirring until sugar dissolves. Stir in bourbon and remaining ingredients. Cover and freeze in a large freezer-proof pitcher. Let stand at room temperature 30 minutes before serving. Yield: 26 cups.   Carol Artall

Atchafalaya Legacy
Melville Woman's Club
Melville, Louisiana

Frozen Orange-Pecan Salad

This frosty salad is a boon for busy cooks, as you can make and freeze it up to a month ahead. Unmold and slice it when ready to serve.

1 (8-ounce) package cream
  cheese, softened
¼ cup orange juice
1 (8-ounce) can crushed
  pineapple, drained
½ cup chopped pecans,
  toasted
½ cup chopped pitted dates

¼ cup chopped maraschino
  cherries
½ teaspoon grated orange rind
1 cup whipping cream
¼ cup sugar
Leaf lettuce
Garnishes: orange slices,
  toasted pecan halves

Beat cream cheese and orange juice in a mixing bowl at medium speed with an electric mixer until fluffy. Stir in pineapple and next 4 ingredients.

Beat whipping cream and sugar at high speed until soft peaks form. Fold whipped cream mixture into cream cheese mixture. Spoon into a lightly oiled 6-cup ring mold or 9- x 5-inch loafpan. Cover and freeze at least 8 hours. Unmold onto a lettuce-lined serving platter. Garnish, if desired. Yield: 10 to 12 servings.

It's About Time: Recipes, Reflections, Realities
National Association Teachers of Family and Consumer Sciences
Bowling Green, Kentucky

Frozen Pineapple Salad

Freeze these creamy little salads in oiled muffin tins or muffin cups lined with aluminum foil baking cups. Then store the individual salads in a plastic zip-top bag in the freezer up to a month.

1 (16-ounce) container sour cream
¾ cup sugar
2 tablespoons fresh lemon juice
⅛ teaspoon salt
1 (8-ounce) can crushed pineapple, drained

½ cup seedless green grapes, halved
¼ cup maraschino cherries, chopped
¼ cup chopped pecans
1 banana, sliced

Stir together first 4 ingredients in a large bowl. Stir in pineapple and remaining ingredients. Spoon mixture into oiled muffin pans. Freeze, uncovered, 10 to 12 hours. Let stand at room temperature 5 minutes before serving. Yield: 12 servings.

The Dining Car
The Service League of Denison, Texas

Mexican Black Bean Salad

1 (15¼-ounce) can whole kernel corn, drained
1 (15-ounce) can black beans, rinsed and drained
1 red bell pepper, chopped
1 small purple onion, chopped
¼ cup chopped fresh cilantro

⅓ cup apple cider vinegar
1½ teaspoons ground cumin
1 teaspoon freshly ground pepper
1 teaspoon minced garlic
1 teaspoon Dijon mustard

Combine first 5 ingredients in a large bowl. Stir together vinegar and remaining 4 ingredients; pour over bean mixture, and toss gently. Cover and let stand at room temperature at least 2 hours before serving. Yield: 6 servings.   Spikell Family

Cookin' with Friends
National Presbyterian School Class of 2000
Washington, D.C.

Green Bean-Mozzarella Salad

½ pound fresh green beans
6 plum tomatoes, sliced
8 ounces mozzarella cheese, cubed
⅓ cup chopped fresh basil
⅓ cup chopped fresh oregano
⅛ teaspoon pepper
½ cup Italian dressing

Wash beans; trim stem ends. Place beans in a large skillet; add cold water to cover. Bring to a boil; reduce heat, and simmer, uncovered, 4 minutes or until crisp-tender. Plunge into ice water to stop the cooking process; drain.

Combine beans, sliced tomatoes, and next 4 ingredients in a large bowl; add dressing, and toss to coat. Cover and chill 1 hour. Yield: 4 servings.   Lori Moses

On Course
Women Associates of the Buffalo Power Squadron
Lancaster, New York

Asparagus Vinaigrette

1 pound fresh asparagus
½ teaspoon salt
1 cup olive oil
⅓ cup white wine vinegar
2 garlic cloves, pressed
2 tablespoons chopped fresh oregano or 2 teaspoons dried oregano
½ teaspoon salt
½ teaspoon pepper
½ teaspoon dry mustard

Snap off tough ends of asparagus. Place asparagus in a large skillet; add ½ teaspoon salt and cold water to cover. Bring to a boil; reduce heat, and simmer, uncovered, 5 minutes or until crisp-tender. Plunge asparagus into ice water to stop the cooking process; drain. Arrange in an 8-inch square dish. Combine oil and remaining 6 ingredients in a jar; cover tightly, and shake vigorously. Pour over asparagus. Cover and chill 2 to 3 hours. Yield: 4 to 6 servings.   Irma and John Sjo

Wildcat Valley: Recipes & Remembrances
Keats Lions Club
Manhattan, Kansas

Minted Fennel Salad with Olives

Our mint-kissed fennel salad begs to be served as a crisp and pleasing accompaniment with a grilled lamb entrée.

2 medium fennel bulbs (about 1 pound each)
1 cup loosely packed fresh mint leaves
¾ cup chopped Mediterranean-style olives (we tested with kalamata)
¼ cup chopped purple onion
3 tablespoons fresh lemon juice
3 tablespoons olive oil
2 teaspoons grated lemon rind
½ teaspoon salt
¼ teaspoon pepper

Trim stems and base from fennel bulbs, reserving fronds. Remove tough outer layer from each bulb. Cut each bulb in half through base. Cut out the small, pyramid-shaped core from each half. Place cored fennel, cut side down, and slice crosswise into 4 thick slices. Slice lengthwise into ¼-inch-wide strips. Chop enough of the reserved fronds to measure 1 tablespoon.

Combine fennel strips, fronds, mint, olives, and onion in a large bowl; toss gently.

Stir together lemon juice and remaining 4 ingredients in a small bowl. Pour over fennel mixture, and toss gently. Cover and chill up to 3 hours. Yield: 8 to 10 servings.

Note: It's important that this salad does not chill longer than 3 hours because the mint leaves begin to wilt. If you would like to prepare it in advance, combine all the other ingredients, and add the mint 3 hours before serving.

Breakfast in Cairo, Dinner in Rome
International School of Minnesota Foundation
Eden Prairie, Minnesota

Tabbouleh Salad

Tabbouleh is a Middle Eastern dish made of bulghur wheat, tomatoes, onions, parsley, mint, lemon juice, and olive oil. Our unusual version goes a step further with the crisp addition of corn, carrot, and celery.

1 cup bulghur wheat
1 cup hot water
3 green onions, thinly sliced (⅓ cup)
2 carrots, chopped (1 cup)
2 medium tomatoes, seeded and diced (3 cups)
1 medium cucumber, peeled, seeded, and chopped (1½ cups)

1 celery rib, thinly sliced (¾ cup)
½ cup frozen whole kernel corn, thawed
⅓ cup chopped fresh parsley
⅓ cup chopped fresh mint
Lemon-Basil Dressing

Stir together bulghur wheat and hot water in a large bowl; let stand 30 minutes. Drain. Stir in green onions and next 7 ingredients. Add Lemon-Basil Dressing, and toss well. Cover and chill 8 hours. Yield: 9 servings.

Lemon-Basil Dressing

⅓ cup olive oil
¼ cup fresh lemon juice
¼ cup chopped fresh basil
2 garlic cloves, minced

1 teaspoon salt
½ teaspoon sugar
½ teaspoon dry mustard

Combine all ingredients, stirring well. Yield: about 1 cup.

Past and Present Meatless Treasures
Kaneohe Seventh-day Adventist Church
Kaneohe, Hawaii

Apple, Chicken, and Wild Rice Salad

2½ cups apple juice
8 skinned and boned chicken
  breast halves
⅔ cup water
½ cup uncooked instant wild
  rice
1½ cups seedless green grapes,
  halved
¾ cup slivered almonds,
  toasted
½ cup chopped celery
1 cup mayonnaise
½ teaspoon seasoned salt
¼ teaspoon ground cinnamon

Bring apple juice to a boil in a Dutch oven over medium heat. Add chicken; cover, reduce heat, and simmer 30 minutes or until tender. Cool chicken completely. Chop chicken, and set aside.

Bring water to a boil in a medium saucepan; add rice. Cover, reduce heat, and simmer 5 minutes; drain. Combine chicken, rice, grapes, almonds, and celery in a bowl. Stir together mayonnaise, seasoned salt, and cinnamon. Spoon over chicken mixture; toss to coat. Cover and chill 8 hours. Yield: 8 servings.

Cooks of the Green Door
The League of Catholic Women
Minneapolis, Minnesota

Rodeo Coleslaw

We rounded up green and red cabbage, carrot, and green and red bell peppers to create this multicolored slaw. Apple cider vinegar and cumin kick up the combo.

½ cup sugar
⅔ cup apple cider vinegar
½ cup olive oil
2 to 3 teaspoons celery seeds
1 tablespoon ground cumin
1 small cabbage, shredded
1 small red cabbage, shredded
2 large carrots, shredded
1 medium-size green bell
  pepper, chopped
1 medium-size red bell pepper,
  chopped
1 small onion, chopped
1 teaspoon salt
½ teaspoon freshly ground
  pepper

Combine first 5 ingredients in a small saucepan. Bring to a boil, stirring until sugar dissolves. Remove from heat, and set aside.

Combine cabbages and next 4 ingredients in a large bowl. Stir in dressing mixture, salt, and pepper. Cover and chill 8 hours. Stir just before serving. Yield: 14 to 16 servings.

Seasons of Santa Fe
Kitchen Angels
Santa Fe, New Mexico

Island Salsa

Island magic casts its spell over this tropical blend of fresh pineapple, mango, and kiwifruit. Spoon it over grilled fish or pork. Try the new kiwifruit with a golden flesh for a change of attitude.

1 cup chopped fresh pineapple
1 cup chopped mango
   (about 2)
1 cup chopped yellow or red
   bell pepper
⅔ cup chopped kiwifruit
   (about 2)
½ cup finely chopped purple
   onion

¼ cup finely chopped fresh
   cilantro
1 teaspoon fresh lime juice
½ teaspoon minced serrano
   chile with seeds
¼ teaspoon salt
⅛ teaspoon ground white
   pepper

Combine all ingredients in a bowl, stirring gently. Cover and chill 3 hours. Yield: 4 cups.

Bravo! Recipes, Legends & Lore
University Musical Society
Ann Arbor, Michigan

Quick and Easy Raspberry Vinaigrette

½ cup raspberry vinegar
½ cup olive oil
1 tablespoon Dijon mustard
½ tablespoon minced garlic
¼ teaspoon salt
¼ teaspoon pepper

Whisk together all ingredients in a small bowl. Cover and chill. Serve over mixed salad greens. Yield: 1 cup.

Vintage Virginia: A History of Good Taste
The Virginia Dietetic Association
Centreville, Virginia

Lemon-Mango Soup

4 medium-size ripe mangoes, cubed
4 to 6 tablespoons fresh lemon juice
1 cup whipping cream
1 to 2 tablespoons grated lemon rind, divided
Garnishes: fresh raspberries, fresh mint sprigs

Process mango and lemon juice in a food processor until smooth. Remove about 3 tablespoons mango puree, and set aside. Stir whipping cream and 2 to 3 teaspoons lemon rind into remaining mango puree. Cover and chill.

Ladle chilled soup into individual soup bowls. Top each serving evenly with reserved puree. Swirl soup and mango puree together, using the tip of a knife. Sprinkle desired amount of remaining lemon rind over each serving. Garnish, if desired. Yield: 3 cups.

Note: For ease in preparation, grate the rind from lemons before juicing them.

Dining by Design: Stylish Recipes, Savory Settings
The Junior League of Pasadena, California

Wild Berry Soup

Fresh berries are blended with yogurt and sweetened with an orange-ginger sauce splashed with white Zinfandel wine.

2 cups quartered fresh
  strawberries
1 cup fresh blueberries
1 cup fresh raspberries
½ cup pineapple juice

1 (32-ounce) container vanilla
  yogurt
1 cup heavy whipping cream
⅓ cup honey
Orange-Ginger Sauce

Process first 4 ingredients in a blender until smooth. Press berry mixture through a wire-mesh stainer into a large bowl, discarding seeds. Stir in yogurt and remaining ingredients. Cover and chill 3 hours. Yield: 8 cups.

Orange-Ginger Sauce

½ cup fresh orange juice
½ cup white Zinfandel or
  blush wine

2 tablespoons honey
2 slices fresh ginger

Bring all ingredients to a boil in a small saucepan over medium-high heat. Reduce heat, and simmer, uncovered, 10 minutes or until juice mixture is reduced by half. Discard ginger. Cool. Yield: ½ cup.

The Kosher Palette
Joseph Kushner Hebrew Academy
Livingston, New Jersey

Hawaiian Loaf

You'll want to let this bread sit for a day after it's baked to allow the flavors to meld and to slice the bread more easily. Just let it cool completely, wrap it in plastic wrap, and chill it overnight. Take the bread out about a half hour before slicing with a serrated knife. It's worth the wait!

1 cup butter or margarine, softened
2 cups sugar
4 large eggs
3 ripe bananas, mashed (about 1 cup)
4 cups all-purpose flour
2 teaspoons baking powder
1 teaspoon baking soda
¾ teaspoon salt
1 (20-ounce) can crushed pineapple in heavy syrup, undrained
1 cup flaked coconut

Beat butter at medium speed with an electric mixer until creamy; gradually add sugar, beating well. Add eggs; beat well. Stir in banana.

Combine flour, baking powder, baking soda, and salt. Gradually add flour mixture to butter mixture, beating just until smooth. Fold in pineapple and coconut. Spoon batter into 2 greased and floured 9- x 5-inch loafpans.

Bake at 350° for 60 to 65 minutes or until a wooden pick inserted in center comes out clean. Cool in pans on a wire rack 15 minutes. Remove loaves from pans, and cool completely on wire rack. Yield: 2 loaves.

Katie B. Burns

Down Home Dining in Mississippi
Mississippi Homemaker Volunteers, Inc.
Water Valley, Mississippi

Bourbon Brownies

Dense and fudgy brownies are splashed with bourbon while hot from the oven and allowed to cool to let the flavor soak in. Then they're frosted twice—once with a creamy white almond frosting, then again with melted chocolate morsels.

2 large eggs
⅓ cup vegetable oil
¼ cup water
1 (21-ounce) package
   family-style brownie mix
   (we tested with Duncan
   Hines)
1 cup chopped pecans

⅓ cup bourbon
½ cup butter or margarine,
   softened
2¼ cups sifted powdered sugar
1 teaspoon almond extract
1 cup (6 ounces) semisweet
   chocolate morsels
1 tablespoon shortening

Line a 13- x 9-inch pan with aluminum foil; lightly grease foil, and set aside.

Beat eggs, oil, and water at medium speed with an electric mixer 1 minute. Gradually add brownie mix, beating well. Stir in pecans. Pour batter into prepared pan. Bake at 350° for 28 minutes. Sprinkle bourbon evenly over hot brownie layer. Chill 1 hour. Remove brownie layer from pan. Remove foil, and place brownie layer on an ungreased baking sheet.

Beat butter at medium speed until creamy; add powdered sugar and almond extract, beating until smooth. Spread frosting over brownie layer. Chill 1 hour.

Combine chocolate morsels and shortening in a microwave-safe bowl; microwave at HIGH 1½ to 2 minutes or until melted, stirring until smooth. Cool 5 minutes, and spread over frosting layer. Chill 30 minutes. Cut into bars. Yield: 4 dozen.

Tapestry: A Weaving of Food, Culture and Tradition
The Junior Welfare League of Rock Hill, South Carolina

Peach Pizza

If you're looking for something different for dessert, try this sweet interpretation of pizza. You'll find a creamy cheese and almond spread, fresh peach slices, and fragrant peach glaze nestled atop a yeast dough crust.

2 (3-ounce) packages cream cheese, softened
⅓ cup ricotta cheese
⅓ cup sifted powdered sugar
¼ teaspoon almond extract
⅛ teaspoon ground nutmeg
¼ cup chopped sliced natural almonds
1 (¼-ounce) envelope active dry yeast
¼ cup warm water (100° to 110°)
1½ cups all-purpose flour, divided

⅓ cup butter or margarine, softened
¼ cup sugar
¼ teaspoon salt
5½ cups peeled, sliced fresh ripe peaches (about 10 medium), divided
1 cup water
2 tablespoons lemon juice, divided
¾ cup sugar
2½ tablespoons cornstarch
¼ teaspoon salt

Beat cream cheese at medium speed with an electric mixer until creamy; add ricotta cheese, beating well. Add powdered sugar, almond extract, and nutmeg, beating well. Stir in almonds and set aside.

Combine yeast and warm water in a 1-cup glass measuring cup; let stand 5 minutes. Combine yeast mixture, 1 cup flour, butter, ¼ cup sugar, and ¼ teaspoon salt in a large mixing bowl; beat at medium speed until well blended. Gradually stir in enough remaining ½ cup flour to make a soft dough. Turn dough out onto a lightly floured surface, and knead until smooth and elastic (about 5 minutes).

Press dough into a greased 15-inch pizza pan. Bake at 375° for 10 minutes or until lightly browned. Remove from oven, and spread evenly with cream cheese mixture. Bake 5 more minutes.

Mash 1 cup sliced peaches in a medium saucepan; add water and 1 tablespoon lemon juice. Combine ¾ cup sugar, cornstarch, and ¼ teaspoon salt; stir into peach mixture. Bring mixture to a boil; reduce heat, and cook over medium-low heat 15 minutes, stirring constantly. Remove from heat, and cool 5 minutes.

Combine 4½ cups sliced peaches and remaining 1 tablespoon lemon juice; arrange over cream cheese mixture. Pour peach sauce over peach slices, spreading with a spatula. Chill 2 hours. Cut into wedges. Yield: 8 to 10 servings. Nash Hanna

A Peach Flavored Past
Altrusa International, Inc., of Palisade, Colorado

Cherry Thing

Convenient ingredients such as cherry pie filling and whipped topping make this rave-winning dessert easy to create under time constraints. It's just the ticket for your next family reunion, church picnic, or potluck supper.

1½ cups all-purpose flour
2 tablespoons powdered sugar
¾ cup butter or margarine,
　softened
¾ cup chopped pecans
2 (21-ounce) cans cherry pie
　filling

1 teaspoon almond extract
1 teaspoon vanilla extract
1 (8-ounce) package cream
　cheese, softened
2 cups sifted powdered sugar
1 (12-ounce) container frozen
　whipped topping, thawed

Combine flour and 2 tablespoons powdered sugar in a large bowl; cut butter into flour mixture with a pastry blender until crumbly. Add pecans, and press mixture into an ungreased 13- x 9-inch baking dish. Bake at 350° for 20 to 25 minutes or until lightly browned. Cool completely in dish on a wire rack. Meanwhile, stir together pie filling and flavorings in a large bowl; set aside.

Beat cream cheese and 2 cups powdered sugar at medium speed with an electric mixer until creamy. Fold in whipped topping. Spread cream cheese mixture over cooled crust. Spread pie filling mixture over cream cheese mixture. Cover and chill at least 8 hours. Yield: 15 servings. Barbara Rasmussen

Menus & Memories
The University of Oklahoma Women's Association
Norman, Oklahoma

Chocolate-Hazelnut Truffle in Custard Sauce

Sinfully rich slices of melt-in-your-mouth chocolate truffle imbued with orange liqueur and toasted hazelnuts are cushioned on dessert plates by a velvety custard sauce.

4 (4-ounce) semisweet chocolate bars, broken (we tested with Ghirardelli)
1 cup heavy whipping cream
¼ cup butter, softened
4 egg yolks
¾ cup sifted powdered sugar

1 cup coarsely chopped hazelnuts, toasted
3 tablespoons orange liqueur or orange juice
Custard Sauce

Line an 8½- x 4½-inch loafpan with heavy-duty aluminum foil; set aside.

Combine chocolate, whipping cream, and butter in a 2-quart saucepan; cook over medium heat 5 minutes or until chocolate melts, stirring often. Remove from heat; add egg yolks, 1 at a time, whisking after each addition. Cook over medium-low heat, stirring constantly, 2 to 3 minutes or until thermometer registers 160°. Stir in powdered sugar, chopped hazelnuts, and liqueur. Pour into prepared loafpan. Cover and freeze 8 hours. Uncover and invert onto a serving platter; remove foil. Slice loaf with a hot knife. Serve with Custard Sauce. Yield: 16 servings.

Custard Sauce

Serve extra sauce with your favorite fruit or berries. Keep refrigerated up to 2 days.

2 cups heavy whipping cream
½ cup sugar
2 teaspoons cornstarch

6 egg yolks
2 teaspoons vanilla extract

Bring whipping cream just to a boil in a 2-quart saucepan over medium heat. Combine sugar and cornstarch in a medium bowl. Add egg yolks; beat at medium speed with an electric mixer until thick and pale. Gradually stir about one-fourth of hot whipping cream into yolks; add yolk mixture to remaining whipping cream, stirring constantly. Cook over low heat, stirring constantly, until thermometer registers 160° and custard thickens and coats a spoon. Stir in vanilla. Cover and chill 8 hours. Yield: 3 cups.

Oh My Stars! Recipes That Shine
The Junior League of Roanoke Valley, Virginia

Cookies and Cream Freeze

For a double java jolt, use coffee ice cream instead of vanilla.

28 cream-filled chocolate sandwich cookies, finely crushed
¼ cup butter or margarine, softened
½ gallon vanilla ice cream, softened
½ cup cold strongly brewed coffee
6 tablespoons butter or margarine

1 cup sugar
1 (5-ounce) can evaporated milk
4 (1-ounce) semisweet chocolate squares
1 teaspoon vanilla extract
1 (16-ounce) container frozen whipped topping, thawed
1 cup chopped pecans, toasted

Stir together cookie crumbs and ¼ cup softened butter; spread in a 13- x 9-inch pan. Freeze 20 minutes or until firm. Stir together ice cream and coffee until smooth. Spoon into frozen crust. Cover and freeze 2 hours.

Melt 6 tablespoons butter in a small saucepan. Add sugar, milk, and chocolate. Bring to a boil over medium heat, stirring constantly. Reduce heat to low, and cook 1 minute, stirring constantly. Remove from heat, and stir in vanilla. Cool completely.

Drizzle chocolate sauce over ice cream mixture. Cover and freeze at least 4 hours or until firm. Let stand at room temperature 20 minutes before serving. Top with whipped topping, and sprinkle with nuts. To serve, cut ice cream into squares, and serve immediately. Yield: 15 servings.   Elizabeth G. Cook

Blended Blessings
First Presbyterian Church
Salisbury, North Carolina

Mocha Pound Cake Freeze

1 (10.75-ounce) loaf frozen
   pound cake
2 cups whipping cream
⅓ cup sugar
1 tablespoon instant coffee
   granules

1 tablespoon cold water
2 English toffee candy bars,
   crushed (we tested with Skor)

Slice pound cake horizontally to make 3 layers; set aside.

Beat whipping cream at high speed with an electric mixer until foamy; gradually add sugar, beating until soft peaks form. Transfer half of whipped cream (about 2 cups) to a bowl; cover and chill.

Dissolve coffee granules in cold water, and add to remaining half of whipped cream. Spread mixture evenly between cake layers. Freeze layers 20 to 25 minutes or until firm.

Cover top and sides of cake with remaining whipped cream. Sprinkle top with candy. Freeze at least 8 hours. Remove from freezer 10 minutes before serving. Yield: 8 servings.   Suzanne Mendoza

"NOT" Just Desserts
St. Isidore Parish—Administration Commission
Bloomingdale, Illinois

Crème de Menthe Ice Cream Pie

2 cups chocolate wafer crumbs
⅓ cup butter or margarine,
   softened
½ gallon vanilla ice cream,
   softened

6 tablespoons green crème de
   menthe
1 cup fudge sauce

Stir together crumbs and butter; press mixture in bottom of a 10-inch pieplate. Cover and freeze 30 minutes.

Stir together ice cream and crème de menthe. Spoon into prepared crust. Cover and freeze 8 hours. Serve with fudge sauce. Yield: 1 (10-inch) pie.   Sandy Sloan

Angels in the Kitchen
Grace Episcopal Church
Anderson, South Carolina

Key Lime Pie with Chocolate Crust

If you can't find fresh Key limes, the bottled juice stands in nicely. Use regular limes or lemons for the rind.

1 (9-ounce) package chocolate wafer cookies

3 tablespoons sugar

3 tablespoons butter or margarine

3 egg yolks

2 (14-ounce) cans sweetened condensed milk

2 teaspoons grated Key lime rind

¾ cup plus 2 tablespoons freshly squeezed Key lime juice

1 cup whipping cream, whipped

Garnish: Key lime slices

Process chocolate wafers, sugar, and butter in food processor to form coarse crumbs. Press mixture in bottom and up sides of a greased 9-inch springform pan. Bake, uncovered, at 350° for 12 minutes. Cool completely in pan on a wire rack.

Whisk egg yolks in a medium bowl until thick and pale. Stir in condensed milk. Gradually add lime rind and juice, stirring constantly. Pour mixture into cooled crust. Bake at 350° for 34 to 36 minutes or until set. Remove to wire rack, and cool completely. Cover and chill 8 to 10 hours.

Remove sides of pan. Spread whipped cream over pie. Garnish, if desired. Yield: 1 (9-inch) pie.

Meet Us in the Kitchen
The Junior League of St. Louis, Missouri

Frozen Lime Torte

Pint amounts of the lime sherbet, lemon sorbet, and frozen vanilla yogurt might be tricky to find in your area, but not to worry. Simply measure out 2 cups from larger containers and indulge in the leftover for snacking.

1¼ cups graham cracker crumbs
¼ cup butter or margarine, melted
2 tablespoons sugar
¼ cup flaked coconut

1 pint lime sherbet, softened
1 tablespoon Key lime juice
1 pint lemon sorbet, softened
1 pint frozen vanilla yogurt, softened

Stir together crumbs, butter, and sugar; firmly press mixture in bottom and up sides of a 9-inch pieplate. Freeze 15 minutes.

Meanwhile, bake coconut in a shallow pan at 350°, stirring occasionally, 5 to 6 minutes or until toasted; set aside.

Beat lime sherbet and lime juice at medium speed with an electric mixer until smooth. Add lemon sorbet and vanilla yogurt; beat until smooth. Spoon mixture into crust. Sprinkle with coconut. Cover and freeze 4 hours. Let stand at room temperature 15 minutes before serving. Yield: 1 (9-inch) torte.

Simple Pleasures: From Our Table to Yours
Arab Mothers' Club
Arab, Alabama

Quick & Easy Recipes

Mango and Prosciutto, page 36

Bacon Appetizers

Only 4 ingredients, but put together just so, they pack a wallop of first-course pleasure.

1 pound bacon	1 cup mayonnaise
1¾ cups (7 ounces) shredded Gouda cheese	½ (16-ounce) package cocktail rye bread, lightly toasted

Cook bacon in a large skillet until crisp; remove bacon, and drain on paper towels. Crumble bacon.

Combine bacon, cheese, and mayonnaise in a large bowl. Spread mixture on rye bread slices. Place on ungreased baking sheets. Bake at 350° for 7 minutes or until cheese is bubbly. Serve warm. Yield: 2 dozen.

Look Who Came to Dinner
The Junior Auxiliary of Amory, Mississippi

Mango and Prosciutto

½ pound prosciutto, thinly sliced	Lime wedges
4 ripe mangoes, peeled and cut into 1-inch pieces	

Cut prosciutto into strips; wrap around mango pieces. Secure with wooden picks. Serve with lime wedges. Yield: 3 dozen.

A Century of Serving
The Junior Board of Christiana Care, Inc.
Wilmington, Delaware

Spiced Holiday Pecans

Pecan halves get a toasting and a bit of spice, courtesy of cinnamon, red pepper, and hot sauce. Store them in an airtight container, or give them to your neighbor as a holiday remembrance.

3 tablespoons butter or
   margarine, melted
3 tablespoons Worcestershire
   sauce
1 teaspoon salt

½ teaspoon ground red pepper
½ teaspoon ground cinnamon
Dash of hot sauce
4 cups pecan halves

Stir together first 6 ingredients in a bowl. Add pecans, and toss gently to coat. Place in an ungreased 15- x 10-inch jellyroll pan.

Bake at 300° for 25 to 28 minutes, stirring twice. Cool completely. Store in an airtight container. Yield: 4 cups.   Ione Morris

We're Cooking Up Something New:
50 Years of Music, History, and Food
Wichita Falls Symphony League
Wichita Falls, Texas

Rarin'-to-Go Tea

Lemonade and almond extract thrust this tea blend into thirst-quenching action.

4 cups boiling water
5 tea bags
3¼ cups cold water
1 cup sugar

1 (6-ounce) can frozen
   lemonade concentrate,
   thawed and undiluted
1 teaspoon almond extract

Pour boiling water over tea bags; cover and steep 5 minutes. Remove tea bags from water, squeezing gently. Add sugar, stirring until sugar dissolves. Add cold water and remaining ingredients in a large pitcher; chill. Serve over ice. Yield: 7 cups.   Lauri Pearman

Diamond Delights
Diamond Hill Elementary School
Abbeville, South Carolina

Spiced Cider Punch

4 cups water
¾ cup sugar
¾ cup firmly packed brown
   sugar

4 (2-inch) cinnamon sticks
4 cups fresh orange juice
3 cups apple cider
1½ cups fresh lemon juice

Combine first 4 ingredients in a large saucepan. Bring to a boil; reduce heat, and simmer, uncovered, 5 minutes. Discard cinnamon sticks. Add orange juice, cider, and lemon juice to pan. Cook until thoroughly heated (do not boil). Serve warm or chilled. Yield: 14 cups.   Eloise Scott

Down Home Dining in Mississippi
Mississippi Homemaker Volunteers, Inc.
Water Valley, Mississippi

Peach Frosty

Fresh summer peaches lend their juicy goodness to this chilly, ginger-spiced blend for two.

Sugar
1 cup peeled, sliced fresh
   peaches
½ cup milk

6 tablespoons sugar
½ teaspoon ground ginger
1 teaspoon vanilla extract
1 cup vanilla ice cream

Dip rims of 2 (8-ounce) glasses into water, and then into sugar. Chill.

Process peaches and next 4 ingredients in a blender until smooth. Add ice cream, and process until smooth. Pour into prepared glasses. Serve immediately. Yield: 2 cups.   Mickey Toley

A Peach Flavored Past
Altrusa International, Inc. of Palisade, Colorado

Easy Banana Pancakes

Easy does it when flipping these airy cakes. They come together in a flash, thanks to biscuit mix and mashed bananas.

2 cups biscuit mix
1 cup milk
2 ripe bananas, mashed

2 large eggs, lightly beaten
Maple syrup or fruit topping

Combine first 4 ingredients in a medium bowl, stirring just until dry ingredients are moistened.

Pour about ¼ cup batter for each pancake onto a hot, lightly greased griddle. Cook pancakes until tops are covered with small bubbles and edges look cooked; turn and cook other side. Serve immediately with syrup or fruit topping. Yield: 16 pancakes.   Rick Lewis

Blended Blessings
First Presbyterian Church
Salisbury, North Carolina

French Bread with Pesto and Sun-Dried Tomatoes

Slices of French bread slathered with a cream cheese blend of pesto and dried tomatoes partner a salad, soup, or stew perfectly.

1 (8-ounce) package cream
  cheese, softened
1 (14-ounce) loaf French bread,
  cut in half horizontally

1 (3.5-ounce) jar pesto
1 (8-ounce) jar dried tomatoes
  in oil, drained

Spread cream cheese over cut sides of bread halves. Spread pesto over cream cheese; top with dried tomatoes. Place bread halves on an ungreased baking sheet. Bake at 400° for 5 minutes or until thoroughly heated. Cut into 2-inch slices, and serve warm. Yield: about 14 servings.   Kristin Dwelle Hurst

Beyond Cotton Country
The Junior League of Morgan County
Decatur, Alabama

Chez Betty's Housemade Corn Muffins

1¼ cups all-purpose flour
⅔ cup yellow cornmeal
⅓ cup sugar
1 tablespoon baking powder

½ teaspoon salt
1 cup milk
⅓ cup canola oil

Combine first 5 ingredients in a large bowl; make a well in center of mixture. Add milk and oil to dry ingredients, stirring just until moistened. Spoon batter by level tablespoonfuls into lightly greased miniature (1¾-inch) muffin pans. Bake at 425° for 13 minutes or until golden. Remove from pans immediately, and cool on wire racks. Yield: 2½ dozen.

Always in Season
The Junior League of Salt Lake City, Utah

Simple Dinner Rolls

Divine describes these easy dinner rolls. A rich combination of sour cream plus pancake and waffle mix creates the base, while toasted sesame seeds top these little wonders.

1 (8-ounce) container sour
　cream
1 large egg, lightly beaten
2 cups pancake and waffle mix
　(we used Aunt Jemima)

2 tablespoons sesame seeds,
　toasted

Stir together sour cream and egg in a medium bowl. Add pancake mix, stirring just until moistened. Drop by heaping tablespoonfuls onto greased baking sheets. Sprinkle with sesame seeds. Bake at 375° for 10 to 12 minutes or until lightly browned. Serve warm. Yield: 22 rolls.　　　　　　　　　　　　　　　　　　　　　Aileen Gabat

Flavors of the Tenderloin
Sidewalk Clean-Up, Recycling & Urban Beautification (SCRUB)
San Francisco, California

Crescent Cheese Twists

1 (8-ounce) can refrigerated
crescent rolls

2 teaspoons butter or
margarine, melted

2 tablespoons finely shredded
Cheddar cheese

¼ teaspoon garlic salt

Unroll crescent rolls, and separate into 4 rectangles; press perforations to seal. Brush 1 side of 2 rectangles with butter. Sprinkle with cheese and garlic salt. Arrange remaining 2 rectangles over prepared rectangles. Using a pizza cutter, cut each rectangle crosswise into 10 (½-inch-wide) strips. Twist each strip 5 or 6 times, and arrange on an ungreased baking sheet, securing ends by pressing to baking sheet. Bake at 375° for 10 to 12 minutes or until lightly browned. Serve warm. Yield: 20 twists.

Vintage Virginia: A History of Good Taste
The Virginia Dietetic Association
Centreville, Virginia

Midnight Breakfast

Pork sausage, eggs, and cheese reinvent themselves for this breakfast fare that strikes the right chord anytime of day.

1 pound ground mild pork
sausage

1 (4-ounce) can mushroom
stems and pieces, drained

2 cups (8 ounces) shredded
Cheddar cheese

8 large eggs, beaten

Cook sausage in a large skillet, stirring until it crumbles and is no longer pink; drain.

Layer sausage, mushrooms, and cheese in a greased 11- x 7-inch baking dish. Pour beaten egg over mixture. Bake, uncovered, at 350° for 22 to 24 minutes. Yield: 6 to 8 servings.   Charlotte Tubb

Look Who Came to Dinner
The Junior Auxiliary of Amory, Mississippi

Oven-Fried Halibut

A coating of crisp dry breadcrumbs and quick baking at high heat on an already hot pan make this oven-fried halibut extra crispy.

½ cup fine, dry breadcrumbs
   (store-bought)
½ teaspoon lemon pepper
½ teaspoon garlic salt with
   parsley
½ teaspoon paprika

4 (6-ounce) halibut fillets
½ cup milk
2 tablespoons butter or
   margarine, melted
Lemon wedges

Stir together first 4 ingredients in a small bowl.

Dip fillets in milk, and dredge in breadcrumb mixture, turning to coat completely.

Lightly coat a 15- x 10-inch jellyroll pan with oil; heat pan at 500° for 3 minutes or until pan is very hot. Carefully arrange fillets on hot pan, and drizzle with melted butter. Bake fillets at 500° for 7 to 8 minutes or until fish flakes with a fork. Serve fillets with lemon wedges. Yield: 4 servings.   Sue Young

Blest Recipes
Our Redeemer Lutheran Church
Chugiak, Alaska

Salmon with Oriental Mahogany Sauce

Our distinctive sauce gets its mahogany color and captivating character from a blending of whole-berry cranberry sauce, soy sauce, honey, and garlic.

2 pounds (1-inch-thick) salmon
   fillets
1 cup whole-berry cranberry
   sauce
¼ cup honey

¼ cup soy sauce
2 garlic cloves, minced
¼ teaspoon pepper
Garnish: chopped fresh parsley

Remove and discard skin from salmon; place salmon in a lightly greased 13- x 9-inch baking dish.

Stir together cranberry sauce and next 4 ingredients in a small bowl. Pour half of sauce (about ¾ cup) over salmon, spreading to coat. Reserve remaining sauce.

Bake, uncovered, at 375° for 20 to 25 minutes or until fish flakes with a fork.

Cook reserved sauce in a saucepan over medium heat until thoroughly heated. Serve with fish. Garnish, if desired. Yield: 4 servings.

Yuletide on Hilton Head: A Heritage of Island Flavors
United Way of Beaufort County
Hilton Head Island, South Carolina

Shrimp with Artichokes

1 pound unpeeled,
  medium-size fresh shrimp
½ cup butter or margarine
1 (0.6-ounce) envelope zesty
  Italian-style dressing mix

1 (8-ounce) package sliced
  fresh mushrooms
1 (6½-ounce) jar marinated
  artichoke hearts, undrained
Hot cooked fettuccine

Peel shrimp, and devein, if desired. Set aside.

Melt butter in a large skillet over medium heat; add dressing mix, and stir until dressing mix dissolves. Add mushrooms and artichoke hearts, and cook 3 to 5 minutes or until mushrooms are tender. Add shrimp, and cook 4 to 5 minutes or just until shrimp turn pink. Pour shrimp mixture over pasta, and toss well. Serve immediately. Yield: 4 servings.

Mary Rogers

Angels in the Kitchen Cookbook
Community Presbyterian Church
Celebration, Florida

Alexander's Pecan Chicken

Since this recipe cooks a dozen chicken breast halves in batches, it may not be possible to get exactly the same size breasts. Just adjust your cooking time up or down slightly if chicken breast halves vary in size.

3 cups pecans, finely chopped
1 cup fine, dry breadcrumbs (store-bought)
1 teaspoon chopped fresh parsley
½ teaspoon salt
⅛ teaspoon ground red pepper

12 (6-ounce) skinned and boned chicken breast halves
½ cup butter or margarine, melted and divided
3 tablespoons vegetable oil, divided
Garnish: fresh parsley sprigs

Stir together first 5 ingredients in a small bowl.

Brush chicken with 2 tablespoons melted butter. Dredge chicken in pecan mixture, pressing gently to coat.

Heat 2 tablespoons butter and 1 tablespoon oil in a large skillet over medium-high heat until hot. Add 4 chicken breast halves, and cook 2 minutes on each side or until browned. Remove chicken to an ungreased baking sheet. Wipe skillet clean with a paper towel. Repeat procedure twice with remaining butter, oil, and chicken breast halves.

Bake at 350° for 15 to 17 minutes or until done. Garnish, if desired. Yield: 12 servings.

Oh My Stars! Recipes That Shine
The Junior League of Roanoke Valley, Virginia

Crispy Onion Baked Chicken

A marriage of French onion soup mix and breadcrumbs adds crunch and crispness to this moist mayonnaise-coated chicken.

1 cup fine, dry breadcrumbs (store-bought)
1 (1.4-ounce) envelope dry onion soup mix (we used Knorr)

⅓ cup mayonnaise
4 skinned and boned chicken breast halves

Combine breadcrumbs and soup mix in a large zip-top plastic bag; seal and shake well. Brush chicken breasts with mayonnaise; place breasts, 1 at a time, in bag. Seal and shake to coat. Arrange chicken on an ungreased rack in a broiler pan. Bake at 425° for 20 to 25 minutes or until done. Yield: 4 servings.   Dorothy Pinzker

"NOT" Just Desserts
St. Isidore Parish—Administration Commission
Bloomingdale, Illinois

Amen Ramen Chicken

Popular ramen noodle soup mix reigns supreme in this tasty one-dish chicken invention.

2 teaspoons vegetable oil	1¾ cups water
1 pound skinned and boned chicken breast halves, cut into ¼-inch strips (about 3 chicken breast halves)	1 (4½-ounce) jar mushrooms, drained
	3 tablespoons soy sauce
2 cups fresh broccoli florets	2 (3-ounce) packages ramen chicken noodle soup mix

Heat oil in a large nonstick skillet over medium-high heat until hot. Add chicken strips, and cook 5 minutes or until done, stirring often. Add broccoli and next 3 ingredients. Stir in 1 flavor packet from soup mix (reserve remaining flavor packet for another use). Bring to a boil; break noodles from both packages of soup mix in half, and add to skillet. Cover, reduce heat, and simmer 5 to 7 minutes or until broccoli and noodles are tender, stirring occasionally. Yield: 4 servings.

It's a Snap!
The Haven of Grace
St. Louis, Missouri

Oriental Nectar Chicken

12 chicken drumsticks
1 cup apricot nectar
1½ tablespoons soy sauce

1 tablespoon white vinegar
¼ teaspoon Chinese five spice
Hot cooked rice

Place chicken on a lightly greased rack in a broiler pan. Broil 3 inches from heat 5 minutes on each side or until browned. Place in an ungreased 13- x 9-inch baking dish.

Stir together apricot nectar and next 3 ingredients; pour over chicken. Bake, uncovered, at 350° for 35 minutes. Serve over rice. Yield: 6 servings.

A Taste Tour
Gingko Twig of Muhlenberg Hospital, Plainfield, New Jersey
Westfield, New Jersey

Roquefort Filets Mignons with Brandy

Beef tenderloin steaks are set apart with a headstrong dose of brandy and Roquefort cheese.

4 (6-ounce) beef tenderloin
   steaks (1 inch thick)
¼ teaspoon salt
¼ teaspoon freshly ground
   pepper
3 tablespoons butter or
   margarine

1 (14½-ounce) can beef broth
¾ cup brandy
1 tablespoon chopped fresh
   rosemary
1 cup crumbled Roquefort
   cheese

Sprinkle steaks with salt and pepper. Melt butter in a large nonstick skillet over medium-high heat; add steaks, and cook 4 to 5 minutes on each side (medium rare) or to desired degree of doneness. Remove steaks to a serving platter; keep warm. Add beef broth, brandy, and rosemary to skillet, stirring to loosen particles from bottom of pan. Bring to a boil; boil 5 to 6 minutes or until sauce is reduced to 1 cup. Pour over steaks. Sprinkle with cheese. Yield: 4 servings.

Settings on the Dock of the Bay
ASSISTANCE LEAGUE® of the Bay Area
Houston, Texas

Italian Meatballs

Make these meatballs when you have time, then freeze them in an airtight container up to a month. To create a supper on the go, simply reheat them in your favorite spaghetti sauce and serve over hot cooked pasta.

4 pounds ground pork
2 pounds ground sirloin
5 large eggs, lightly beaten
2 cups soft breadcrumbs
     (homemade)
1 cup freshly grated Parmesan
     cheese

⅓ cup chopped fresh parsley
6 garlic cloves, minced
1 teaspoon salt
½ teaspoon freshly ground
     pepper

Combine all ingredients in a large bowl, and mix lightly. Shape mixture into 1½-inch balls. Place meatballs on baking sheets lined with aluminum foil and coated with cooking spray. Bake at 400° for 18 to 20 minutes or until meatballs are done. Serve immediately, or freeze in airtight containers up to 1 month. Yield: about 9 dozen meatballs (20 to 22 servings). Christine Maggio

Taste Buds–A Collection of Treasured Recipes
Alliance of the Illinois State Dental Society
Springfield, Illinois

Pork Tenderloin Diane

1 (1-pound) pork tenderloin, cut into 10 pieces
2 teaspoons lemon pepper
2 tablespoons butter
2 tablespoons fresh lemon juice
1 tablespoon Worcestershire sauce
1 teaspoon Dijon mustard
1 tablespoon finely chopped fresh parsley or chives

Place meat between 2 sheets of heavy-duty plastic wrap, and flatten to 1-inch thickness, using a meat mallet or rolling pin. Sprinkle both sides of meat with lemon pepper.

Melt butter in a large skillet over medium-high heat. Add meat, and cook 3 to 4 minutes on each side or until done. Transfer to a serving platter, and keep warm.

Add lemon juice, Worcestershire sauce, and mustard to skillet; cook, stirring constantly, until thoroughly heated. Pour sauce over meat, and sprinkle with parsley or chives. Serve immediately. Yield: 4 servings.

Note: If you don't have a skillet large enough to cook all the meat at once, use a smaller skillet, and cook the meat in 2 batches, using 1 tablespoon of butter per batch.

Twice Treasured Recipes
The Bargain Box, Inc.
Hilton Head Island, South Carolina

10-Minute Spicy Black Bean Chili

Chili in mere minutes is what this recipe is all about. To keep things flexible, use whichever type of canned tomatoes you have on hand, such as Mexican-style stewed tomatoes, to vary the batch.

¾ **pound ground beef**
1 **tablespoon chili powder**
1 **(19-ounce) can black beans, rinsed and drained**

1 **(14½-ounce) can crushed tomatoes, undrained**
1 **(8-ounce) jar hot salsa**

Cook ground beef in a large skillet over medium-high heat, stirring until it crumbles and is no longer pink. Drain well. Add chili powder, and cook, stirring constantly, 3 minutes. Add beans, tomatoes, and salsa; bring to a boil. Cover, reduce heat, and simmer 5 minutes, stirring occasionally. Yield: 4 cups.   Mary Taulbee

McInnis Bobcat Favorites
McInnis Elementary PTA
DeLeon Springs, Florida

Orange-Glazed Ham Steak

Dinner can't get much quicker and easier than this. Simply stir together a little orange marmalade and Dijon mustard, baste a ham steak, and grill away.

¼ **cup orange marmalade**
1 **teaspoon Dijon mustard**

1 **pound cooked center-cut ham steak**

Stir together marmalade and mustard in a small bowl. Grill ham steak, covered with grill lid, over medium-high heat (350° to 400°) about 3 minutes on each side or until thoroughly heated, turning and basting once with glaze. Yield: 4 servings.

A Sunsational Encore
The Junior League of Greater Orlando, Florida

"Eggstra" Special Spaghetti

Here's a dish similar to spaghetti carbonara. If you can't find process American cheese in your grocer's dairy case, check the deli counter.

8 ounces uncooked spaghetti
8 slices bacon, cut into ½-inch
  pieces
½ cup chopped onion
4 large eggs, lightly beaten

4 ounces process American
  cheese, shredded
Garnishes: chopped fresh
  parsley, chopped fresh chives

Cook spaghetti according to package directions; keep warm.

Cook bacon in a large nonstick skillet until crisp; remove bacon, and drain on paper towels, reserving drippings in skillet. Sauté onion in hot drippings until tender. Add spaghetti and bacon to skillet; stir in eggs and cheese. Cook until eggs are set and cheese melts, stirring often. Garnish, if desired. Yield: 4 servings.

Picnics, Potlucks & Prizewinners
Indiana 4-H Foundation, Inc.
Indianapolis, Indiana

Linguine with Pepper Breadcrumbs

½ cup butter, divided
1½ cups soft breadcrumbs
  (homemade)
2 teaspoons coarsely ground
  pepper

2 (9-ounce) packages
  refrigerated linguine
1 cup grated Romano cheese

Melt 5 tablespoons butter in a large skillet over medium heat. Add breadcrumbs and pepper; cook until breadcrumbs are golden brown, stirring occasionally. Remove from heat, and set aside.

Cook pasta according to package directions. Drain well; place in a serving bowl. Cut remaining 3 tablespoons butter into pieces; add butter and cheese to pasta; toss well. Add breadcrumb mixture; toss well. Serve immediately. Yield: 6 to 8 servings.   Lorraine Lesinski

On Course
Women Associates of the Buffalo Power Squadron
Lancaster, New York

Tortellini Salad

2 (9-ounce) packages
  refrigerated cheese-filled
  tortellini
1 (12-ounce) jar marinated
  artichoke hearts, drained
  and sliced
1 (8-ounce) jar dried tomatoes
  in oil, undrained and
  chopped

1 tablespoon fresh lemon juice
2 garlic cloves, crushed
½ teaspoon salt
1 teaspoon pepper

Cook pasta according to package directions; rinse with cold water, and drain well. Combine artichoke hearts and remaining 5 ingredients in a large bowl. Add pasta, and toss gently. Cover and chill 2 to 4 hours before serving. Yield: 8 servings.   The Franceschini Family

Heaven's Bounty
Long Beach Catholic School Parents' Club
Long Beach, New York

Honey-Herb Salad Dressing

¼ cup white wine vinegar
¼ cup honey
2 tablespoons chopped fresh
  basil or mint
1 tablespoon minced green
  onion

¼ teaspoon salt
¼ teaspoon freshly ground
  pepper

Whisk together all ingredients in a bowl. Serve over salad greens or fresh fruit. Yield: ½ cup.   Marg and Ken Waldhauser

North Country Cooking
51st National Square Dance Convention
Champlin, Minnesota

Couscous Amandine

2 cups water
1 (10-ounce) package couscous
½ cup raisins
½ teaspoon salt
½ cup slivered almonds,
   toasted

¼ cup chopped fresh parsley
2 tablespoons olive oil
½ teaspoon ground cinnamon

Bring water to a boil in a medium saucepan; stir in couscous, raisins, and salt. Cover, remove from heat, and let stand 5 minutes. Fluff couscous mixture with a fork.

Stir in almonds and remaining ingredients. Serve immediately. Yield: 8 to 10 servings.

What Can I Bring?
The Junior League of Northern Virginia
McLean, Virginia

Oven-Roasted Asparagus with Thyme

Oven roasting the asparagus with olive oil, garlic, and a hint of thyme heightens the subtle, delicate essence of the vegetable.

1½ pounds fresh asparagus
1 large garlic clove, halved
2 teaspoons olive oil
½ teaspoon salt

¼ teaspoon freshly ground
   pepper
¼ teaspoon dried thyme

Snap off tough ends of asparagus. Rub cut sides of garlic over bottom and sides of an ungreased 13- x 9-inch baking dish. Place asparagus and garlic in dish. Drizzle with olive oil. Sprinkle with salt, pepper, and thyme; toss gently. Bake, uncovered, at 400° for 20 minutes, stirring once. Yield: 4 servings.   Elizabeth Morrison Pilgrim

Beyond Cotton Country
The Junior League of Morgan County
Decatur, Alabama

Broccoli-Rice Casserole

2 (10-ounce) packages frozen
  broccoli florets
2 cups cooked rice
1 (10¾-ounce) can cream of
  mushroom soup, undiluted

½ (15-ounce) jar process
  cheese spread
3 tablespoons saltine cracker
  crumbs

Place broccoli in a 2-quart microwave-safe baking dish. Cover and microwave at HIGH 8 to 10 minutes or until crisp-tender; drain.

While broccoli cooks, stir together rice, soup, and cheese spread in a large bowl. Stir in broccoli. Wipe dish dry, and coat with cooking spray. Pour mixture into casserole; sprinkle with cracker crumbs. Microwave, uncovered, at HIGH 8 to 10 minutes or until thoroughly heated. Yield: 6 servings.

Simple Pleasures: From Our Table to Yours
Arab Mothers' Club
Arab, Alabama

Zesty Tomato Treats

Summer tomatoes at their peak make this recipe soar. It's a BLT sans the bread.

6 medium tomatoes
12 lettuce leaves
½ cup mayonnaise
½ cup sour cream

2 tablespoons finely chopped
  onion
6 slices bacon, cooked and
  crumbled

Slice tomatoes in half crosswise. Slice off rounded ends of tomatoes so halves sit upright, large cut sides up. Arrange lettuce leaves on a serving platter; top each leaf with a tomato half.

Stir together mayonnaise, sour cream, and onion in a small bowl. Spread the mayonnaise mixture evenly over each tomato half, and sprinkle with bacon. Yield: 12 servings.

More Enchanted Eating from the West Shore
Friends of the Symphony
Muskegon, Michigan

Creamed Corn

Freshly grated Parmesan cheese and ground red pepper zap this creamed corn recipe with unexpected flair.

4 (10-ounce) packages frozen whole kernel corn, thawed
2 cups whipping cream
2 tablespoons sugar
1 teaspoon salt
⅛ teaspoon ground red pepper
2 tablespoons butter
2 tablespoons all-purpose flour
¾ cup freshly grated Parmesan cheese, divided

Combine first 5 ingredients in a large saucepan. Bring to a boil over medium heat, stirring occasionally. Reduce heat, and simmer, uncovered, 5 minutes.

Meanwhile, microwave butter in a microwave-safe dish at HIGH 45 to 50 seconds or until melted. Add flour, stirring until smooth. Stir into corn mixture; remove from heat. Stir in ½ cup cheese. Pour mixture into an ungreased 11- x 7-inch baking dish; sprinkle with remaining ¼ cup cheese. Broil 5½ inches from heat 4 to 5 minutes or until cheese melts. Yield: 8 servings.   Pat Hicks

Savor the Flavor: Delightfully Vegetarian
Portland Adventist Community Services
Portland, Oregon

Golden Carrots Supreme

¾ cup chicken broth
¼ cup butter or margarine
2 teaspoons sugar
1 teaspoon salt
⅛ teaspoon pepper
5 cups sliced carrot (about 2 pounds)
¼ cup chopped fresh parsley
2 teaspoons lemon juice

Bring chicken broth to a boil in a large saucepan over medium-high heat. Add butter, sugar, salt, and pepper; stir until butter melts. Add carrot; cover and cook 10 minutes or until carrot is crisp-tender. Stir in parsley and lemon juice. Yield: 8 servings.

Twice Treasured Recipes
The Bargain Box, Inc.
Hilton Head Island, South Carolina

Macadamia Yams

1 (29-ounce) can yams, drained
⅓ cup chopped macadamia
   nuts
⅓ cup firmly packed brown
   sugar
⅓ cup flaked coconut
3 tablespoons all-purpose flour
3 tablespoons butter or
   margarine, melted

Place yams in an ungreased 1-quart baking dish. Combine nuts and remaining 4 ingredients, stirring until mixture is crumbly. Sprinkle nut mixture over yams. Bake, uncovered, at 350° for 35 minutes. Yield: 4 servings.   Anastasia Ferreira-Harrington

Ofukuro No Aji: Favorite Recipes from Mama's Kitchen
Hōkūlani Cultural Exchange Committee
(Hōkūlani Elementary School)
Honolulu, Hawaii

Apple Sauté with Calvados

Calvados is a dry apple brandy named for the Normandy region of France where it's made. It pairs especially well with this homestyle apple dish.

6 tablespoons butter, divided
6 Gala apples, peeled and
   thinly sliced, divided
½ cup firmly packed brown
   sugar
⅔ cup Calvados

Melt 2 tablespoons butter in a large nonstick skillet over medium-high heat; place one-third of apple slices in a single layer in skillet, and cook 4 minutes on each side or until browned. Remove from skillet. Repeat procedure twice with remaining butter and apple slices.

Reduce heat to medium; add brown sugar to any butter remaining in skillet, stirring until sugar dissolves. Add Calvados, and bring to a boil; cook, stirring constantly, 5 minutes. Reduce heat to low, and add apple slices to skillet; cook 5 minutes or until thoroughly heated. Serve immediately. Yield: 7 servings.   Barbi Smith

Divine Offerings: Recipes and Hints for the Kitchen
St. Charles Presbyterian Women
St. Charles, Missouri

Peanut Butter Squares

4 cups sifted powdered sugar
1 (5⅓-ounce) package graham
  crackers, crushed (about
  1⅔ cups)
1 cup creamy peanut butter

1 cup butter or margarine,
  melted
1 cup (6 ounces) semisweet
  chocolate morsels, melted

Stir together first 4 ingredients in a medium bowl. Firmly press mixture into an ungreased 13- x 9-inch pan. Spread melted chocolate evenly over cracker layer.

Let stand at room temperature 2 hours or until chocolate is set. Cut into squares. Yield: 2 dozen.   Forest Bryant

A Little DAPS of This . . . A Little DAPS of That
Dallas Area Parkinsonism Society (DAPS)
Dallas, Texas

Roscoe's Special

Not to worry–there should be plenty of extra chocolate sauce to save for another important occasion, such as a midnight snack.

2 cups firmly packed brown
  sugar
1 (5-ounce) can evaporated
  milk
½ cup butter or margarine

2 (1-ounce) unsweetened
  chocolate squares
6 slices pound cake, toasted
1 pint vanilla ice cream

Combine first 4 ingredients in a small saucepan. Cook over medium heat, stirring constantly, until sugar dissolves and sauce is smooth. Place pound cake on dessert plates; top with a scoop of ice cream. Serve sauce warm over pound cake and ice cream. Yield: 2¼ cups.

Note: Sauce can be stored in refrigerator up to 1 week.

Tapestry: A Weaving of Food, Culture and Tradition
The Junior Welfare League of Rock Hill, South Carolina

Appetizers & Beverages

Mustard-Dill Pancakes with Smoked Salmon and Caviar, page 64

Buttery Brown Sugar Dip for Fruit

1 cup chopped pecans, toasted
1 cup butter
1¾ cups firmly packed light
  brown sugar

1 cup whipping cream
Sliced apples
Sliced pears
Lemon juice

Spread pecans in an ungreased 15- x 10-inch jellyroll pan. Bake at 350° for 6 minutes or until toasted; set aside.

Melt butter in a heavy saucepan over medium heat. Add brown sugar and whipping cream, and cook, stirring constantly, until sugar dissolves. Stir in toasted pecans.

Serve dip warm with apple and pear slices sprinkled with lemon juice. Yield: about 3½ cups. Lynn M. Connette

Olivet Heritage Cookbook
Olivet Presbyterian Church
Charlottesville, Virginia

Chutney Pie

1 (8-ounce) package cream
  cheese
2 cups (8 ounces) shredded
  sharp Cheddar cheese
1 teaspoon curry powder

1 tablespoon dry sherry
⅔ cup chutney (we used Major
  Grey)
½ cup chopped green onions

Process first 4 ingredients in a food processor 30 seconds or until smooth, stopping to scrape down sides.

Line a 9-inch pieplate with plastic wrap; firmly press cheese mixture into pieplate. Cover and chill 1 hour.

Just before serving, unmold cheese mixture onto a serving platter; remove plastic wrap. Spread chutney over cheese mixture, and sprinkle with green onions. Serve with crackers. Yield: 10 to 12 appetizer servings. Joyce and Beril Susman

A Little DAPS of This . . . A Little DAPS of That
Dallas Area Parkinsonism Society (DAPS)
Dallas, Texas

Baked Crab, Brie, and Artichoke Dip

Create a lasting impression by serving this special-occasion fare in a hollowed sourdough bread round. The melding of flavors such as Vidalia onion, spinach, artichoke, and Brie makes this dip memorable.

½ (10-ounce) package frozen chopped spinach, thawed and drained
½ cup canned artichoke hearts, drained and coarsely chopped
1 (15-ounce) round Brie
1 medium leek
1 medium Vidalia onion, finely chopped
6 large garlic cloves, minced
2 tablespoons olive oil
½ cup whipping cream
¼ cup dry white wine
1 pound fresh jumbo lump crabmeat, drained
3 tablespoons finely chopped fresh parsley
2 tablespoons finely chopped fresh dill
1 tablespoon finely chopped fresh tarragon
1 teaspoon Dijon mustard
1 teaspoon hot sauce
½ teaspoon pepper

Press spinach and artichoke hearts between layers of paper towels to remove excess moisture; set aside.

Remove and discard rind from cheese with a vegetable peeler. Cut cheese into ¼-inch pieces; set aside.

Remove roots, outer leaves, and tops from leek, leaving only white part. Cut in half lengthwise. Cut each half crosswise to form 1-inch-thick strips. Cut strips into 1-inch pieces. Rinse with cold water; drain.

Sauté leek, onion, and garlic in hot oil in a large skillet over medium-high heat 5 minutes or until tender. Stir in spinach and artichoke. Add whipping cream and wine; cook over high heat, stirring constantly, 5 minutes or until liquid evaporates. Remove from heat; add cheese, stirring until cheese melts.

Combine crabmeat and remaining 6 ingredients in a large bowl; stir well. Add hot cheese mixture; stir well. Spoon into a lightly greased 1½-quart soufflé dish. Bake at 425° for 20 minutes or until golden. Serve with crackers or thin toasted French baguette slices. Yield: 5 cups.

Susan Mason

From Black Tie to Blackeyed Peas: Savannah's Savory Secrets
St. Joseph's Foundation of Savannah, Inc.
Savannah, Georgia

Tony Caputo's Red Pesto

Dried tomatoes give this pesto its ruby hue and intense tomato flavor. Give it a second life by tossing with hot cooked pasta.

1⅔ cups (3 ounces) dried
   tomatoes
¼ cup grated Parmesan cheese
1 cup loosely packed fresh
   Italian parsley

4 garlic cloves
¾ cup extra-virgin olive oil
Toasted French baguette slices

   Place dried tomatoes in a small bowl; add boiling water to cover, and let stand 5 minutes. Drain and pat dry. Place tomatoes, cheese, parsley, and garlic in food processor bowl. With processor running, slowly pour oil through food chute, processing until smooth. Serve with toasted French baguette slices. Yield: 1⅔ cups.

Always in Season
The Junior League of Salt Lake City, Utah

Roasted Portobello Appetizer

4 medium-size fresh portobello
   mushrooms (about 4 ounces
   each)
½ cup Italian dressing

⅓ cup chopped dried tomatoes
   in oil, drained
1 (3-ounce) package goat
   cheese, crumbled

   Cut stems off mushrooms near caps. Place stems and mushroom caps, stem side down, in an ungreased 15- x 10-inch jellyroll pan lined with aluminum foil. Pour dressing over mushroom stems and caps. Cover and chill 8 hours.

   Bake mushrooms, uncovered, at 400° for 10 minutes. Remove from oven. Turn mushroom caps over. Remove stems from pan, and coarsely chop. Combine chopped stems and tomatoes. Spoon tomato mixture into mushroom caps; sprinkle with goat cheese. Bake 10 more minutes. Serve warm. Yield: 4 appetizers.   Rebecca Lando

The Heart of Pittsburgh
Sacred Heart Elementary School PTG
Pittsburgh, Pennsylvania

Corn and Black Bean Tortilla Cakes

Turn these tortilla cakes into lunch by teaming them with a crisp side salad. The satisfying cakes are brimming with black beans, corn, and 2 cheeses.

1 (15-ounce) can black beans, rinsed and drained
1 cup frozen whole kernel corn, thawed
1 cup finely chopped purple onion
1½ cups (6 ounces) shredded extra-sharp Cheddar cheese
1½ cups (6 ounces) shredded Monterey Jack cheese
12 (6-inch) flour tortillas
1 tablespoon olive oil
¼ teaspoon ground red pepper

Stir together first 3 ingredients in a medium bowl. Combine Cheddar cheese and Monterey Jack cheese in another bowl.

Place 3 tortillas on a large ungreased baking sheet. Top each tortilla with ⅓ cup bean mixture and ⅓ cup cheese mixture. Repeat layers twice to make 3 "stacks," using remaining bean mixture, cheese mixture, and tortillas, ending with a tortilla.

Combine olive oil and pepper in a small bowl; brush over top tortillas. Bake at 450° for 10 minutes or until golden. Cut each stack into 6 wedges. Yield: 6 appetizer servings.   Lynn Weber

Menus & Memories
The University of Oklahoma Women's Association
Norman, Oklahoma

Crostini with Wild Mushroom Ragoût

Excite your taste buds with shiitake mushrooms. These wild mushrooms have a rich and woodsy character and a meaty texture.

½ loaf French baguette, cut into 24 slices
2 tablespoons olive oil
2 garlic cloves, halved
5 ounces fresh shiitake and button mushrooms (shiitake stems removed)
1 tablespoon unsalted butter
2 teaspoons olive oil

1 small onion, chopped
3 garlic cloves, minced
1 tablespoon chopped fresh parsley
1 tablespoon chopped fresh thyme
½ teaspoon salt
¼ teaspoon pepper
½ cup dry white wine

Arrange bread slices on an ungreased baking sheet. Drizzle with 2 tablespoons olive oil. Rub cut sides of 2 garlic cloves over both sides of bread slices.

Bake at 350° for 6 to 8 minutes or until crisp and golden brown. Cool completely on a wire rack.

Cut mushrooms into 2-inch pieces. Melt butter in a large skillet over medium heat. Add 2 teaspoons olive oil, and heat until hot. Add onion, and sauté 2 minutes. Add mushrooms; increase heat to medium-high, and sauté 3 minutes or until mushrooms are tender.

Stir in garlic and next 4 ingredients. Add wine, and cook 3 to 4 minutes or until liquid evaporates. To serve, spoon mushroom mixture evenly onto bread slices. Yield: 24 appetizers.

Sounds Delicious: The Flavor of Atlanta in Food & Music
Atlanta Symphony Orchestra
Atlanta, Georgia

Hot Cheese Puffs

Golden flaky phyllo pastry encases the special feta cheese and mint filling of these puffs. Just one bite and you'll be happy this recipe makes a bunch.

2 large eggs
2 cups (8 ounces) crumbled
   feta cheese
1 (8-ounce) package cream
   cheese, softened
¼ cup chopped fresh parsley

¼ cup chopped green onions
½ teaspoon dried mint
16 sheets frozen phyllo pastry,
   thawed in refrigerator
1 cup butter or margarine,
   melted

Process first 3 ingredients in a blender or food processor until smooth, stopping to scrape down sides. Add parsley, green onions, and mint; blend until smooth. Chill 1 hour.

Place 1 phyllo sheet on a large work surface (keep remaining phyllo covered). Brush phyllo with melted butter. Top with another phyllo sheet, and brush with butter. Cut layered phyllo sheets lengthwise into 6 (2-inch) strips. Place 1 teaspoon cheese filling on 1 short end of each strip.

Working with 1 strip at a time, fold bottom corner over cheese filling, forming a triangle. Continue folding back and forth to end of strip. Lightly brush phyllo triangle with butter to seal. Repeat procedure with remaining phyllo, butter, and cheese filling. Place on ungreased baking sheets. Bake at 375° for 23 minutes or until lightly browned. Serve warm. Yield: 4 dozen.   Donna Goodman

Note: These appetizers can be frozen up to 2 weeks before baking. Store in an airtight container. Thaw overnight in refrigerator in airtight container. Bake as directed above.

Blended Blessings
First Presbyterian Church
Salisbury, North Carolina

Sausage and Cheese Tartlets

Our cheese tarts may be small, but they pack a spicy wallop, thanks to pork sausage, olives, and Ranch-style dressing.

1 pound mild ground pork sausage
1¼ cups (5 ounces) shredded Monterey Jack cheese
1¼ cups (5 ounces) shredded sharp Cheddar cheese
1 (8-ounce) bottle Ranch-style dressing

1 (4¼-ounce) can chopped ripe olives, drained
1 teaspoon ground red pepper
5 (2.1-ounce) packages frozen mini phyllo tart shells, thawed in refrigerator

Cook sausage in a large skillet, stirring until it crumbles and is no longer pink; drain. Combine sausage, cheeses, and next 3 ingredients in a large bowl. Fill each shell with a heaping teaspoon of sausage mixture, and place on ungreased baking sheets. Bake at 350° for 8 to 10 minutes or until cheeses melt. Serve warm. Yield: about 6 dozen.

Creating a Stir
The Fayette County Medical Auxiliary
Lexington, Kentucky

Mustard-Dill Pancakes with Smoked Salmon and Caviar

1 cup all-purpose flour
2 teaspoons baking powder
1 large egg
1¼ cups milk
3 tablespoons Dijon mustard
1 tablespoon mustard seeds
3 tablespoons butter or margarine, melted

2 tablespoons chopped fresh dill
1 pound thinly sliced smoked salmon
½ cup sour cream
1 (4-ounce) jar red or black caviar
Garnish: fresh dill sprigs

Combine flour and baking powder in a large bowl; set aside.

Whisk together egg and next 3 ingredients; add to flour mixture, whisking just until dry ingredients are moistened. Stir in butter and dill. Cover and chill 1 hour.

For each pancake, pour about ½ tablespoon batter onto a hot, lightly greased griddle. Cook pancakes until tops are covered with bubbles and edges look cooked (about 1½ minutes); turn and cook other side. Keep warm. Repeat with remaining batter.

To serve, top each pancake with salmon, sour cream, and caviar. Garnish, if desired. Yield: 52 appetizers.   Wolfle Family

Cookin' with Friends
National Presbyterian School Class of 2000
Washington, D.C.

Profiteroles with Smoked Salmon

½ pound smoked salmon, cut
   into thin strips
½ cup minced purple onion
½ cup sour cream
¼ cup minced fresh dill

½ cup water
3 tablespoons unsalted butter
¾ cup all-purpose flour
¼ teaspoon salt
2 large eggs

Combine first 4 ingredients in a small bowl; stir well. Cover and chill.

Combine water and butter in a medium saucepan; bring to a boil over medium-high heat. Add flour and salt all at once, stirring vigorously until mixture leaves sides of pan and forms a smooth ball. Remove from heat, and cool 3 to 4 minutes. Add eggs, 1 at a time, beating thoroughly with a wooden spoon after each addition; continue beating until dough is smooth.

Drop dough by rounded teaspoonfuls 2 inches apart on an ungreased baking sheet. Bake at 425° for 5 minutes. Reduce oven temperature to 375°, and bake 15 minutes. Remove from baking sheet, and cool on a wire rack.

Cut top off each cream puff; pull out and discard soft dough inside. Fill bottom halves with 2 to 3 tablespoons of filling; cover with top halves. Serve immediately. Yield: 1 dozen.   Barbara Bonney

Cooking with Music: Celebrating the Tastes and Traditions of the Boston Symphony Orchestra
Boston Symphony Association of Volunteers
Boston, Massachusetts

Crab Quesadillas

Quesadillas make great use of imitation crabmeat, but if you want to take them uptown, use the same amount of fresh lump crabmeat.

1 (8-ounce) package imitation crabmeat, chopped
1 (6.5-ounce) package garlic-and-herb soft spreadable cheese, softened (we used Alouette)
1 (4.5-ounce) can chopped green chiles, drained
1 (4¼-ounce) can chopped ripe olives, drained
3 green onions, chopped
12 (8-inch) flour tortillas
2 tablespoons butter or margarine, melted

Combine first 5 ingredients in a large bowl. Spread about ½ cup crabmeat mixture on 6 tortillas. Top with remaining 6 tortillas; place on 2 greased baking sheets. Brush tops of tortillas with melted butter. Bake at 375° for 12 to 14 minutes or until tortillas are lightly browned. Cut each quesadilla into 6 wedges. Serve with salsa and guacamole. Yield: 12 appetizer servings.

Lighthouse Secrets: A Collection of Recipes from the Nation's Oldest City
The Junior Service League of St. Augustine, Florida

Cheesy Crab Tarts

1 tablespoon butter or margarine
¼ cup finely chopped onion
1 (8-ounce) package cream cheese
2 cups (8 ounces) shredded Cheddar cheese
½ pound fresh lump crabmeat, drained
¼ cup chopped fresh parsley
½ teaspoon hot sauce
45 frozen mini phyllo tart shells, thawed in refrigerator

Combine butter and onion in a small microwave-safe bowl. Microwave, uncovered, at HIGH 45 seconds to 1 minute or until onion is tender.

Microwave cream cheese in a microwave-safe dish on HIGH 50 seconds, stirring once after 25 seconds. Combine cream cheese and onion mixture, stirring well. Stir in Cheddar cheese, crabmeat, parsley, and hot sauce.

Spoon crabmeat mixture evenly into phyllo shells. Place on an ungreased baking sheet. Bake at 350° for 15 minutes or until thoroughly heated. Yield: 45 appetizers.

Splendor in the Bluegrass
The Junior League of Louisville, Kentucky

Marinated Shrimp Wrapped in Pea Pods

1½ **cups olive oil**
¼ **cup sherry vinegar**
¼ **cup chopped fresh parsley**
2 **tablespoons chopped fresh rosemary**
2 **tablespoons chopped shallots**
1 **garlic clove, crushed**
2 **teaspoons salt**
½ **teaspoon sugar**

¼ **teaspoon freshly ground pepper**
1½ **tablespoons Dijon mustard**
1 **tablespoon fresh lemon juice**
7½ **cups water**
2½ **pounds unpeeled, medium-size fresh shrimp**
½ **pound fresh snow pea pods**

Combine first 11 ingredients in a large heavy-duty zip-top plastic bag. Seal bag securely, and shake vigorously.

Bring water to a boil; add shrimp, and cook 3 to 5 minutes or just until shrimp turn pink. Drain and rinse with cold water. Chill. Peel shrimp, and devein. Add shrimp to marinade in bag. Seal bag securely; chill 8 hours, turning bag occasionally.

Cook snow peas in boiling water 30 seconds; drain. Plunge into ice water to stop the cooking process; drain.

Drain shrimp, discarding marinade. Wrap 1 snow pea around each shrimp horizontally, and secure with a wooden pick. Yield: about 8 dozen appetizers.

Flavors of the Gardens
Callaway Gardens
Pine Mountain, Georgia

Shrimp with Feta Cheese

Turn the tables on this hearty appetizer by serving generous portions with rice, pasta, or a loaf of crusty bread to create dinner.

1½ pounds large fresh shrimp, peeled and deveined
½ teaspoon salt
¼ teaspoon freshly ground pepper
½ cup olive oil, divided
1 medium onion, chopped
1 bunch green onions, minced
2 garlic cloves, minced
3 tablespoons chopped fresh basil

1 tablespoon dried oregano
4 tomatoes, peeled, seeded, and chopped
½ cup white wine
1 teaspoon sugar
1 teaspoon freshly ground pepper
2 cups (8 ounces) crumbled feta cheese
5 tablespoons chopped fresh Italian parsley

Sprinkle shrimp with salt and ¼ teaspoon pepper. Sauté shrimp in ¼ cup hot oil in a large skillet over medium-high heat 5 minutes or until opaque. Remove shrimp from pan; set aside, and keep warm.

Add remaining ¼ cup oil to skillet. Sauté onion in hot oil over medium heat 5 minutes. Add green onions, garlic, basil, and oregano, and sauté 4 more minutes. Add tomato, wine, and sugar; simmer, uncovered, 8 to 10 minutes or until slightly thickened. Stir in 1 teaspoon pepper.

Divide half of tomato mixture among 8 (4-ounce) ramekins. Place shrimp over tomato mixture in ramekins. Spoon remaining tomato mixture over shrimp. Sprinkle with feta cheese. Bake at 400° for 10 minutes or until cheese melts and shrimp turn pink. Sprinkle with parsley. Yield: 8 servings.   Diane Kondos

Flavor It Greek! A Celebration of Food, Faith and Family
Philoptochos Society of Holy Trinity Greek Orthodox Church
Portland, Oregon

Tropical Crunch Granola

5 cups uncooked regular oats
1 cup flaked coconut
½ cup macadamia nuts,
  chopped
½ cup sunflower kernels
½ cup wheat germ

¼ cup sesame seeds
⅓ cup honey
¼ cup vegetable oil
½ cup chopped dried mango
½ cup raisins

Combine first 6 ingredients in a large bowl. Stir together honey and oil. Add honey mixture to oat mixture, stirring well. Spoon mixture onto 2 ungreased 15- x 10-inch jellyroll pans. Bake at 300° for 35 to 40 minutes or until golden, stirring every 10 minutes. Cool completely in pans on wire racks. Place in a large bowl. Stir in mango and raisins. Store in an airtight container up to 2 weeks, or freeze up to 3 months. Yield: 8 cups.

Flavors of Hawaii
Child and Family Service Guild
Honolulu, Hawaii

Cappuccino

Sweeten this coffee-house specialty to suit your palate.

2 cups strong brewed coffee
2 cups milk
1 tablespoon sugar
1 tablespoon cocoa

2 tablespoons brandy
2 tablespoons crème de cacao
Garnishes: whipped cream,
  cinnamon sticks

Combine first 4 ingredients in a saucepan; bring to a boil over medium-high heat. Remove from heat; stir in brandy and crème de cacao. Serve immediately. Garnish, if desired. Yield: 4½ cups.

Black Tie & Boots Optional
Colleyville Woman's Club
Colleyville, Texas

Frozen Cappuccinos

2 cups ice cubes
1 cup brewed espresso or
   strong brewed coffee, chilled
¼ cup half-and-half
3 tablespoons sugar
¼ cup coffee liqueur
¼ teaspoon ground cinnamon
Ground cinnamon

Process first 6 ingredients in a blender until smooth. Pour into tall serving glasses. Sprinkle with cinnamon. Serve immediately. Yield: 3 cups.

A Sunsational Encore
The Junior League of Greater Orlando, Florida

Tropical Smoothie

Pick ripe banana, mango, and pineapple that are at their peak of sweetness to showcase this thick smoothie.

1 ripe banana, sliced
1 medium mango, cubed
   (about 1 cup)
1 cup cubed fresh pineapple
1 cup unsweetened pineapple
   juice, chilled
½ cup canned light coconut
   milk, chilled
1 teaspoon fresh lime juice

Arrange first 3 ingredients in a single layer on a baking sheet lined with plastic wrap. Place in freezer 30 minutes or until frozen solid.

Process frozen fruit, pineapple juice, coconut milk, and lime juice in a blender until thick and smooth, stopping to scrape down sides. Serve immediately. Yield: 3 cups.   Bea Westin

. . . And It Was Very Good
Temple Emeth
Teaneck, New Jersey

Summer Iced Tea

6 tea bags
4 cups boiling water
1½ cups sugar
10 cups water
1 cup pineapple juice
1 (6-ounce) can frozen lemonade concentrate, thawed and undiluted

1 (6-ounce) can frozen orange juice concentrate, thawed and undiluted
Garnish: fresh mint sprigs

Steep tea bags in boiling water 5 minutes; discard tea bags. Add sugar to tea, and stir until sugar dissolves. Combine steeped tea, water, and next 3 ingredients in a 1-gallon pitcher; stir well. Serve over ice. Garnish, if desired. Yield: 16 cups.

Simple Pleasures: From Our Table to Yours
Arab Mothers' Club
Arab, Alabama

Zahna Juice

Spin this orange juice and fresh fruit combo into a frosty sipper by freezing the fruit before blending.

1 ripe banana, thickly sliced
⅓ cup fresh pineapple chunks
8 fresh strawberries

1 cup orange juice
2 tablespoons honey
Ice cubes

Process first 5 ingredients in a blender until smooth, stopping to scrape down sides. Add ice to 5-cup level; process until smooth. Serve immediately. Yield: 5 cups.   Annie Zahniser

Cooking with Class
Forest Hills Elementary School PTO
Lake Oswego, Oregon

Watermelon Margaritas

If your melon is not at its peak, just add a bit more sugar to sweeten the experience.

3 cups peeled, seeded, and
   cubed watermelon
Lime wedge
Salt
½ cup tequila
¼ cup orange liqueur

1 tablespoon sugar
2 tablespoons lime juice
2 cups ice cubes
Garnishes: fresh lime slices,
   fresh orange slices

Place watermelon in a large heavy-duty zip-top plastic bag; seal bag securely, and freeze 2 hours.

Rub rim of each cocktail glass with lime wedge. Place salt in a saucer; spin rim of each glass in salt. Set prepared glasses aside.

Process frozen watermelon, tequila, and next 3 ingredients in a blender until smooth, stopping to scrape down sides. Add ice, and process until blended. Pour into prepared glasses. Garnish, if desired. Yield: 5 cups.   Andrea M. Siderakis

The Western New York Federal Court Centennial Cookbook
U.S. District Court, Western District of New York
Buffalo, New York

Cranberry Punch

Spike interest in this punch by using 1 liter of vodka instead of the ginger ale.

1 (64-ounce) bottle cranberry
  juice, chilled
1 (2-liter) bottle ginger ale,
  chilled

1 (46-ounce) can pineapple
  juice, chilled
1 (7.5-ounce) container frozen
  lemon juice, thawed

Combine all ingredients in a large punch bowl. Serve immediately. Yield: 23 cups.

Sunnie Raccuglia

Jubilee 2000 Recipe Collection
St. Alphonsus Liguori Parish—Hospitality Committee
Prospect Heights, Illinois

Special Party Punch

No need for a run to the store for superfine sugar to prepare this punch. Simply process the same amount of regular sugar in a food processor until very fine.

2 (25.4-ounce) bottles sauterne,
  chilled
1 (46-ounce) can pineapple
  juice, chilled
¾ cup superfine sugar

½ cup fresh lemon juice,
  chilled
1 (1-liter) bottle club soda,
  chilled

Combine first 4 ingredients in a punch bowl; stir until sugar dissolves. Stir in club soda just before serving. Serve immediately. Yield: 17½ cups.

Vintage Virginia: A History of Good Taste
The Virginia Dietetic Association
Centreville, Virginia

Mocha Cappuccino Punch

We couldn't wait so we sampled this creamy punch before adding the club soda. We prized its mocha magic either way.

2 tablespoons instant coffee granules
¼ teaspoon ground cinnamon
1 cup hot water
1 (14-ounce) can fat-free sweetened condensed milk
½ cup chocolate syrup
4 cups milk or half-and-half
¼ cup coffee liqueur
1 quart coffee ice cream or chocolate ice cream
2 cups club soda, chilled
Garnishes: ground cinnamon, cocoa

Combine coffee granules, cinnamon, and water in a bowl; stir until coffee granules dissolve. Stir in condensed milk and chocolate syrup. Cover and chill.

Combine coffee mixture, milk, and liqueur in a punch bowl; stir well. Scoop ice cream into coffee mixture. Stir in club soda just before serving. Garnish, if desired. Yield: 14 cups.

Picnics, Potlucks & Prizewinners
Indiana 4-H Foundation, Inc.
Indianapolis, Indiana

Breads

Cinnamon Twists, page 91

Sour Cream 'n' Chive Biscuits

Snippets of fresh chives fleck these tender sour cream biscuits with their green goodness.

2 cups all-purpose flour
2 teaspoons baking powder
¼ teaspoon baking soda
¾ teaspoon salt

⅓ cup shortening
¾ cup sour cream
⅓ cup chopped fresh chives
¼ cup milk

Stir together first 4 ingredients in a bowl. Cut shortening into flour mixture with a pastry blender until crumbly. Combine sour cream, chives, and milk. Add sour cream mixture to dry ingredients, stirring until dry ingredients are moistened.

Turn dough out onto a lightly floured surface, and knead 3 or 4 times.

Pat or roll dough to ¾-inch thickness; cut with a 2-inch round cutter, and place on an ungreased baking sheet. Bake at 450° for 9 minutes. Yield: 1 dozen.   Rose Marie Kaminski

Gifts from Our Heart
Mercy Special Learning Center
Allentown, Pennsylvania

Baked Donut Holes

These miniature breakfast bites look like tiny muffins in appearance and texture. Serve them just as soon as they're brushed with melted butter and rolled in cinnamon-sugar.

¼ cup shortening
1 cup sugar
2 large eggs
3 cups all-purpose flour
4 teaspoons baking powder
1 teaspoon salt

1 teaspoon ground nutmeg
1 cup milk
½ cup butter or margarine,
   melted
6 tablespoons sugar
1 tablespoon ground cinnamon

Beat shortening and 1 cup sugar at medium speed with an electric mixer until creamy. Add eggs, and beat well.

Combine flour and next 3 ingredients; add to sugar mixture alternately with milk, beginning and ending with flour mixture. Spoon batter by level tablespoonfuls into lightly greased miniature (1¾-inch) muffin pans.

Bake at 425° for 10 minutes. Remove from pans, and place on wire racks. Brush tops of warm donut holes with melted butter.

Combine 6 tablespoons sugar and cinnamon in a small bowl. Roll tops of warm donut holes in cinnamon mixture. Serve warm. Yield: 3½ dozen.

Specialties of the Haus
TCM International, Inc.
Indianapolis, Indiana

African Butternut Squash Fritters

Enhance these golden-hued squash fritters with a generous dusting of powdered sugar before serving.

1 small butternut squash	2 tablespoons sugar
1½ cups all-purpose flour	1 large egg
1½ teaspoons baking powder	½ cup milk
½ teaspoon salt	Vegetable oil

Prick squash several times with a knife. Microwave at HIGH 2 minutes; slice in half, and remove seeds and pulp. Place squash, cut side down, in a 13- x 9-inch pan. Pour water in pan to a depth of ½ inch. Bake, uncovered, at 400° for 45 minutes or until tender. Drain squash. Scoop out and mash pulp; cool completely. Measure ½ cup pulp, reserving remaining pulp for another use.

Combine flour and next 3 ingredients. Combine squash, egg, and milk in a bowl; add to flour mixture, stirring just until dry ingredients are moistened.

Pour oil to a depth of 2 inches into a large heavy skillet. Heat to 375°. Drop batter in batches by heaping teaspoonfuls into hot oil. Fry 2 to 3 minutes or until golden. Drain. Serve warm. Yield: 20 fritters.

A Thyme to Remember
Dallas County Medical Society Alliance
Dallas, Texas

Applesauce Spice Muffins

Here's a mini-muffin recipe that'll work around your busy schedule. Once you mix the batter, store in the refrigerator in an airtight container up to a week, or bake into muffins immediately.

4 cups all-purpose flour	2 cups sugar
2 teaspoons baking soda	2 large eggs
1 teaspoon salt	2 cups applesauce
1 tablespoon ground cinnamon	1 cup chopped pecans
2 teaspoons ground allspice	¼ cup sifted powdered sugar
½ teaspoon ground cloves	
1 cup butter or margarine, softened	

Stir together first 6 ingredients in a large bowl; make a well in center of mixture.

Beat butter at medium speed with an electric mixer until creamy; gradually add 2 cups sugar, beating well. Add eggs, 1 at a time, beating well after each addition. Stir in applesauce. Add applesauce mixture to dry ingredients, stirring just until moistened. Fold in pecans. Spoon into greased miniature (1¾-inch) muffin pans, filling two-thirds full.

Bake at 350° for 14 to 16 minutes. Remove from pans immediately, and cool on wire racks. Sprinkle with powdered sugar. Yield: 6 dozen.

Black Tie & Boots Optional
Colleyville Woman's Club
Colleyville, Texas

Tex-Mex Muffins

These rustic muffins will accent a mellow bowl of soup or stand up to a hearty, full-bodied stew or gumbo.

1 cup all-purpose flour	1 tablespoon chopped green
2 tablespoons sugar	bell pepper
1 tablespoon baking powder	½ teaspoon caraway seeds
1 teaspoon salt	1 large egg, lightly beaten
1 cup cornmeal	1 cup milk
1¾ cups (7 ounces) shredded	3 tablespoons melted butter or
Cheddar cheese, divided	margarine
1 tablespoon finely chopped	1 large egg, lightly beaten
onion	1 tablespoon whipping cream

Combine first 4 ingredients in a large bowl. Add cornmeal, 1½ cups cheese, and next 3 ingredients; stir well. Make a well in center of mixture.

Stir together 1 egg, milk, and butter; add to dry ingredients, stirring just until moistened. Spoon into greased muffin pans, filling three-fourths full.

Combine remaining ¼ cup cheese, egg, and whipping cream in a small bowl; stir well. Place 1 teaspoon cheese mixture over batter in each cup. Bake at 375° for 16 to 18 minutes. Remove from pans immediately; cool on wire racks. Yield: 16 muffins.

Picnics, Potlucks & Prizewinners
Indiana 4-H Foundation, Inc.
Indianapolis, Indiana

Tex-Mex Waffles

We think these southwestern-inspired cornmeal waffles are perfect for a brunch or lunch. They're stoked with plenty of chopped bell pepper and green onions.

½ small red bell pepper, chopped (½ cup)
½ small green bell pepper, chopped (½ cup)
3 small green onions, chopped (½ cup)
1 teaspoon vegetable oil
1 cup all-purpose flour
1 cup yellow cornmeal
1 tablespoon baking powder

¼ teaspoon salt
3 large eggs
1 (8-ounce) container plain yogurt
½ cup milk
⅓ cup butter or margarine, melted
Melted jalapeño pepper jelly
Shredded Cheddar cheese

Sauté first 3 ingredients in hot oil in a small skillet 5 minutes or until tender. Set aside.

Combine flour and next 3 ingredients. Combine eggs and next 3 ingredients in a bowl; add to flour mixture, stirring just until dry ingredients are moistened. Stir in vegetable mixture.

Spread 1¼ cups batter onto a preheated, oiled waffle iron; spread batter to edges. Bake until lightly browned. Repeat procedure with remaining batter. Serve waffles with pepper jelly and cheese. Yield: 12 (4-inch) waffles.

Settings on the Dock of the Bay
ASSISTANCE LEAGUE® of the Bay Area
Houston, Texas

Apple Coffee Cake

A cinnamon-apple-pecan filling hides in the middle of this tender tube-pan cake.

1 baking apple, peeled and chopped
½ cup chopped pecans
½ cup firmly packed brown sugar
2 teaspoons ground cinnamon
½ cup butter or margarine, softened
1 cup sugar
2 large eggs
2 cups all-purpose flour
1 teaspoon baking powder
1 teaspoon baking soda
½ teaspoon salt
1 (8-ounce) container sour cream
1 teaspoon vanilla extract

Combine first 4 ingredients in a small bowl; set apple mixture aside.

Beat butter at medium speed with an electric mixer until creamy; gradually add 1 cup sugar, beating well. Add eggs, 1 at a time, beating after each addition.

Combine flour, baking powder, soda, and salt; add to butter mixture alternately with sour cream, beginning and ending with flour mixture. Mix at low speed after each addition until blended. Stir in vanilla.

Pour half of batter into a greased 10-inch tube pan. Sprinkle with half of apple mixture. Add remaining batter, and top with remaining apple mixture. Bake at 375° for 30 to 35 minutes or until a wooden pick inserted in center comes out clean. Cool 30 minutes in pan on a wire rack. Remove cake from pan, and cool completely on wire rack. Yield: 1 (10-inch) coffee cake.   Phyllis Crook

Alaska's Best
Alaska Telephone Pioneers
Anchorage, Alaska

Blueberry Bundt Coffee Cake

Moist fresh blueberries dance about this tender sour cream cake while a ribbon of cinnamon, brown sugar, and pecans meanders through the center of each slice.

½ cup butter or margarine, softened
¾ cup sugar
2 large eggs
1 teaspoon vanilla extract
1 (8-ounce) container sour cream
2 cups all-purpose flour
1 teaspoon baking powder
1 teaspoon baking soda

¼ teaspoon salt
1½ cups fresh blueberries
2 tablespoons butter or margarine
½ cup firmly packed brown sugar
2 tablespoons all-purpose flour
1 tablespoon ground cinnamon
½ cup chopped pecans

Beat ½ cup butter at medium speed with an electric mixer until creamy; gradually add ¾ cup sugar, beating well. Add eggs and vanilla, beating until blended. Stir in sour cream.

Combine 2 cups flour, baking powder, soda, and salt; add to butter mixture, and beat at low speed just until blended. Stir in blueberries.

Combine 2 tablespoons butter and next 3 ingredients with a pastry blender until crumbly; stir in pecans. Spread half of batter in a greased 12-cup Bundt pan. Spoon brown sugar mixture evenly over batter. Top with remaining batter. Bake at 350° for 45 to 50 minutes. Cool in pan on a wire rack 5 minutes; invert onto a serving plate. Serve warm. Yield: 1 (10-inch) coffee cake.

A Taste of Washington State
Washington Bed & Breakfast Guild
Seattle, Washington

Marbled Apricot Bread

Dried apricots, golden raisins, and walnuts are swirled with an orange-cream cheese mixture throughout this dense bread.

1 cup dried apricots, chopped
½ cup golden raisins
2 (3-ounce) packages cream cheese, softened
⅓ cup sugar
1 large egg
1 tablespoon grated orange rind
¼ cup butter or margarine, softened

1 cup sugar
½ cup firmly packed light brown sugar
1 large egg
2 cups all-purpose flour
2 teaspoons baking powder
½ teaspoon baking soda
½ teaspoon salt
¾ cup orange juice
½ cup chopped walnuts

Combine apricots and raisins in a medium bowl. Add boiling water to cover. Let stand 15 minutes; drain well, pressing between paper towels to remove excess moisture.

Process cream cheese and next 3 ingredients in a food processor until smooth, stopping to scrape down sides.

Beat butter at medium speed with an electric mixer about 2 minutes or until creamy. Gradually add 1 cup sugar and brown sugar, beating 5 to 7 minutes. Add egg, beating just until yellow disappears.

Combine flour and next 3 ingredients; add to butter mixture alternately with orange juice, beginning and ending with flour mixture. Beat at low speed until blended after each addition. Stir in apricots, raisins, and walnuts.

Divide two-thirds of batter among 4 greased 5¾- x 3¼-inch loaf-pans. Spoon cream cheese mixture evenly over batter in pans; top evenly with remaining one-third of batter. Swirl batter and cream cheese mixture gently with a knife. Bake at 350° for 43 minutes or until a wooden pick inserted in center comes out clean. Cool in pans on wire racks 10 minutes. Remove from pans, and cool completely on wire racks. Store loaves in refrigerator. Yield: 4 loaves.

Café Weller . . . Tastes to Remember
Apple Corps of the Weller Health Education Center
Easton, Pennsylvania

French Honey Bread

This recipe sifts the flour with the spices to help distribute them throughout every bite of this chewy and intensely flavored bread. Slather each slice with honey butter.

3 cups all-purpose flour
1 teaspoon baking soda
¼ teaspoon salt
1 teaspoon ground cinnamon
½ teaspoon ground nutmeg
½ teaspoon ground cloves

¾ cup honey
1 (5-ounce) can evaporated milk
⅓ cup milk
¼ cup firmly packed brown sugar

Combine first 6 ingredients; sift together. Stir together honey, evaporated milk, milk, and brown sugar. Add honey mixture to flour mixture; stir until blended. Pour into a greased and floured 9- x 5-inch loafpan.

Bake at 325° for 1 hour and 15 to 20 minutes or until a wooden pick inserted in center comes out clean. Cool in pan on a wire rack 5 minutes. Remove from pan, and cool completely on wire rack. Store loaf in an airtight container for 24 hours before serving. Yield: 1 loaf.

Joey Grathwol

Tried and True from Riverview
Riverview Hospital Auxiliary
Wisconsin Rapids, Wisconsin

Garlic and Artichoke Bread

1 (6-ounce) jar marinated artichoke hearts, undrained
1 (16-ounce) loaf frozen white bread dough, thawed
1¼ cups freshly grated Parmesan cheese, divided

4 garlic cloves, minced
1½ teaspoons dried basil
1½ teaspoons dried oregano

Drain artichoke hearts, reserving marinade. Coarsely chop artichoke hearts; set aside.

Roll dough into an 18- x 12-inch rectangle on a lightly floured surface. Let stand 5 minutes. Brush 3 tablespoons reserved marinade evenly over dough, leaving a 1-inch margin at sides.

Combine chopped artichoke, 1 cup Parmesan cheese, and remaining 3 ingredients; stir well. Sprinkle evenly over dough, leaving a 1-inch margin at sides.

Roll up dough, jellyroll fashion, starting at long side; pinch seam to seal. Place roll, seam side down, on a large greased baking sheet; shape into a ring, and pinch ends together to seal. Brush ring with remaining reserved marinade.

Cover and let rise in a warm place (85°) free from drafts, 30 minutes or until doubled in bulk. Bake at 375° for 15 minutes; sprinkle with remaining ¼ cup Parmesan cheese. Bake 10 more minutes or until golden. Transfer to a wire rack to cool. Yield: 1 loaf.

A Taste Tour
Gingko Twig of Muhlenberg Hospital, Plainfield, New Jersey
Westfield, New Jersey

Carrot Bread

Here's a wholesome whole wheat bread laced with the goodness of carrot, honey, and molasses. Try this walnut-studded wonder with your favorite soup.

¾ cup water
2¼ cups bread flour
1 cup whole wheat flour
1 tablespoon instant nonfat dry
   milk powder
1½ teaspoons salt

1 cup grated carrot
6 tablespoons honey
2 tablespoons molasses
¼ cup chopped walnuts
1 (¼-ounce) envelope active
   dry yeast

Combine all ingredients in order given in a 2-pound capacity bread machine according to manufacturer's instructions. Select bake cycle; start machine.

Remove bread from pan, and cool completely on a wire rack. Yield: 1 (1½-pound) loaf.

Danielle Mazza

Sesquicentennially Delicious
Western Pennsylvania Hospital
Pittsburgh, Pennsylvania

King Cake

King Cake, as colorful as New Orleans, is a fitting end to any traditional Mardi Gras celebration. Don't forget to insert a tiny plastic baby doll into the cake before frosting. Legend has it the doll brings good luck—and the recipient brings the King Cake to the next year's festivities.

4¾ cups all-purpose flour, divided	¾ cup milk
1 cup sugar, divided	½ cup water
1½ teaspoons salt	2 large eggs
2 (¼-ounce) envelopes rapid-rise yeast	1 tablespoon ground cinnamon
¾ cup butter or margarine, divided	2 cups sifted powdered sugar
	3 tablespoons milk
	Colored Sugars

Combine 1½ cups flour, ¼ cup sugar, salt, and yeast in a large bowl.

Melt ½ cup butter in a small saucepan over low heat. Add ¾ cup milk and water, and heat until hot (120° to 130°). Add milk mixture to flour mixture, and beat at medium speed with an electric mixer 2 minutes. Add eggs, beating well. Stir in remaining 3¼ cups flour. Turn dough out onto a well-floured surface, and knead until smooth and elastic (about 10 minutes). Place in a well-greased bowl, turning to grease top.

Cover and let rise in a warm place (85°), free from drafts, 45 minutes or until doubled in bulk.

Stir together remaining ¾ cup sugar and cinnamon.

Punch dough down, and divide into 3 portions. Roll each portion into a 28- x 4-inch rectangle. Melt remaining ¼ cup butter; brush evenly over rectangles. Sprinkle each rectangle with ¼ cup sugar mixture.

Roll up each rectangle, jellyroll fashion, beginning with long side, making long ropes; braid ropes. Place braid on a greased baking sheet; shape braid into an oval. Pinch loose ends to seal.

Cover and let rise in a warm place (85°), free from drafts, 15 minutes or until doubled in bulk.

Bake at 375° for 18 to 20 minutes or until golden. Transfer to a wire rack to cool completely.

Combine powdered sugar and 3 tablespoons milk in a small bowl, stirring until smooth. Drizzle over cake, and sprinkle with Colored Sugars. Yield: 1 cake.

Colored Sugars

1½ cups sugar, divided
8 drops each green, yellow,
   and blue liquid food coloring

16 drops red liquid food
   coloring

Combine ½ cup sugar and 8 drops of green food coloring in a plastic bag. Shake vigorously to evenly mix sugar with coloring. Combine ½ cup sugar with 8 drops of yellow food coloring, and follow same procedure. Combine remaining ½ cup sugar, 8 drops of blue food coloring, and 16 drops of red food coloring to make purple sugar following same procedure. Yield: ½ cup each of green, yellow, and purple sugars.   Murline Jackson Murray

Note: To make King Cake ahead, follow directions through stirring in all flour. (Do not knead dough.) Cover and chill 24 hours. Punch dough down, and proceed as directed. (The braided oval will take longer to double in bulk.)

Atchafalaya Legacy
Melville Woman's Club
Melville, Louisiana

Norwegian Christmas Bread

The predominant flavor of this traditional holiday bread comes from cardamom. Whole cardamom is much more fragrant than ground cardamom, but if the whole form isn't available, you can use 1 to 2 teaspoons ground cardamom.

Whole cardamom pods
1 (¼-ounce) envelope active dry yeast
¼ cup warm water (100° to 110°)
9 to 9¼ cups all-purpose flour, divided
1 cup sugar
2 cups milk
1 cup butter or margarine, melted

1 teaspoon salt
3 large eggs, beaten
1½ cups golden raisins
½ cup chopped red or green candied cherries
½ cup chopped red or green candied pineapple
½ cup coarsely chopped pecans

Place whole cardamom pods in a mortar; use a pestle to crack pods open. Discard pod fragments from the brown or black seeds, and crush seeds with pestle to equal 2 teaspoons. Set seeds aside.

Combine yeast and warm water in a 1-cup glass measuring cup; let stand 5 minutes.

Combine yeast mixture, 2 cups flour, and next 4 ingredients in a large mixing bowl; beat at medium speed with an electric mixer 2 minutes. Beat in cardamom and eggs. Stir in fruit and pecans. Gradually stir in enough of remaining 7¼ cups flour to make a soft dough.

Turn dough out onto a well-floured surface, and knead until smooth and elastic (about 10 minutes). Place in a well-greased bowl, turning to grease top.

Cover and let rise in a warm place (85°), free from drafts, 1 hour and 15 minutes or until doubled in bulk.

Punch dough down, and divide in half; roll 1 portion of dough into a 14- x 7-inch rectangle. Roll up dough, starting at short end, pressing firmly to eliminate air pockets; pinch ends to seal. Place dough, seam side down, in a well-greased 9- x 5-inch loafpan. Repeat procedure with remaining portion of dough.

Cover and let rise in a warm place, free from drafts, 25 minutes or until doubled in bulk.

Bake at 350° for 30 minutes. Shield loaves with aluminum foil to prevent excessive browning. Bake 20 more minutes or until loaves sound hollow when tapped. Remove bread from pans immediately; cool on wire racks. Yield: 2 loaves. Betty Hilliard

Keittokirja: Kaleva Centennial Cookbook
Project Kaleva/Kaleva Historical Society
Kaleva, Michigan

Rapid Italian Herb Bread

1½ cups water (115° to 125°)
2 tablespoons shortening
3 tablespoons sugar
1½ teaspoons salt
4 cups bread flour
3 tablespoons instant nonfat
   dry milk powder

1½ teaspoons dried marjoram
1½ teaspoons dried basil
1½ teaspoons dried thyme
2 teaspoons rapid-rise yeast

Combine all ingredients in order given in a 2-pound capacity bread machine according to manufacturer's instructions. Select rapid bake cycle; start machine.

Remove bread from pan, and cool completely on a wire rack. Yield: 1 (2-pound) loaf. Aleja Estronza

Deborah Heart and Lung Center
75th Anniversary National Cookbook
Deborah Hospital Foundation
Browns Mills, New Jersey

Authentic Italian Figassa

Use this bread as the gourmet base for your next homemade pizza. It resembles focaccia in appearance and texture.

3½ cups all-purpose flour, divided

1 teaspoon salt

1 (¼-ounce) envelope active dry yeast

1½ cups warm water (100° to 110°)

2 tablespoons olive oil

2 teaspoons kosher salt

Combine 1½ cups flour, 1 teaspoon salt, and yeast in a large bowl. Add water, stirring until combined (dough will be very sticky). Gradually stir in remaining 2 cups flour to make a soft dough.

Turn dough out onto a floured surface, and knead until smooth and elastic (about 4 minutes), adding more flour, if necessary. Place in a well-greased bowl, turning to grease top.

Cover and let rise in a warm place (85°), free from drafts, 40 minutes or until doubled in bulk.

Punch dough down, and place in a lightly greased 16½- x 12-inch sheet pan (see Note). Press dough evenly to fit pan. Using fingertips, make indentations all over dough; brush evenly with olive oil, and sprinkle evenly with kosher salt.

Cover loosely, and let rise in a warm place, free from drafts, 40 minutes or until doubled in bulk.

Bake at 375° for 25 to 30 minutes or until golden. Cut or tear into squares. Yield: 1 loaf.   Caterina deLandro and Madeline Doll

Variation: Just before baking, sprinkle 3 cups chopped green onions over dough.

Note: We tested with a 16½- x 12-inch sheet pan to create a crisp crust. If you don't have this pan, prepare it in a 15- x 10-inch jellyroll pan, and it will be just a little bit thicker.

Sharing Our Best
Bull Run Parent Teacher Club
Sandy, Oregon

Cinnamon Twists

C'mon baby, and do the twist with these two-toned treats. They're sure to please the young and young-at-heart with their cinnamon and brown sugar sweetness.

1 (¼-ounce) envelope active dry yeast
¾ cup warm water (100° to 110°), divided
½ cup warm milk (100° to 110°)
4 to 4½ cups all-purpose flour, divided
¼ cup sugar

1½ teaspoons salt
¼ cup butter or margarine, softened
1 large egg
¼ cup butter or margarine, melted
½ cup firmly packed light brown sugar
4 teaspoons ground cinnamon

Combine yeast and ¼ cup warm water in a 1-cup glass measuring cup; let stand 5 minutes.

Combine yeast mixture, remaining ½ cup warm water, milk, 2 cups flour, and next 4 ingredients; beat at medium speed with an electric mixer until well blended. Gradually stir in enough of remaining 2½ cups flour to make a soft dough.

Turn dough out onto a well-floured surface, and knead until smooth and elastic (6 to 8 minutes). Place in a well-greased bowl, turning to grease top.

Cover and let rise in a warm place (85°), free from drafts, 1 hour or until doubled in bulk. Punch dough down. Roll dough into a 16- x 12-inch rectangle. Brush with melted butter.

Combine brown sugar and cinnamon; sprinkle over rectangle. Let dough rest 6 minutes. Cut lengthwise into 3 (16- x 4-inch) strips. Cut each strip crosswise into 16 (4- x 1-inch) pieces. Twist each piece, and place on greased baking sheets.

Cover and let rise in a warm place, free from drafts, 30 minutes or until doubled in bulk.

Bake at 350° for 13 to 15 minutes or until golden. Serve warm. Yield: 4 dozen.

Regina Charlton

Alaska's Best
Alaska Telephone Pioneers
Anchorage, Alaska

Spicy Hot Cross Buns

Hot cross buns are traditionally served on Good Friday, but you'll want to serve these slightly sweet buns year-round. The "spicy" in the title comes from five different spices stirred into the yeast mixture.

2 (¼-ounce) envelopes active dry yeast
½ cup warm water (100° to 110°)
6 to 7 cups all-purpose flour, divided
1 cup warm mashed potatoes (100° to 110°)
½ cup milk
½ cup butter, melted and cooled
⅓ cup sugar
⅓ cup firmly packed brown sugar
2 large eggs
1 teaspoon salt
2 teaspoons ground cinnamon

1 teaspoon ground allspice
1 teaspoon ground nutmeg
¼ teaspoon ground cloves
¼ teaspoon ground mace (optional)
1 cup raisins
3 tablespoons warm water
3 tablespoons rum
½ cup candied citron, minced
½ cup milk
⅓ cup sugar
3 tablespoons butter, softened
1 tablespoon milk
2 tablespoons fresh lemon juice
3 cups sifted powdered sugar

Combine yeast and ½ cup warm water in a 1-cup glass measuring cup; let stand 5 minutes.

Process yeast mixture, 1½ cups flour, potato, next 10 ingredients, and mace, if desired, in a food processor until blended. Transfer dough to a large bowl; cover and let stand 30 minutes.

Meanwhile, combine raisins, 3 tablespoons warm water, and rum in a small bowl; let stand 30 minutes.

Add raisin mixture, citron, and enough of remaining 5½ cups flour to make a soft dough, beating at medium speed with an electric mixer. Place dough in a well-greased bowl, turning to grease top. Cover and let rise in a warm place (85°), free from drafts, 1 hour or until dough is doubled in bulk.

Punch dough down, and divide into 20 portions; roll each portion into a ball. Place 1 inch apart on a greased baking sheet.

Cover and let rise in a warm place, free from drafts, 30 to 40 minutes or until doubled in bulk. Bake at 350° for 18 minutes or until golden.

Combine ½ cup milk and ⅓ cup sugar in a saucepan; bring to a boil, and boil, stirring constantly, until reduced to ¼ cup. Brush buns immediately with glaze. Brush again in 2 minutes. Cool completely.

Combine 3 tablespoons butter, 1 tablespoon milk, and lemon juice in a small bowl; stir well. Gradually add powdered sugar, stirring after each addition until smooth. Spoon frosting into a pastry bag fitted with a #4 round plain tip. Pipe frosting onto each bun in form of a cross. Yield: 20 buns.   Dottie Dueltgen

Recipes from the Kitchens of Family & Friends
Gresham Women of Elks
Gresham, Oregon

Herb Cheddar Rolls

2 (¼-ounce) envelopes active
   dry yeast
¾ cup warm water (100° to 110°)
¾ cup warm milk (100° to 110°)
¼ cup vegetable oil
¼ cup sugar
1 tablespoon salt

4 to 4½ cups all-purpose flour
¼ cup grated Romano cheese
3 tablespoons (¾ ounce)
   shredded sharp Cheddar
   cheese
1½ tablespoons dried Italian
   seasoning

Combine yeast and warm water in a 2-cup glass measuring cup; let stand 5 minutes.

Combine yeast mixture, milk, oil, sugar, salt, and 2 cups flour in a large mixing bowl; beat at medium speed with an electric mixer until well blended. Gradually stir in enough of remaining 2½ cups flour to make a soft dough. Place in a well-greased bowl, turning to grease top.

Cover and let rise in a warm place (85°), free from drafts, 45 minutes or until doubled in bulk.

Punch dough down; turn out onto a lightly floured surface, and knead until smooth and elastic (about 3 minutes). Roll dough into a 12- x 8-inch rectangle; sprinkle with cheeses and Italian seasoning. Roll up dough, jellyroll fashion, starting at short side. Slice dough into ¾-inch slices; place slices, cut side down, in a lightly greased 13- x 9-inch pan. Cover and let rise in a warm place, free from drafts, 40 minutes or until doubled in bulk.

Bake at 400° for 18 to 20 minutes or until lightly browned. Cool slightly in pan on a wire rack. Serve warm. Yield: 15 rolls.

Splendor in the Bluegrass
The Junior League of Louisville, Kentucky

Ballpark Soft Pretzels

Serve these golden pretzels warm with a spicy mustard for dipping. If you crave a sweet version, bake them without egg or salt, and after they've cooled, lightly brush them with butter and generously sprinkle with cinnamon-sugar.

1 (¼-ounce) envelope active dry yeast	1 tablespoon sugar
1½ cups warm water (100° to 110°)	1 teaspoon salt
	1 large egg, lightly beaten
4 cups all-purpose flour	Coarse salt (we tested with kosher)

Combine yeast and warm water in a 2-cup glass measuring cup; let stand 5 minutes.

Combine yeast mixture, flour, sugar, and 1 teaspoon salt in a large bowl, stirring until a soft dough forms.

Turn dough out onto a floured surface, and knead until smooth and elastic (5 to 7 minutes).

Divide dough into 12 equal portions. Roll each portion into a 20-inch-long rope. Twist each rope into a pretzel shape. Place about 1½ inches apart on a lightly greased baking sheet. Brush dough with egg; sprinkle with coarse salt. Cover loosely, and let rise in a warm place (85°), free from drafts, 40 minutes or until doubled in bulk. Bake at 425° for 12 minutes or until lightly browned. Serve warm, or cool on wire racks. Yield: 1 dozen.

A Thyme to Remember
Dallas County Medical Society Alliance
Dallas, Texas

Cakes

Peach Melba Shortcakes, page 119

Aunt Lillian's Crumb Cake

Toasted flakes of coconut, bits of walnuts, and spicy cinnamon adorn each slice of this buttery sour cream cake. Brew a pot of strong coffee or tea to accompany each satisfying bite.

½ cup butter or margarine, softened
1½ cups sugar, divided
2 large eggs
1 (8-ounce) container sour cream
1 teaspoon vanilla extract

1½ cups all-purpose flour
1 teaspoon baking soda
¼ teaspoon salt
¼ cup chopped walnuts
2 tablespoons flaked coconut
2 teaspoons ground cinnamon

Beat butter at medium speed with an electric mixer until creamy. Gradually add 1 cup sugar, beating well. Add eggs, 1 at a time, beating until blended after each addition. Add sour cream and vanilla; beat well.

Combine flour, soda, and salt in a medium bowl; add to butter mixture, and beat until blended. Spread half of batter in a greased 8-inch square pan (batter will be thick).

Combine remaining ½ cup sugar, walnuts, coconut, and cinnamon in a small bowl. Sprinkle half of sugar mixture over batter; spread with remaining batter, and sprinkle with remaining sugar mixture. Swirl sugar mixture and batter gently with a knife.

Bake at 350° for 30 to 35 minutes. Serve warm, or cool completely in pan on a wire rack. Yield: 9 servings.   Pam Kasper

Wildcat Valley: Recipes & Remembrances
Keats Lions Club
Manhattan, Kansas

Blake's Chocolate Cake

1 (18.25-ounce) package German chocolate cake mix (we tested with Pillsbury Moist Supreme)
3 large eggs
1¼ cups water
⅓ cup vegetable oil

1 cup (6 ounces) semisweet chocolate morsels
1 (14-ounce) can sweetened condensed milk
⅓ cup caramel topping
1 (12-ounce) container frozen whipped topping, thawed

Prepare cake mix according to package directions, using eggs, water, and oil. Pour batter into a greased 13- x 9-inch pan.

Bake at 350° for 10 minutes. Sprinkle with chocolate morsels. Bake 20 more minutes or until a wooden pick inserted in center comes out clean.

Remove cake from oven; poke holes in cake with handle of a wooden spoon. Pour sweetened condensed milk evenly over cake. Cool completely in pan on a wire rack. Drizzle with caramel topping. Dollop with whipped topping before serving. Store in refrigerator. Yield: 15 servings.   Blake Selzler

Cooking with Class
Timber Lake Booster Club
Timber Lake, South Dakota

Quick Cinnamon Cake

Greet your kids with an after-school treat. They'll welcome the familiar cinnamon scent of this simple snack cake. Serve each slice with a glass of cold milk. Add variety by adding ½ cup of chopped pecans to the batter.

⅓ cup shortening
1 cup sugar
2 large eggs
2 cups all-purpose flour
2 teaspoons baking powder
1 teaspoon salt

¾ cup milk
1 teaspoon vanilla extract
½ cup butter or margarine, melted
3 tablespoons sugar
1 tablespoon ground cinnamon

Beat shortening and 1 cup sugar at medium speed with an electric mixer until fluffy. Add eggs, 1 at a time, beating after each addition.

Combine flour, baking powder, and salt; add to shortening mixture alternately with milk and vanilla, beginning and ending with flour mixture. Pour batter into a greased 13- x 9-inch pan. Pour melted butter over batter.

Combine 3 tablespoons sugar and cinnamon; sprinkle over batter.

Bake at 375° for 28 to 30 minutes or until a wooden pick inserted in center of cake comes out clean. Cool in pan on a wire rack. Yield: 15 servings.

Lighthouse Secrets: A Collection of Recipes from the Nation's Oldest City
The Junior Service League of St. Augustine, Florida

Pumpkin Pie Cake

Herald the harvest with this easy-to-make pumpkin cake. It boasts a yellow cake base, pumpkin pie filling, and cinnamon crumb topping.

1 (18.25-ounce) package yellow cake mix (we tested with Duncan Hines)
½ cup butter, softened
1 large egg
1 (30-ounce) can pumpkin
1 cup sugar

3 large eggs
⅔ cup evaporated milk
2 teaspoons ground cinnamon
1 cup chopped pecans
½ cup sugar
¼ cup butter or margarine, melted

Reserve 1 cup cake mix; set aside. Combine remaining cake mix, ½ cup butter, and 1 egg; beat at medium speed with an electric mixer until a soft dough forms. Press mixture in a greased and floured 13- x 9-inch pan.

Stir together pumpkin and next 4 ingredients, and pour over dough in pan.

Combine reserved cake mix, pecans, ½ cup sugar, and melted butter in a small bowl, stirring until crumbly. Sprinkle pecan mixture over pumpkin mixture.

Bake at 350° for 1 hour and 15 minutes (center of cake will not be completely set). Cool cake completely in pan on a wire rack. Yield: 15 servings.
John D. Kossman

Sharing Our Best
The Arrangement Hair Salon
Columbus, Ohio

Double Lemon Cake

Pucker up for this lemony delight. Fresh lemon juice, lemon rind, and a citrusy splash of lemon extract will draw compliments.

¾ cup sugar
1 tablespoon grated lemon rind
¾ cup unsalted butter or
   margarine, softened
3 large eggs
1½ cups sifted cake flour

1 teaspoon baking powder
Pinch of salt
1 teaspoon lemon extract
⅔ cup sifted powdered sugar
⅓ cup fresh lemon juice
Lemon Frosting

Process ¾ cup sugar and lemon rind in a food processor until rind is almost as fine as sugar. Beat butter at medium speed with an electric mixer until creamy. Gradually add sugar mixture, beating well. Add eggs, 1 at a time, beating after each addition.

Combine flour, baking powder, and salt. Add to butter mixture, beating well (batter will be thick). Stir in lemon extract. Spoon batter into a greased and floured 8-inch springform pan.

Bake at 350° for 23 to 25 minutes or until a wooden pick inserted in center comes out clean. Whisk together powdered sugar and lemon juice in a small bowl. Brush glaze over warm cake. Cool in pan on a wire rack 10 minutes. Remove sides of springform pan, and cool completely. Spread Lemon Frosting over cake. Yield: 1 (8-inch) cake.

Lemon Frosting

1½ cups sifted powdered sugar
1½ tablespoons unsalted butter
   or margarine, softened
Pinch of salt

2 teaspoons grated lemon rind
2 tablespoons fresh lemon
   juice

Combine all ingredients in a small mixing bowl; beat at low speed with an electric mixer until smooth. Yield: ½ cup.

A Thyme to Remember
Dallas County Medical Society Alliance
Dallas, Texas

Souffléed Truffle Cake

4 (4-ounce) semisweet
   chocolate bars (we tested
   with Ghirardelli)
½ cup unsalted butter
4 egg yolks, lightly beaten
2 tablespoons brandy
1 tablespoon all-purpose flour
4 egg whites

⅛ teaspoon cream of tartar
⅛ teaspoon salt
1 cup heavy whipping cream
4 egg yolks
⅓ cup sugar
2 tablespoons brandy
Powdered sugar (optional)

Grease and flour an 8-inch springform pan; set aside.

Combine chocolate and butter in a heavy saucepan over low heat. Cook until chocolate and butter melt, stirring often. Remove from heat, and let stand 5 to 10 minutes.

Combine about 1 cup chocolate mixture, 4 egg yolks, 2 tablespoons brandy, and flour; stir well. Add to remaining chocolate mixture, stirring well.

Beat egg whites, cream of tartar, and salt at high speed with an electric mixer until stiff peaks form.

Stir about one-third of beaten egg white into chocolate mixture. Gently fold remaining egg white into batter. Spoon batter into prepared pan.

Bake at 425° for 20 minutes (center will not test done). Cool in pan on a wire rack. Cover and chill at least 8 hours.

Whisk together whipping cream, 4 egg yolks, and ⅓ cup sugar in a small saucepan. Cook over medium-low heat, stirring constantly with a wooden spoon, 8 to 10 minutes or until thickened and mixture coats back of spoon. (Do not boil.) Remove from heat; pour through a wire mesh strainer into a bowl. Stir in 2 tablespoons brandy.

Carefully remove sides of springform pan. Lightly sprinkle top of cake with powdered sugar, if desired. Cut cake into wedges, and serve with warm brandy sauce. Yield: 1 (8-inch) cake.

Art Fare: A Commemorative Celebration of Art & Food
The Toledo Museum of Art Aides
Toledo, Ohio

Blueberry-Lemon Cake

1 (18.25-ounce) package lemon
   cake mix (we tested with
   Betty Crocker Super Moist)
½ cup fresh orange juice
½ cup water
⅓ cup vegetable oil
3 large eggs
1½ cups fresh blueberries
1 tablespoon grated orange
   rind
1 tablespoon grated lemon rind
Citrus Cream Cheese Frosting

Combine first 5 ingredients in a mixing bowl; beat at medium speed with an electric mixer 2 minutes. Fold in blueberries, orange rind, and lemon rind. Pour batter into 2 greased and floured 8-inch round cakepans.

Bake at 350° for 30 minutes or until a wooden pick inserted in center comes out clean. Cool in pans on wire racks 10 minutes; remove from pans, and cool on wire racks.

Spread Citrus Cream Cheese Frosting between layers and on top and sides of cake. Store cake in refrigerator. Yield: 1 (2-layer) cake.

Citrus Cream Cheese Frosting

¼ cup butter, softened
1 (3-ounce) package cream
   cheese, softened
1 tablespoon fresh orange juice
¼ teaspoon vanilla extract
3½ cups sifted powdered
   sugar, divided
½ cup whipping cream
2 tablespoons grated orange
   rind
1 tablespoon grated lemon rind

Beat butter and cream cheese at medium speed with an electric mixer until creamy. Add orange juice and vanilla; beat until blended. Gradually add 2 cups powdered sugar, beating at low speed until fluffy.

Beat whipping cream at medium speed until foamy. Gradually add remaining 1½ cups powdered sugar, beating until soft peaks form. Stir in orange rind and lemon rind. Add to butter mixture, and beat at low speed until blended. Yield: 3¾ cups.

Splendor in the Bluegrass
The Junior League of Louisville, Kentucky

Lemon Platinum Cake

8 large eggs
1 teaspoon cream of tartar
½ teaspoon salt
1 cup sugar
1 cup all-purpose flour

2 teaspoons grated lemon rind
⅓ cup fresh lemon juice
Filling
2 cups whipping cream

Separate 8 eggs, discarding 1 egg yolk. Set remaining 7 egg yolks aside.

Beat 8 egg whites, cream of tartar, and salt in a large mixing bowl at high speed with an electric mixer until foamy. Add sugar, 1 tablespoon at a time, beating until stiff peaks form and sugar dissolves (2 to 4 minutes). Set aside.

Beat reserved 7 egg yolks at high speed 1 minute. Add flour, lemon rind, and lemon juice; beat 1 minute or until thick and pale. Fold into beaten egg white. Pour batter into an ungreased 10-inch tube pan, spreading evenly in pan. Bake at 325° for 40 to 45 minutes or until cake springs back when lightly touched. Invert tube pan; cool cake 1 hour and 15 minutes. Gently loosen cake from sides of pan, using a narrow metal spatula; remove cake from pan.

Reserve ½ cup filling; set aside. Slice cake horizontally into 3 layers. Spread remaining filling between layers of cake. Beat whipping cream until soft peaks form. Fold ½ cup whipped cream into reserved filling. Fold mixture into remaining whipped cream. Spread on top and sides of cake. Store cake in refrigerator up to 1 week. Yield: 1 (10-inch) cake.   Colville-Hemsley Family

Filling

1 cup sugar
¼ cup cornstarch
⅛ teaspoon salt
1¼ cups water
2 egg yolks

1 tablespoon butter
2 teaspoons grated lemon rind
3 tablespoons fresh lemon
   juice

Combine sugar, cornstarch, and salt in a small saucepan. Gradually stir in water. Cook over medium heat, stirring constantly, until mixture comes to a boil and thickens. Remove from heat.

Beat egg yolks until thick and pale. Gradually stir about one-fourth of hot mixture into yolks; add yolk mixture to remaining hot mixture, stirring constantly. Stir in butter, lemon rind, and lemon juice. Cover and chill filling 1 hour. Yield: 2 cups.

Cookin' with Friends
National Presbyterian School Class of 2000
Washington, D.C.

Chocolate Carrot Cake

¾ cup chopped pecans
1½ cups butter, melted
4 large eggs
1 tablespoon vanilla extract
2 cups all-purpose flour
2 cups sugar
½ cup cocoa

1 teaspoon baking powder
1 teaspoon baking soda
¼ teaspoon salt
2 cups shredded carrot
1 cup crushed pineapple, undrained
Frosting

Bake pecans in a shallow pan at 350°, stirring occasionally, 5 minutes or until toasted. Set aside.

Beat butter, eggs, and vanilla at medium speed with an electric mixer until blended. Combine flour and next 5 ingredients. Add to egg mixture; beat well. Stir in carrot and pineapple. Pour into 3 (9-inch) greased and floured cakepans. Bake at 350° for 35 minutes. Cool in pans on wire racks 10 minutes; remove from pans. Cool on racks. Spread frosting between layers and on top and sides of cake. Sprinkle with pecans. Store cake in refrigerator. Yield: 1 (3-layer) cake.

Frosting

2 (8-ounce) packages cream
   cheese, softened
½ cup butter, softened
3 cups sifted powdered sugar

1 cup flaked coconut
2 teaspoons lemon juice
2 teaspoons vanilla extract

Beat cream cheese and butter at medium speed with an electric mixer until creamy. Gradually add sugar and remaining ingredients, beating well. Yield: 4 cups.   Pat Miller

Blest Recipes
Our Redeemer Lutheran Church
Chugiak, Alaska

The Best Marble Cake

Slather this swirled two-toned cake with your own chocolate buttercream frosting to make it even more delicious.

1 cup shortening	½ teaspoon salt
3 cups sugar	1 cup buttermilk
6 large eggs	1 teaspoon vanilla extract
3 cups sifted cake flour	1 (5.5-ounce) can chocolate
½ teaspoon baking soda	syrup

Beat shortening at medium speed with an electric mixer about 2 minutes or until fluffy. Gradually add sugar, beating 5 to 7 minutes. Add eggs, 1 at a time, beating just until yellow disappears.

Combine flour, soda, and salt; add to shortening mixture alternately with buttermilk, beginning and ending with flour mixture. Beat at low speed just until blended after each addition. Stir in vanilla. Pour half of batter into a greased and floured 10-inch tube pan. Add chocolate syrup to remaining half of batter. Spoon chocolate batter over plain batter. Swirl batter gently with a knife.

Bake at 350° for 1 hour or until a long wooden pick inserted in center of cake comes out clean. Cool in pan on a wire rack 10 to 15 minutes; remove from pan, and cool completely on wire rack. Yield: 1 (10-inch) cake.   Anita Chadwell

Sharing Recipes from Green Road Baptist Church
Green Road Baptist Church
Green Road, Kentucky

Chocolate Fudge Cake

Chocolate morsels abound in a cream cheese mixture nestled between layers of dark chocolate cake.

3 cups all-purpose flour
2¼ cups sugar
½ cup cocoa
1 cup buttermilk
1 cup hot water or coffee
1 cup vegetable oil
2 large eggs
1 teaspoon vanilla extract
¼ teaspoon salt
½ cup chopped pecans
   (optional)

1 (8-ounce) package cream
   cheese, softened
1 large egg
¼ cup sugar
1 cup (6 ounces) semisweet
   chocolate morsels
1 teaspoon vanilla extract
Glaze

Combine first 9 ingredients in a large mixing bowl; beat at medium speed with an electric mixer until blended. Stir in pecans, if desired.

Beat cream cheese and egg at medium speed until creamy; gradually add ¼ cup sugar, beating well. Stir in chocolate morsels and 1 teaspoon vanilla.

Pour half of batter into a greased and floured 10-inch tube pan. Spoon cream cheese mixture evenly over batter. Pour remaining batter over cream cheese mixture.

Bake at 350° for 60 to 65 minutes or until a long wooden pick inserted in center comes out clean. Cool in pan on a wire rack 15 minutes; remove from pan, and cool completely on wire rack. Drizzle glaze over cake. Yield: 1 (10-inch) cake.

Glaze

1 cup sifted powdered sugar
2 tablespoons cocoa
2 tablespoons butter, melted

2 tablespoons milk
1 teaspoon vanilla extract

Combine all ingredients in a small bowl; stir with a wire whisk until smooth. Yield: ½ cup.   Mary Clark

Feeding the Flock
St. Philips Episcopal Church
Topeka, Kansas

Butterscotch-Pumpkin Cake

Bake this cake when leaves are falling and there's a nip in the air. Butterscotch morsels, cinnamon, nutmeg, and pumpkin reflect the flavors of the season.

1 cup (6 ounces) butterscotch morsels
2 cups all-purpose flour
1¾ cups sugar
1 tablespoon baking powder
1 teaspoon salt
1½ teaspoons ground cinnamon
½ teaspoon ground nutmeg
1 cup canned mashed pumpkin
½ cup vegetable oil
3 large eggs
1 teaspoon vanilla extract
Powdered sugar

Microwave morsels in a small glass bowl on HIGH 30 to 60 seconds or until melted, stirring once. Cool.

Combine flour and next 5 ingredients in a medium bowl. Stir together melted morsels, pumpkin, and next 3 ingredients in a large bowl. Add flour mixture, stirring until well blended. Pour batter into a greased 12-cup Bundt pan.

Bake at 350° for 35 to 37 minutes or until a long wooden pick inserted in center comes out clean. Cool in pan on a wire rack 15 minutes; remove from pan, and cool completely on wire rack. Sprinkle with powdered sugar. Yield: 1 (10-inch) cake.   Jeanette Campbell

Wildcat Valley: Recipes & Remembrances
Keats Lions Club
Manhattan, Kansas

Harvey Wallbanger Cake

We don't know if there's a gentleman named Harvey Wallbanger, but we do know that the moniker refers to a sweet cocktail made of Galliano (anise liqueur), vodka, and orange juice.

4 large eggs
¾ cup vegetable oil
1 (18.25-ounce) package yellow cake mix (we tested with Duncan Hines)
1 (3.4-ounce) package French vanilla instant pudding mix
1 cup Galliano
¼ cup vodka
¼ cup orange juice
1½ cups sifted powdered sugar
2 teaspoons Galliano
2 teaspoons vodka
2 to 2½ teaspoons orange juice

Combine first 7 ingredients in a large mixing bowl; beat at medium speed with an electric mixer 2 minutes. Pour batter into a greased and floured 12-cup Bundt pan.

Bake at 350° for 45 minutes or until a long wooden pick inserted in center comes out clean. Cool in pan on a wire rack 10 minutes; remove cake from pan, and place on wire rack.

Stir together powdered sugar, 2 teaspoons Galliano, 2 teaspoons vodka, and enough orange juice to make a good drizzling consistency. Drizzle glaze over warm cake. Cool completely on wire rack. Cover and let stand overnight. Yield: 1 (10-inch) cake.   Joyce Stephens

202's Totally Tempting Treasures
American Legion Auxiliary Green-Pierce Unit 202
Wichita Falls, Texas

Apricot-Pecan Pound Cake

Apricot baby food and sour cream make this cake tender and terrific. It's a stand-alone winner, but add the Butterscotch Icing if you're looking for a different type of topper.

1 cup butter, softened
3 cups sugar
1 (6-ounce) jar apricot baby food
6 large eggs, separated
3 cups all-purpose flour
½ teaspoon baking soda
½ teaspoon salt
1 (8-ounce) container sour cream
1 cup chopped pecans
1½ teaspoons all-purpose flour
2 teaspoons maple flavoring or dry sherry
1 teaspoon lemon extract
1 teaspoon vanilla extract
Butterscotch Icing

Beat butter and sugar at medium speed with an electric mixer until creamy. Add apricots, and beat until blended. Add egg yolks, 1 at a time, beating well after each addition.

Combine 3 cups flour, soda, and salt; add to butter mixture alternately with sour cream, beginning and ending with flour mixture. Toss pecans with 1½ teaspoons flour. Stir pecan mixture and flavorings into batter.

Beat egg whites at medium speed until stiff peaks form. Fold beaten egg white into batter. Spoon batter into a greased and floured 10-inch tube pan. Bake at 300° for 1½ hours. Cool in pan on a wire rack 10 minutes; remove from pan, and cool completely on wire rack. Frost top and sides of cake with Butterscotch Icing. Yield: 1 (10-inch) cake.

Butterscotch Icing

2 cups sifted powdered sugar
½ cup butterscotch morsels, melted
½ cup butter, softened
3 tablespoons apricot nectar

Combine all ingredients in a mixing bowl. Beat at medium speed with an electric mixer until spreading consistency. Yield: 2 cups.

Vintage Virginia: A History of Good Taste
The Virginia Dietetic Association
Centreville, Virginia

Caramel-Nut Pound Cake

There's no real caramel in this cake, but there's a pound of brown sugar and lots of butter that blend together and fool you into thinking there's lots of caramel.

1 cup butter, softened	3 cups all-purpose flour
½ cup shortening	½ teaspoon baking powder
1 (16-ounce) package light	½ teaspoon salt
brown sugar	1 cup milk
1 cup sugar	1 teaspoon vanilla extract
5 large eggs	1 cup walnuts, finely chopped

Beat butter and shortening at medium speed with an electric mixer 2 minutes or until creamy. Gradually add sugars, beating 5 to 7 minutes. Add eggs, 1 at a time, beating just until yellow disappears.

Combine flour, baking powder, and salt; add to butter mixture alternately with milk, beginning and ending with flour mixture. Mix at low speed after each addition just until blended. Stir in vanilla and walnuts.

Pour batter into a greased and floured 10-inch tube pan. Bake at 325° for 1 hour and 15 to 20 minutes or until a long wooden pick inserted in center comes out clean. Cool in pan on a wire rack 15 minutes; remove from pan, and cool completely on wire rack. Yield: 1 (10-inch) cake.

From Black Tie to Blackeyed Peas: Savannah's Savory Secrets
St. Joseph's Foundation of Savannah, Inc.
Savannah, Georgia

Lemon Pound Cake

Here's a tried-and-true tip from our Test Kitchens. Grate the lemon rind from a fresh lemon before squeezing the juice. You'll find it much easier to handle. For an extra treat, serve slices of this melt-in-your-mouth pound cake with the peach sauce.

6 to 8 fresh ripe peaches	½ teaspoon baking powder
½ cup sugar	¾ cup milk
½ cup peach schnapps	2 teaspoons grated lemon rind
1 cup butter, softened	3 tablespoons fresh lemon juice
2 cups sugar	
5 large eggs	1 tablespoon lemon extract
3½ cups all-purpose flour	1 tablespoon vanilla extract

Peel and slice peaches. Stir in ½ cup sugar and peach schnapps. Cover and chill.

Beat butter at medium speed with an electric mixer about 2 minutes or until creamy. Gradually add 2 cups sugar, beating 5 to 7 minutes. Add eggs, 1 at a time, beating just until yellow disappears.

Combine flour and baking powder. Combine milk, lemon rind, and lemon juice, stirring well. Add flour mixture to butter mixture alternately with milk mixture, beginning and ending with flour mixture. Beat at low speed just until blended after each addition. Stir in flavorings. Pour batter into a greased 12-cup Bundt pan.

Bake at 325° for 1 hour and 5 minutes or until a long wooden pick inserted in center comes out clean. Cool in pan on a wire rack 10 to 15 minutes; remove from pan, and cool on wire rack. Serve with chilled peach mixture. Yield: 1 (10-inch) cake.

Chautauqua Celebrations
Wythe Arts Council, Ltd.
Wytheville, Virginia

Hot Milk Sponge Cake

Here's a simple vanilla sponge cake that's oh so satisfying either alone for a snack, topped with ice cream and fudge topping, or even turned into a shortcake.

4 large eggs	½ teaspoon salt
2 cups sugar	1 cup milk
2 cups all-purpose flour	¼ cup butter
2 teaspoons baking powder	

Line a 10-inch tube pan with wax paper; set aside.

Beat eggs at medium speed with an electric mixer 8 minutes or until thick and pale. Gradually add sugar, beating until very thick.

Stir together flour, baking powder, and salt; set aside. Combine milk and butter in a small saucepan; cook over low heat, stirring constantly, just until butter melts.

Add dry ingredients to egg mixture, beating well. Slowly add milk mixture, beating until blended. Pour batter into prepared pan.

Bake at 350° for 35 minutes or until a long wooden pick inserted in center of cake comes out clean. Cool in pan on a wire rack 10 to 15 minutes; remove from pan, and peel off wax paper. Cool completely on wire rack. Yield: 1 (10-inch) cake.   Mattie Mahanes

Olivet Heritage Cookbook
Olivet Presbyterian Church
Charlottesville, Virginia

Luscious Almond Cheesecake

1¼ cups crushed vanilla wafers
¾ cup finely chopped blanched
   almonds
¼ cup sugar
⅓ cup butter, melted
4 (8-ounce) packages cream
   cheese, softened
1¼ cups sugar
4 large eggs

1½ teaspoons almond extract
1 teaspoon vanilla extract
1 (16-ounce) container sour
   cream
¼ cup sifted powdered sugar
1 teaspoon vanilla extract
2 tablespoons sliced blanched
   almonds, toasted

Combine first 4 ingredients in a bowl; stir well. Firmly press mixture in an ungreased 10-inch springform pan. Bake at 350° for 8 minutes. Cool in pan on a wire rack.

Beat cream cheese at medium speed with an electric mixer until creamy; gradually add 1¼ cups sugar, beating well. Add eggs, 1 at a time, beating after each addition. Stir in almond extract and 1 teaspoon vanilla. Pour batter into prepared pan.

Bake at 350° for 55 to 60 minutes or until almost set. Cool in pan on a wire rack 15 minutes. Stir together sour cream, powdered sugar, and 1 teaspoon vanilla. Spread sour cream mixture over cheesecake. Cool to room temperature in pan on wire rack. Cover and chill 8 hours. Remove sides of pan, and sprinkle with toasted almonds. Yield: 14 servings.

Tnyla Smith

Panthers' Pantry
Children's Educational Foundation
Madera, California

Caramel Apple Cheesecake

Carnival flavors cap this cheesecake and make it as luscious to look at as it is to eat.

1 (21-ounce) can apple pie filling	½ cup sugar
1 (9-ounce) graham cracker crust	2 large eggs
2 (8-ounce) packages cream cheese, softened	¼ teaspoon vanilla extract
	¼ cup caramel topping
	10 pecan halves
	2 tablespoons chopped pecans

Reserve ¾ cup pie filling (about 10 apple slices). Spoon remaining pie filling into crust.

Beat cream cheese at medium speed with an electric mixer until creamy; gradually add sugar, beating well. Add eggs, 1 at a time, beating well after each addition. Stir in vanilla. Pour cream cheese mixture over pie filling.

Bake at 350° for 30 to 35 minutes or until set. Cool completely in pan on a wire rack.

Combine reserved pie filling and caramel topping in a small saucepan. Cook over medium heat 1 minute, stirring constantly. Remove apple slices with a slotted spoon, and set aside. Spread caramel mixture over cheesecake. Arrange apple slices around outer edge of cheesecake. Place pecan halves between apple slices, and sprinkle with chopped pecans. Cover and chill 8 hours. Yield: 8 servings.   Brandon Puckett

Sharing Our Best
Poyen Assembly of God Youth Ministry
Poyen, Arkansas

Café au Lait Cheesecake

1¾ cups chocolate wafer crumbs (about 30 cookies)
⅓ cup butter, melted
2 (1-ounce) squares semisweet chocolate, chopped
2 tablespoons water
1½ tablespoons instant coffee granules
2 tablespoons coffee liqueur
3 (8-ounce) packages cream cheese, softened
1 cup sugar
4 large eggs, lightly beaten
2 tablespoons all-purpose flour
1½ teaspoons vanilla extract

Process cookies in a food processor until fine crumbs form. Combine chocolate wafer crumbs and butter. Firmly press mixture in bottom and 1½ inches up sides of an ungreased 9-inch springform pan. Chill.

Combine chocolate, water, and coffee granules in a small saucepan. Cook over low heat, stirring constantly, until chocolate melts and mixture is smooth. Remove from heat; stir in liqueur. Cool completely.

Beat cream cheese at medium speed with an electric mixer until creamy; gradually add sugar, beating well. Add eggs, beating well. Stir in flour and vanilla. Reserve 2 cups cream cheese mixture; cover and chill.

Combine remaining cream cheese mixture and chocolate mixture, stirring well. Pour into prepared crust.

Bake at 350° for 30 minutes. (Center will not be completely set.) Carefully spread reserved cream cheese mixture over cheesecake. Bake 30 to 35 more minutes or until cheesecake is set. Cool to room temperature in pan on a wire rack. Cover and chill 8 hours. Remove sides of pan. Yield: 12 servings.

Meet Us in the Kitchen
The Junior League of St. Louis, Missouri

Chocolate Malt Cheesecake

1 cup graham cracker crumbs
⅓ cup butter, softened
¼ cup sugar
3 (8-ounce) packages cream
  cheese, softened
1 (14-ounce) can sweetened
  condensed milk

¾ cup chocolate malt powder
1 teaspoon vanilla extract
4 large eggs
1 cup (6 ounces) semisweet
  chocolate mini-morsels

Combine first 3 ingredients in a bowl; stir well. Firmly press mixture in bottom of a 9-inch springform pan coated with cooking spray. Bake at 350° for 8 minutes. Cool in pan on a wire rack.

Beat cream cheese and condensed milk at medium speed with an electric mixer until creamy. Add malt powder and vanilla; beat until blended. Add eggs, 1 at a time, beating just until blended after each addition. Fold in chocolate morsels. Spoon batter into prepared crust.

Bake at 300° for 55 minutes (center will not be completely set). Turn oven off; leave cake in oven 45 minutes. Run knife around edge of pan to release sides. Cool completely on a wire rack; cover and chill at least 8 hours. Remove sides of pan when ready to serve. Yield: 12 servings.

It's About Time: Recipes, Reflections, Realities
National Association Teachers of Family and Consumer Sciences
Bowling Green, Kentucky

Peanut Butter Cheesecake

Discover chunks of peanut butter and chocolate chips throughout each smooth slice of this nut lover's cheesecake. Sprinkle it with chopped peanuts for good measure.

1½ cups graham cracker crumbs
⅓ cup butter or margarine, melted
5 (8-ounce) packages cream cheese, softened
1½ cups sugar
¾ cup creamy peanut butter
2 teaspoons vanilla extract
3 large eggs
1 cup (6 ounces) peanut butter morsels
1 cup (6 ounces) semisweet chocolate morsels
1 (8-ounce) container sour cream
½ cup sifted powdered sugar
3 tablespoons creamy peanut butter
½ cup finely chopped unsalted peanuts

Stir together graham cracker crumbs and melted butter. Firmly press mixture in bottom and 1 inch up sides of a 10-inch springform pan. Bake at 350° for 5 minutes; cool in pan on a wire rack.

Beat cream cheese at high speed with an electric mixer until creamy; gradually add 1½ cups sugar, beating well. Add ¾ cup peanut butter and vanilla, beating until blended. Add eggs, 1 at a time, beating until blended after each addition. Stir in morsels. Pour batter into prepared pan.

Bake at 350° for 55 minutes to 1 hour or until cheesecake is almost set. Remove from oven; cool in pan on wire rack 15 minutes.

Meanwhile, stir together sour cream, powdered sugar, and 3 tablespoons peanut butter. Spread sour cream mixture over top of cheesecake; sprinkle with peanuts. Run knife around edge of pan to release sides; cool to room temperature. Cover and chill at least 8 hours. Remove sides of pan. Yield: 14 servings.   Teresa Austin

Sharing Our Best
Poyen Assembly of God Youth Ministry
Poyen, Arkansas

Chocolate-Zucchini Roll

3 large eggs
1 teaspoon vanilla extract
¾ cup all-purpose flour
1 teaspoon baking soda
¼ teaspoon salt
¾ cup sugar
½ cup cocoa
1 teaspoon ground cinnamon
1 cup peeled, shredded
    zucchini (about 1 small)

Powdered sugar
1 (8-ounce) package cream
    cheese, softened
¼ cup butter or margarine,
    softened
2 teaspoons vanilla extract
1 cup sifted powdered sugar
Additional sifted powdered
    sugar

Grease a 15- x 10-inch jellyroll pan. Line with wax paper; grease wax paper. Set aside.

Beat eggs and 1 teaspoon vanilla at medium speed with an electric mixer until blended. Stir together flour and next 5 ingredients. Add to egg mixture, beating well. Stir in zucchini. Spread batter into prepared pan.

Bake at 350° for 12 to 14 minutes or until cake springs back when lightly touched. Sift powdered sugar in a 15- x 10-inch rectangle on a cloth towel. When cake is done, immediately loosen from sides of pan, and turn out onto sugared towel. Peel off wax paper. Starting with narrow end, roll up cake and towel together; cool completely on a wire rack, seam side down.

Beat cream cheese, butter, and 2 teaspoons vanilla until fluffy. Slowly add 1 cup powdered sugar, beating well. Unroll cooled cake; remove towel, and spread filling over cake to within 1 inch from edges. Roll up cake and filling; place seam side down on a serving plate. Dust with additional powdered sugar. Chill at least 1 hour. Yield: 1 filled cake roll (5 to 6 servings).

Janice Johnson

Feeding the Flock
St. Philips Episcopal Church
Topeka, Kansas

Orange Cupcakes

Get ready to become addicted to these mini muffinlike morsels. The recipe makes quite a few because it's hard to stop eating after one or two.

½ cup butter
2 cups sugar
3 large eggs, separated
3 cups all-purpose flour
2 teaspoons baking powder
1 cup milk
1 teaspoon lemon extract
1 teaspoon vanilla extract

2 cups sugar
1 tablespoon grated orange rind
⅔ cup fresh orange juice
2 tablespoons grated lemon rind
⅓ cup fresh lemon juice

Beat butter at medium speed with an electric mixer until creamy; gradually add 2 cups sugar, beating well. Add egg yolks, 1 at a time, beating well after each addition.

Combine flour and baking powder; add to butter mixture alternately with milk, beginning and ending with flour mixture. Beat at low speed until blended after each addition. Stir in flavorings; set aside.

Beat egg whites at high speed until stiff peaks form. Gently fold beaten egg whites into batter. Spoon batter into greased miniature (1¾-inch) muffin pans, filling two-thirds full.

Bake at 375° for 10 to 12 minutes or until a wooden pick inserted in center comes out clean.

Stir together 2 cups sugar and remaining 4 ingredients in a small bowl. Remove cupcakes from pan 1 at a time. Drop each cupcake into juice mixture; remove with slotted spoon. Place cupcakes on wire racks over wax paper; cool completely. Yield: 6 dozen.   Ida Garth

Olivet Heritage Cookbook
Olivet Presbyterian Church
Charlottesville, Virginia

Peach Melba Shortcakes

1¼ cups sifted cake flour
1 teaspoon baking powder
½ teaspoon baking soda
¼ teaspoon salt
½ cup unsalted butter, softened
½ cup sugar
2 large eggs
1 teaspoon vanilla extract
½ cup buttermilk

Powdered sugar
4 large fresh ripe peaches, peeled and sliced
1 cup fresh raspberries
⅓ cup sugar
1 (10-ounce) package frozen raspberries in syrup, thawed
1½ cups whipping cream
2 teaspoons vanilla extract
2 tablespoons sugar

Stir together first 4 ingredients in a large bowl; set aside.

Beat butter and ½ cup sugar at medium speed with an electric mixer until creamy. Add eggs, 1 at a time, beating well after each addition. Stir in 1 teaspoon vanilla. Stir in flour mixture and buttermilk.

Place 8 (3¾-inch) tart pans (measured across the top) with removable bottoms on an ungreased baking sheet; coat with cooking spray. Spoon batter evenly into tart pans.

Bake at 350° for 20 to 22 minutes or until a wooden pick inserted in center comes out clean. Remove pans from baking sheet, and cool on a wire rack 5 minutes. Release shortcakes from tart pans, and cool completely on wire rack.

Cut cakes in half horizontally with a serrated knife. Sift powdered sugar over cake tops.

Combine peaches and fresh raspberries in a medium bowl; stir in ⅓ cup sugar. Set aside until juices form. Process frozen raspberries in a food processor bowl until smooth. Press raspberries through a wire-mesh strainer into a bowl, using the back of a spoon. Discard pulp and seeds. Set puree aside.

Beat whipping cream and 2 teaspoons vanilla at high speed until foamy; gradually add 2 tablespoons sugar, beating cream until soft peaks form.

Place cake bottoms on individual serving plates. Top each with peach mixture. Spoon whipped cream over peaches; replace cake tops. Top with any remaining whipped cream, if desired. Spoon raspberry puree around cakes. Yield: 8 servings.

Always in Season
The Junior League of Salt Lake City, Utah

Grandma's Strawberry-Brown Sugar Shortcake

4 cups fresh strawberries, sliced
½ cup firmly packed light brown sugar, divided
1¼ cups all-purpose flour
1 teaspoon baking powder
¼ teaspoon baking soda
¼ teaspoon salt
1 teaspoon grated orange rind
½ teaspoon ground cinnamon
⅓ cup butter
⅔ cup buttermilk
¾ cup heavy whipping cream

Combine strawberries and ¼ cup brown sugar; stir gently. Set aside.

Stir together 2 tablespoons brown sugar, flour, and next 5 ingredients. Cut butter into flour mixture with a pastry blender until crumbly; add buttermilk, stirring until dry ingredients are moistened. Turn dough out onto a lightly floured surface; knead 3 or 4 times. Pat or roll dough to ¾-inch thickness; cut with a 3-inch round cutter, and place on an ungreased baking sheet.

Bake at 425° for 10 minutes. Remove to a wire rack; cool slightly. Split biscuits in half. Place a biscuit half on each of 5 dessert plates. Spoon strawberries over biscuit halves. Beat cream until foamy; gradually add remaining 2 tablespoons brown sugar, beating until soft peaks form. Top with remaining biscuit halves. Dollop with whipped cream. Yield: 5 servings.   Nancy Massin

Alaska's Best
Alaska Telephone Pioneers
Anchorage, Alaska

Cookies & Candies

Autumn Elegance, page 126

Peanut Butter Burst Cookies

Peanut butter morsels burst forth with their nutty presence throughout each bite of these drop cookies.

1 cup butter or margarine, softened
¾ cup firmly packed light brown sugar
½ cup sugar
1 large egg
½ teaspoon vanilla extract
2 cups all-purpose flour
1 teaspoon baking powder
¼ teaspoon salt
1 (10-ounce) package peanut butter morsels

Beat butter at medium speed with an electric mixer until creamy; gradually add sugars, beating well. Add egg and vanilla; beat well.

Combine flour, baking powder, and salt; gradually add to butter mixture, beating well. Stir in peanut butter morsels.

Drop dough by rounded teaspoonfuls 2 inches apart onto lightly greased baking sheets. Bake at 375° for 7 to 9 minutes or until edges are lightly browned. Cool on baking sheets 2 minutes; remove to wire racks to cool. Yield: about 6 dozen.   Elma Jones

Sharing Recipes from Green Road Baptist Church
Green Road Baptist Church
Green Road, Kentucky

Frosted Carrot Cookies

4 carrots, sliced
¾ cup butter or margarine, softened
¾ cup sugar
1 large egg
1 teaspoon vanilla extract
2½ cups all-purpose flour
2¼ teaspoons baking powder
½ teaspoon salt
1½ cups sifted powdered sugar
2 teaspoons grated orange rind
1½ tablespoons fresh orange juice
1½ teaspoons butter or margarine, melted

Cook carrot in water to cover 10 minutes or until crisp-tender. Mash carrot to equal 1 cup, and set aside.

Beat ¾ cup butter and ¾ cup sugar at medium speed with an electric mixer until creamy. Add egg, and beat well. Stir in mashed carrot and vanilla. Combine flour, baking powder, and salt; stir into butter mixture. Drop dough by heaping teaspoonfuls onto lightly greased baking sheets. Bake at 375° for 12 minutes. Immediately remove to wire racks. Stir together powdered sugar and remaining 3 ingredients in a small bowl; frost warm cookies. Cool completely on wire racks. Yield: 5 dozen.   Lau Yee Fujii

Ofukuro No Aji: Favorite Recipes from Mama's Kitchen
Hōkūlani Cultural Exchange Committee
(Hōkūlani Elementary School)
Honolulu, Hawaii

10-Cup Cookies

Cupfuls of 10 hearty ingredients combine to make these everything-but-the-kitchen-sink cookies.

1 cup sugar
1 cup firmly packed light
  brown sugar
1 cup shortening
1 cup peanut butter
3 large eggs, lightly beaten
1 cup all-purpose flour
1 cup uncooked quick-cooking
  oats

2 teaspoons baking soda
1 teaspoon baking powder
1 cup chopped pecans
1 cup flaked coconut
1 cup raisins
1 cup (6 ounces) semisweet
  chocolate morsels

Combine first 4 ingredients in a large mixing bowl; beat at medium speed with an electric mixer until creamy. Add eggs, beating well.

Combine flour and next 3 ingredients; add to peanut butter mixture, and beat well. Stir in pecans and remaining ingredients.

Drop dough by level tablespoonfuls onto lightly greased baking sheets. Bake at 350° for 10 to 12 minutes or until golden. Immediately remove to wire racks to cool. Yield: 5½ dozen.   Debbie Field

Favorite Recipes
Friends of Memorial Hospital
Weiser, Idaho

Chocolate-Almond Biscotti

Have a cup of coffee ready for dunking these crunchy almond-and chocolate-laden lovelies.

1½ cups all-purpose flour
½ cup cocoa
1½ teaspoons baking powder
½ teaspoon baking soda
⅔ cup sugar
2 large eggs

2 tablespoons butter, softened
1 teaspoon almond extract
1 cup (6 ounces) semisweet chocolate morsels
½ cup chopped or slivered blanched almonds

Stir together first 4 ingredients in a medium bowl; set aside.

Beat sugar, eggs, butter, and almond extract at medium speed with an electric mixer until creamy. Gradually add flour mixture, beating at low speed until blended.

Turn dough out onto a lightly floured surface; lightly flour hands, and knead in chocolate morsels and almonds.

Divide dough in half; shape each portion into a 12- x 2-inch log on a lightly greased baking sheet.

Bake at 350° for 25 minutes. Transfer to a wire rack; cool 5 minutes.

Cut each log diagonally into ½-inch-thick slices with a serrated knife, using a gentle sawing motion; place slices on ungreased baking sheets.

Bake at 350° for 25 minutes. Remove to wire racks to cool. Yield: about 3 dozen.

Everything But the Entrée
The Junior League of Parkersburg, West Virginia

White Chocolate-Cherry Cookies

9 ounces white chocolate, coarsely chopped
1 cup coarsely chopped pecans
1 cup dried tart cherries
1 cup unsalted butter, softened
⅔ cup sugar
⅔ cup firmly packed light brown sugar

2 large eggs
1½ teaspoons vanilla extract
2⅓ cups all-purpose flour
1 teaspoon baking soda
½ teaspoon salt

Line 2 baking sheets with parchment paper; set aside.

Combine first 3 ingredients in a bowl; set aside.

Beat butter and sugars at medium speed with an electric mixer until light and fluffy. Add eggs, 1 at a time, beating after each addition. Stir in vanilla.

Combine flour, baking soda, and salt; add to butter mixture, beating just until blended. Stir in white chocolate mixture.

Shape dough into 1½-inch balls, and place 3 inches apart on prepared baking sheets. Bake at 350° for 13 to 15 minutes or until golden. Remove cookies to wire racks to cool. Yield: 5 dozen.

Dining by Design: Stylish Recipes, Savory Settings
The Junior League of Pasadena, California

Pecan Shortbread Cookies

1 cup unsalted butter, softened
½ cup sugar
½ teaspoon vanilla extract
⅛ teaspoon almond extract
1¾ cups all-purpose flour
⅔ cup pecan pieces, toasted
¼ teaspoon salt

Beat butter at medium speed with an electric mixer until creamy; gradually add sugar, beating well. Stir in flavorings.

Combine flour, pecans, and salt; add to butter mixture, beating well. Cover and chill 1 hour.

Roll dough to ¼-inch thickness on a lightly floured surface. Cut dough with a 2-inch round cookie cutter, and place 1 inch apart on ungreased baking sheets. Chill 10 minutes.

Bake at 325° for 15 to 17 minutes or until edges are lightly browned. Cool 1 minute on baking sheets. Remove to wire racks to cool. Yield: 3 dozen. Deborah Gragnani

Panthers' Pantry
Children's Educational Foundation
Madera, California

Autumn Elegance

Store any pizelles left over in an airtight container to enjoy filled with ice cream or fruit.

6 large eggs
1½ cups sugar
1 cup vegetable oil
1 tablespoon anise extract
3½ cups all-purpose flour
1 teaspoon baking powder
3 fresh ripe peaches, peeled
   and sliced

1 teaspoon vanilla extract
½ (8-ounce) container frozen
   whipped topping, thawed
Garnishes: whipped topping,
   toasted chopped pecans

Whisk eggs, gradually adding sugar. Stir in oil and anise extract.

Combine flour and baking powder; stir into egg mixture (batter will be thick). Spoon 2 tablespoons batter into preheated, oiled pizzelle iron. Cook 1½ to 2 minutes or until lightly browned. Quickly shape warm pizzelles into cones. Place seam side down on a wire rack to cool completely.

Gently stir peaches and vanilla into whipped topping. Spoon evenly into about 17 pizzelle cones. Garnish, if desired. Yield: 17 filled pizzelles plus 14 unfilled pizzelles.
                                                                    Edith Johnson

Note: For best results in rolling cones, remove from hot iron, and roll only 1 pizzelle at a time.

A Peach Flavored Past
Altrusa International, Inc. of Palisade, Colorado

Orange Delight

Plenty of freshly grated orange rind adds citrusy splendor to these lightly frosted bar cookies.

¾ cup butter, softened
1 cup firmly packed light
  brown sugar
½ cup sugar
2 large eggs
½ cup sour cream
1 tablespoon grated orange
  rind
3 cups all-purpose flour

2 teaspoons baking powder
½ teaspoon baking soda
½ teaspoon salt
1 cup chopped pecans
2 cups sifted powdered sugar
1 tablespoon sour cream
1 tablespoon butter, softened
2 teaspoons grated orange rind
1½ tablespoons milk

Beat butter at medium speed with an electric mixer until creamy; add 1 cup brown sugar and ½ cup sugar, beating well. Add eggs, 1 at a time, beating well after each addition. Add ½ cup sour cream and 1 tablespoon orange rind, beating well.

Combine flour and next 3 ingredients; add to butter mixture, beating well. Stir in pecans. Spread dough into a greased 13- x 9-inch pan. Bake at 350° for 23 minutes or until a wooden pick inserted in center comes out clean.

Meanwhile, stir together powdered sugar and next 3 ingredients; add milk, stirring until smooth. Drizzle frosting over warm cookies in pan. Cool completely in pan on a wire rack; cut into bars. Yield: 2 dozen.   June Shook

Savory Secrets
P.E.O. Chapter LR
St. Charles, Missouri

Mocha Fudge Brownie Bites

Chocolate morsels, coffee granules, and coffee liqueur infuse these bite-size beauties with their mocha essence.

1 cup (6 ounces) semisweet
  chocolate morsels
¼ cup butter or margarine
1 tablespoon instant coffee
  granules
1 large egg
1 egg yolk

⅔ cup all-purpose flour
½ cup sugar
⅛ teaspoon baking soda
1 tablespoon coffee liqueur
1 teaspoon vanilla extract
Sifted powdered sugar

Combine chocolate morsels and butter in a medium saucepan; cook over low heat, stirring constantly, until melted. Stir in coffee granules, egg, and egg yolk. Stir in flour and next 4 ingredients. Pour batter into a lightly greased 8-inch square pan.

Bake at 350° for 20 minutes. Cool in pan on a wire rack. Sprinkle brownies with powdered sugar. Cut into bite-size pieces. Yield: 4 dozen. Tonya Baldwin

McInnis Bobcat Favorites
McInnis Elementary PTA
DeLeon Springs, Florida

Macadamia Bars

Beneath the crunchy, crackly meringue topping of these bar cookies lies a chewy chocolate-and-macadamia nut layer.

1 cup butter, softened
2 cups firmly packed light
  brown sugar, divided
2 large eggs, separated
2 teaspoons mint liqueur
1 tablespoon water
2 cups all-purpose flour

¼ teaspoon baking soda
½ teaspoon salt
1 cup (6 ounces) semisweet
  chocolate morsels
1 cup chopped macadamia
  nuts

Beat butter at medium speed with an electric mixer until creamy; gradually add 1 cup brown sugar, beating well. Add egg yolks, beating well; stir in mint liqueur and water.

Combine flour, soda, and salt; add to butter mixture, beating well. Press dough evenly into an ungreased 13- x 9-inch pan. Sprinkle chocolate morsels and nuts evenly over dough; set aside.

Beat egg whites at medium speed until soft peaks form. Gradually add remaining 1 cup brown sugar, beating at high speed until stiff peaks form and sugar dissolves (2 to 4 minutes). Carefully spread over dough. Bake at 325° for 40 to 45 minutes or until meringue is slightly cracked on top. Cool in pan on a wire rack. Cut into bars. Yield: 2 dozen.   Milo Jarvis

Flavors of the Tenderloin
Sidewalk Clean-Up, Recycling & Urban Beautification (SCRUB)
San Francisco, California

Turtle Bars

2 cups all-purpose flour
1½ cups firmly packed light
   brown sugar, divided
½ cup butter, softened

1½ cups chopped pecans
⅔ cup butter
1 (11.5-ounce) package milk
   chocolate morsels

Combine flour and 1 cup brown sugar in a large bowl; cut in ½ cup butter with a pastry blender until crumbly. Press mixture into an ungreased 15- x 10-inch jellyroll pan. Sprinkle with pecans.

Combine ⅔ cup butter and remaining ½ cup brown sugar in a saucepan; cook over medium heat, stirring constantly, until mixture begins to boil. Boil 1 minute, and pour over pecans.

Bake at 350° for 20 to 25 minutes or until firm. Remove pan to a wire rack. Sprinkle immediately with chocolate morsels; let stand 5 minutes, and spread to cover. Cool in pan on wire rack. Cut into bars. Yield: 5 dozen.

Twice Treasured Recipes
The Bargain Box, Inc.
Hilton Head Island, South Carolina

Peanut Butter Fingers

The marriage of peanut butter and chocolate unite in these ultra-rich bars. Savor each one with a tall glass of cold milk.

1 cup all-purpose flour
1 cup uncooked quick-cooking
   oats
½ cup sugar
½ cup firmly packed light
   brown sugar
½ teaspoon baking soda
¼ teaspoon salt
½ cup butter, softened

⅓ cup creamy peanut butter
1 large egg
½ teaspoon vanilla extract
1 cup (6 ounces) semisweet
   chocolate morsels
½ cup sifted powdered sugar
½ cup creamy peanut butter
6 tablespoons milk

Combine first 10 ingredients in a large bowl. Beat at medium speed with an electric mixer until well blended. Firmly press mixture into a greased 13- x 9-inch pan. Bake at 350° for 20 to 22 minutes or until golden. Remove pan to a wire rack; sprinkle immediately with chocolate morsels. Let stand 5 minutes, and spread to cover.

Whisk together powdered sugar, ½ cup peanut butter, and milk in a small bowl. Spoon mixture over melted chocolate layer in pan. Gently swirl chocolate and peanut butter with a knife to create a marbled effect. Cool in pan on wire rack. Cut into bars. Yield: 4 dozen.   Jason Graham

Wildcat Valley: Recipes & Remembrances
Keats Lions Club
Manhattan, Kansas

Fudgy Bonbons

Wrap chocolate kisses in blankets of sweet chocolate dough to create fudgy, chewy candy-cookies.

2 cups (12 ounces) semisweet chocolate morsels
¼ cup butter or margarine
1 (14-ounce) can sweetened condensed milk
2 cups all-purpose flour
1 teaspoon vanilla extract

60 milk chocolate kisses
1 (2-ounce) vanilla candy coating square or white chocolate baking bar
1 teaspoon shortening or vegetable oil

Combine chocolate morsels and butter in a medium saucepan; cook over low heat until morsels and butter melt and mixture is smooth, stirring often. Stir in condensed milk.

Combine chocolate mixture, flour, and vanilla in a medium bowl; stir well.

Shape 1 tablespoon of dough around each chocolate kiss, covering kiss completely. Place 1 inch apart on ungreased baking sheets.

Bake at 350° for 7 minutes. (Cookies will appear soft and shiny, but will firm up as they cool. Do not overbake.) Immediately remove to wire racks to cool.

Place candy coating and shortening in a heavy-duty zip-top plastic bag; seal. Microwave at MEDIUM (50% power) 30 seconds; remove and knead. Repeat process in 30-second intervals until mixture is smooth, about 1½ minutes. Cut a very small hole in the corner of the bag, and drizzle coating over cookies. Let stand until candy coating is firm. Store cookies in an airtight container in a cool place. Yield: 5 dozen.   Carolyn Clark

Note: If you like nuts, use the milk chocolate kisses with almonds.

Panthers' Pantry
Children's Educational Foundation
Madera, California

Chocolate Caramel Candy

1 (11.5-ounce) package milk
  chocolate morsels, divided
1 (11-ounce) package
  butterscotch morsels, divided
¾ cup creamy peanut butter,
  divided
¼ cup butter or margarine

1 cup sugar
¼ cup evaporated milk
1½ cups marshmallow cream
1½ cups salted peanuts
1 teaspoon vanilla extract
1 (14-ounce) package caramels
¼ cup whipping cream

Combine 1 cup chocolate morsels, 1 cup butterscotch morsels, and ¼ cup peanut butter in a small saucepan. Cook over low heat until smooth, stirring constantly. Pour into a greased 13- x 9-inch pan; chill 25 minutes or until set.

Melt butter in a saucepan over medium heat; add sugar and milk. Bring to a boil; reduce heat, and simmer 5 minutes, stirring constantly. Remove from heat; stir in marshmallow cream, ¼ cup peanut butter, peanuts, and vanilla. Spread mixture over layer in pan; chill 25 minutes or until set.

Combine caramels and whipping cream in a saucepan. Cook over low heat until smooth, stirring constantly. Pour over layer in pan; chill 25 minutes or until set.

Combine remaining chocolate morsels, butterscotch morsels, and ¼ cup peanut butter in a saucepan. Cook over low heat until melted, stirring constantly. Pour over layer in pan; chill 2 hours or until set. Cut into 1-inch squares. Store in an airtight container in refrigerator. Yield: about 10 dozen.

Jarech Coriell

Glen Haven Community Cookbook 1999
Glen Haven Area Volunteer Fire Department
Glen Haven, Colorado

Chocolate Pralines

Three ingredients make these pralines a breeze to blend. You'll find that they have a softer texture than traditional pralines, but the same rich, nutty taste.

1 (14-ounce) package milk
  chocolate kisses
1 (14-ounce) can sweetened
  condensed milk

2 cups pecans, coarsely
  chopped

Combine chocolate kisses and condensed milk in a medium saucepan. Cook over medium-low heat 2 minutes or until chocolate kisses melt, stirring often. Remove from heat; stir in pecans. Drop by heaping teaspoonfuls onto wax paper. Cool until firm. Yield: about 3 dozen.   Leslie Wheeler

202's Totally Tempting Treasures
American Legion Auxiliary Green-Pierce Unit 202
Wichita Falls, Texas

White Chocolate-Eggnog Fudge

Eggnog, the traditional holiday beverage, is incorporated into a festive fudge to adorn your cookie tray.

2 cups sugar
¾ cup refrigerated eggnog
½ cup butter
3 (3½-ounce) white chocolate
    candy bars, broken into
    pieces

½ teaspoon freshly grated
    nutmeg
1 cup chopped pecans
1 (7-ounce) jar marshmallow
    cream
½ to 1 teaspoon rum extract

Combine first 3 ingredients in a medium saucepan; cook over medium heat, stirring constantly, until a candy thermometer registers 234° (soft ball stage).

Remove from heat; stir in white chocolate and nutmeg. Stir in pecans, marshmallow cream, and rum extract. Beat with a wooden spoon until blended. Pour into a greased 9-inch pan. Cool completely. Cut into squares. Yield: 2¼ pounds.

Yuletide on Hilton Head: A Heritage of Island Flavors
United Way of Beaufort County
Hilton Head Island, South Carolina

Ebony and Ivory Chocolate Truffles

You can make these candies even more delightful by rolling them in a bit of cocoa. Wear plastic gloves to keep the chocolate from melting onto your fingers.

¾ **cup heavy whipping cream, divided**
1 **tablespoon sugar, divided**
1 **tablespoon butter, divided**
7 **(1-ounce) squares white chocolate, finely chopped**

2 **(4-ounce) semisweet chocolate bars, finely chopped (we tested with Ghirardelli)**
½ **cup cocoa**

Combine ¼ cup whipping cream, ½ tablespoon sugar, and ½ tablespoon butter in a small saucepan; bring just to a simmer over medium heat. Combine cream mixture and white chocolate in a bowl; let stand 5 minutes. Whisk white chocolate mixture until smooth; let stand at room temperature 1 hour.

Meanwhile, combine remaining ½ cup whipping cream, remaining ½ tablespoon sugar, and remaining ½ tablespoon butter in pan; bring just to a simmer over medium heat. Combine whipping cream mixture and semisweet chocolate in a bowl; let stand 5 minutes. Whisk semisweet chocolate mixture until smooth; let stand at room temperature 1 hour.

Chill chocolate mixtures 15 minutes or until very thick, stirring every 5 minutes. Drop white chocolate mixture by level teaspoonfuls onto a baking sheet lined with wax paper. Drop semisweet chocolate mixture by level teaspoons on top of white chocolate mixture. Chill 5 minutes.

Shape mixtures into 1-inch balls, washing hands as necessary. Roll balls in cocoa. Cover and chill up to 1 week, or freeze up to 1 month. Yield: 3 dozen.

Black Tie & Boots Optional
Colleyville Woman's Club
Colleyville, Texas

Orange-Sugared Walnuts

You'll want to make a batch or two of these sugary walnuts during the holidays. Their fresh orange flavor signals the season. Make sure you grate the orange for the rind before juicing.

3 cups sugar
½ cup water
½ cup fresh orange juice

1 pound walnut halves
1 teaspoon grated orange rind

Combine first 3 ingredients in a large heavy saucepan. Cook over low heat, stirring gently, until sugar dissolves. Cover and cook over medium heat 2 to 3 minutes to wash down sugar crystals from sides of pan.

Uncover and cook, stirring constantly, until a candy thermometer registers 238° (soft ball stage). Remove pan from heat, and stir in walnut halves and orange rind with a wooden spoon just until mixture begins to thicken. Pour candy onto greased wax paper. Working rapidly, separate walnuts with 2 forks. Let candy stand until firm. Yield: 2 pounds.   Betty Stringfellow

Cooking Up Memories
The Tazewell County Genealogical and Historical Society
Pekin, Illinois

Desserts

Chocolate Soufflés, page 146

Apple Enchiladas

Here's a sweet treat that's sure to please the whole family. It's easy to prepare, thanks to canned pie filling and store-bought tortillas. Bathe them in a simple cinnamon-sugar sauce and bake until warm and tempting. The fun comes with the addition of whipped cream, ice cream, or shredded Cheddar cheese. To vary the flavor, use a different fruit pie filling.

1 (21-ounce) can apple pie
   filling
6 (8-inch) flour tortillas
1 teaspoon ground cinnamon
½ cup sugar

½ cup firmly packed light
   brown sugar
½ cup water
⅓ cup butter or margarine

Spoon filling down centers of tortillas; sprinkle with cinnamon. Roll up tortillas, and place seam side down in a lightly greased 11- x 7-inch baking dish.

Combine sugar and remaining 3 ingredients in a large saucepan. Bring sugar mixture to a boil; reduce heat, and simmer, uncovered, 3 minutes.

Pour sugar mixture over tortillas, and let stand 30 minutes. Bake at 350° for 20 minutes. Serve with ice cream, whipped cream, or Cheddar cheese. Yield: 6 servings.   Bill Davidson

A Little DAPS of This . . . A Little DAPS of That
Dallas Area Parkinsonism Society (DAPS)
Dallas, Texas

Honey-Wine Baked Apples

6 Gala apples, peeled and
   sliced
¼ cup raisins
½ cup honey
¼ cup butter or margarine,
   melted

½ cup dry white wine
Whipped cream
Ground cinnamon
Chopped pecans

Place apple and raisins in an ungreased 13- x 9-inch baking dish. Drizzle with honey and melted butter. Pour wine over apple mixture in dish.

Bake at 400° for 20 to 25 minutes or until apple is tender. Serve warm with whipped cream, cinnamon, and chopped pecans. Yield: 5 servings.   Cheri Schutt

Homemade with Love
Swanton-Missisquoi Valley Lions Club
Highgate Center, Vermont

Blackberry Grunt

A "grunt" is an old-fashioned dessert comprised of steamed dumplings over fruit. Molasses or maple syrup provided the sweetening power when white sugar was at a premium. Our updated version carries on with time-tested goodness.

4 cups fresh blackberries	¼ teaspoon salt
¾ cup sugar	2 tablespoons sugar
½ cup water	½ cup milk
1 tablespoon butter or margarine	2 tablespoons butter or margarine, melted
1 cup all-purpose flour	Sweetened whipped cream (optional)
1½ teaspoons baking powder	

Combine first 4 ingredients in a 3-quart saucepan. Bring to a boil over medium heat, stirring mixture occasionally. Cover and reduce heat to low.

Meanwhile, combine flour and next 3 ingredients in a bowl. Add milk and melted butter, stirring until smooth. Spoon mixture over berry mixture. Cover and simmer 15 minutes or until a knife inserted in center comes out clean. (Do not remove cover to check dumplings during cooking time.) Serve warm with sweetened whipped cream, if desired. Yield: 8 servings.   Laurie Timm

The Cookbook Tour
Good Shepherd Lutheran Church
Plainview, Minnesota

Pineapple Crisp

Try this pineapple crisp for a delightful and delicious variation on the apple crisp theme.

3 (15¼-ounce) cans pineapple
  chunks, drained
¼ cup sugar
2 tablespoons quick-cooking
  tapioca

1 cup all-purpose flour
1 cup firmly packed light
  brown sugar
½ cup unsalted butter or
  margarine, cut into pieces

Place pineapple in a lightly greased 11- x 7-inch baking dish. Sprinkle with ¼ cup sugar and tapioca; toss lightly.

Combine flour and brown sugar in a medium bowl; cut in butter with a pastry blender until mixture is crumbly. Sprinkle over pineapple mixture. Bake at 375° for 40 minutes or until bubbly. Yield: 8 servings.   Lore Wootton

Favorite Recipes
Friends of Memorial Hospital
Weiser, Idaho

Flan

Slices of custard as smooth as silk revel in caramelized sugar dripping down their sides. Serve the beauties with perfect fresh berries.

2½ cups sugar, divided
4 cups milk

8 large eggs, lightly beaten
1½ teaspoons vanilla extract

Sprinkle 1 cup sugar in a large heavy skillet or saucepan. Cook over medium heat, stirring constantly with a wooden spoon, until sugar melts and turns light brown. Quickly pour hot syrup into a lightly oiled 10-inch (1 piece) tube pan, tilting to coat bottom evenly; set aside. (Syrup will harden and crack as it cools.)

Combine remaining 1½ cups sugar and milk in a large saucepan; cook over medium heat, stirring constantly, until sugar melts and mixture comes to a simmer (do not boil). Remove from heat.

Combine eggs and vanilla in a medium bowl. Gradually stir about one-fourth of hot milk mixture into egg mixture; add egg mixture to remaining hot milk mixture, stirring constantly.

Pour custard into prepared pan. Place pan in a large roasting pan; add hot water to roasting pan to a depth of 1 inch. Bake at 325° for 50 minutes or until a knife inserted in center comes out clean. Remove flan from water; cool completely in tube pan on a wire rack. Cover and chill at least 8 hours. Loosen edges of flan with a spatula; invert onto a rimmed serving plate, letting melted caramelized sugar drizzle over top. Yield: 10 servings.   Chachy Plá

De Nuestra Mesa: Our Food, Wine, and Tradition
New Hope Charities, Inc.
West Palm Beach, Florida

Bon Ton Bread Pudding

Let the good times roll with generous servings of this whiskey sauce-soaked bread pudding.

1 (1-pound) loaf soft French bread	1 cup raisins
3 large eggs	3 tablespoons butter or margarine, melted
2 cups sugar	2 tablespoons vanilla extract
4 cups milk	Whiskey Sauce

Cut bread into 2-inch-thick slices. Arrange slices in an ungreased 13- x 9-inch baking dish.

Whisk together eggs and 1 cup sugar in a large bowl until thick and pale. Add remaining 1 cup sugar and 1 cup milk; whisk until smooth. Gradually stir in remaining 3 cups milk, raisins, melted butter, and vanilla. Pour mixture over bread slices. Cover and chill 1 hour. Uncover and bake at 300° for 65 minutes or until firm. Remove from oven; cool. Cut into squares. Spoon Whiskey Sauce over each serving. Yield: 12 servings.

Whiskey Sauce

1 large egg	½ cup butter or margarine, cut into pieces
1 cup sugar	
¼ cup whiskey	

Whisk together egg, sugar, and whiskey in a small saucepan until smooth. Cook over medium-low heat, whisking constantly, 5 minutes or until thickened. Add butter, and whisk until smooth. Yield: 1¼ cups.

Claire Jackson DuBos

Atchafalaya Legacy
Melville Woman's Club
Melville, Louisiana

French Velvet

Frozen whipped topping and pudding mixes make this dessert easy to make and good to take to your next bring-a-dish affair.

½ cup butter or margarine, softened
1 cup all-purpose flour
1 cup chopped pecans
1 (8-ounce) package cream cheese, softened
1 cup sifted powdered sugar
1 (12-ounce) container frozen whipped topping, thawed and divided

1 (3.9 ounce) package chocolate instant pudding mix
1 (3.4 ounce) package vanilla instant pudding mix
3 cups milk
1 (1.55-ounce) milk chocolate bar, grated

Combine first 3 ingredients; press into an ungreased 13- x 9-inch pan. Bake at 350° for 20 minutes. Cool in pan on a wire rack.

Beat cream cheese, powdered sugar, and 1 cup whipped topping at low speed with an electric mixer until combined. Spread over crust. Chill 30 minutes.

Beat pudding mixes and milk at low speed with mixer until blended; set aside 5 minutes to thicken. Spread over cream cheese mixture. Chill 10 minutes. Top with remaining whipped topping. Sprinkle with grated chocolate. Yield: 15 servings.   Terry Chapman

Feeding the Flock
St. Philips Episcopal Church
Topeka, Kansas

Cinnamon Pudding

2 cups firmly packed light
  brown sugar
1½ cups water
2 tablespoons butter or
  margarine
⅛ teaspoon salt
2 teaspoons vanilla extract,
  divided
2 cups all-purpose flour

1 cup sugar
2 teaspoons baking powder
2 teaspoons ground cinnamon
½ teaspoon salt
1 cup milk
2 tablespoons butter or
  margarine, melted
1 cup chopped pecans

Combine first 4 ingredients in a medium saucepan. Bring to a boil over medium heat, and cook, uncovered, 5 minutes. Remove from heat; stir in 1 teaspoon vanilla. Set syrup aside.

Combine flour and next 4 ingredients in a large bowl; set aside.

Combine milk, melted butter, and remaining 1 teaspoon vanilla in a small bowl. Add milk mixture to flour mixture all at once; stir until well blended. Pour batter into a greased 13- x 9-inch pan; pour syrup carefully over batter. Sprinkle with pecans.

Bake at 350° for 38 to 40 minutes or until edges are golden and pull away from sides of pan. Let stand 5 minutes before serving. Serve warm. Yield: 12 servings.   Rebecca Rollins Boudreaux

Atchafalaya Legacy
Melville Woman's Club
Melville, Louisiana

Lemon Curd Mousse

Lemon mousse richly crafted with butter and whipping cream is elegantly presented in 10-ounce wine goblets. Layer the dessert in smaller wine or parfait glasses for more genteel portions.

½ teaspoon unflavored gelatin
2 teaspoons cold water
1 cup sugar
2 tablespoons grated lemon rind
½ cup fresh lemon juice
6 egg yolks
¾ cup unsalted butter or margarine, cut into small pieces

2 cups heavy whipping cream
12 ounces fresh blueberries (about 2 cups)
1 cup flaked coconut, toasted
Garnish: fresh mint sprigs, blueberries

Sprinkle gelatin over cold water; let stand 10 minutes.

Whisk together sugar, lemon rind, juice, and egg yolks in a heavy saucepan. Add butter. Cook over medium heat, stirring constantly, 10 to 13 minutes or until mixture thickens. (Do not boil.) Remove from heat. Add gelatin mixture to lemon mixture; stir until gelatin dissolves. Spoon mixture into a medium bowl. Cover with plastic wrap, pressing wrap directly onto surface. Chill at least 8 hours.

Beat whipping cream at medium speed with an electric mixer until soft peaks form. Add 1 cup whipped cream to chilled lemon mixture, and beat until smooth.

To assemble, layer about 2 tablespoons blueberries, 2½ tablespoons mousse, 1 tablespoon coconut, and 3 tablespoons whipped cream into each of 8 stemmed 10-ounce wine glasses. Repeat layers with remaining ingredients. Chill until ready to serve. Garnish, if desired. Yield: 8 servings.

More Enchanted Eating from the West Shore
Friends of the Symphony
Muskegon, Michigan

Chocolate Soufflés

1⅓ cups (8 ounces) semisweet
   chocolate morsels
1 tablespoon butter or
   margarine
1 tablespoon all-purpose flour
½ cup fat-free milk

4 egg yolks, lightly beaten
1 tablespoon vanilla extract
4 egg whites
⅛ teaspoon cream of tartar
¼ cup sugar
Sifted powdered sugar

Butter 8 (6-ounce) ramekins; sprinkle lightly with sugar. Place on a baking sheet. Melt chocolate morsels in a heavy saucepan over low heat. Set aside.

Melt butter in a heavy saucepan over low heat; whisk in flour until smooth. Cook 1 minute, whisking constantly. Gradually whisk in milk; cook over medium heat, whisking constantly, until mixture is thickened and bubbly. Remove from heat, and stir in chocolate; whisk until smooth. Gradually whisk in egg yolks and vanilla.

Beat egg whites and cream of tartar at high speed with an electric mixer until foamy. Add ¼ cup sugar, 1 tablespoon at a time, beating until stiff peaks form and sugar dissolves (2 to 4 minutes).

Gently fold egg white mixture into chocolate mixture. Spoon into prepared ramekins. Bake at 375° for 17 minutes. Sprinkle with powdered sugar. If desired, serve with chocolate or caramel sauce. Yield: 8 servings.   Lynn Weber

Note: Soufflés can be frozen before baking. Bake, still frozen, at 375° for 22 to 24 minutes.

Menus & Memories
The University of Oklahoma Women's Association
Norman, Oklahoma

Simple Peach Sorbet

Just 3 ingredients, yet this satiny sorbet carries an intense ripe peach impact that belies its simplicity.

4 or 5 fresh ripe peaches, peeled and chopped	¾ cup sugar
	1 teaspoon fresh lemon juice

Process all ingredients in a blender until smooth, stopping to scrape down sides. Pour mixture into a 9-inch square pan. Cover and freeze 3 hours or until firm.

Remove pan from freezer; let stand 10 minutes. Break frozen mixture into chunks; process in a food processor until smooth. Spoon into individual dessert dishes. Yield: 4 cups.   Kat McKay

A Peach Flavored Past
Altrusa International, Inc., of Palisade, Colorado

Unbelievable Chocolate Ice Cream

Nothing's better on a hot summer day than the cool taste of this soft chocolate ice cream. You'll appreciate the ease of preparation, too.

½ gallon chocolate milk	1 (12-ounce) container frozen whipped topping, thawed
1 (14-ounce) can sweetened condensed milk	2 tablespoons cocoa

Pour all ingredients into freezer container of a 5-quart hand-turned or electric freezer. Freeze according to manufacturer's instructions.

Pack freezer with additional ice and rock salt, and let stand 1 hour before serving. Yield: 1 gallon.   Joan Underwood

Down Home Dining in Mississippi
Mississippi Homemaker Volunteers, Inc.
Water Valley, Mississippi

Chocolate Ice Cream Balls

This sinfully delicious dessert is super easy to make. Look for amaretti cookies in the gourmet section of your supermarket. And if chocolate-chocolate chip ice cream isn't available, simply substitute your favorite chocolate ice cream.

2 cups amaretti cookies
1 pint chocolate-chocolate chip
   ice cream

¾ cup hot fudge topping,
   warmed
¼ cup almond liqueur

Crush cookies in a heavy-duty zip-top plastic bag, using a rolling pin. Shape ice cream into 8 balls, using a small ice cream scoop or spoon. Roll each ball in cookie crumbs, coating evenly. Reserve remaining crumbs. Place balls in an 8- or 9-inch square pan; freeze until firm.

To serve, place 2 balls into each of 4 dessert bowls. Drizzle each serving with 3 tablespoons fudge sauce and 1 tablespoon liqueur. Sprinkle with reserved crumbs. Yield: 4 servings.   Jeanne Koch

St. Andrew's Cooks Again
Presbyterian Women of St. Andrew
Beaumont, Texas

Butterscotch Torte

A slather of orange-tinged butterscotch topping makes oozy, slightly less-than-neat slices of torte, but the great taste makes up for the casual appearance.

1 cup firmly packed light brown sugar
½ cup butter or margarine
½ cup water
¼ cup orange juice
1 large egg, lightly beaten
1 teaspoon vanilla extract
6 large eggs, separated
1½ cups sugar
1 teaspoon baking powder
Dash of salt
2 cups crushed graham crackers
1 cup chopped pecans
2 cups whipping cream
¼ cup sifted powdered sugar

Combine first 6 ingredients in a small saucepan. Bring to a boil over medium heat. Reduce heat, and simmer until slightly thickened, stirring constantly. Set butterscotch topping aside, and cool.

Beat egg yolks at medium speed with an electric mixer until thick and pale. Add 1½ cups sugar, baking powder, and salt.

Beat egg whites until stiff peaks form; fold beaten egg white into yolk mixture. Add graham cracker crumbs and pecans. Spoon into a greased 13- x 9-inch pan. Bake at 325° for 35 minutes. Cool completely in pan on a wire rack.

Beat whipping cream until foamy; gradually add powdered sugar, beating until soft peaks form. Spread whipped cream over torte. Pour butterscotch topping over whipped cream. Cover and chill 1 to 2 hours. Yield: 15 servings.   Donna Boberg

Sharing Our Best
Hackensack American Legion Auxiliary Unit 202
Hackensack, Minnesota

Éclair Torte

A puff pastry is the basis for many fabulous desserts. In this recipe, the pastry forms the crust, encompassing a creamy pudding filling that's crowned with whipped topping and a drizzle of chocolate.

1 cup water
½ cup butter
1 cup all-purpose flour
¼ teaspoon salt
4 large eggs
1 (8-ounce) package cream cheese, softened

2 (3.4-ounce) packages vanilla instant pudding mix
3 cups cold milk
1 (12-ounce) container frozen whipped topping, thawed
Chocolate syrup

Combine water and butter in a medium saucepan; bring to a boil. Add flour and salt, all at once, stirring vigorously over medium-high heat until mixture leaves sides of pan and forms a smooth ball. Remove from heat, and cool 4 to 5 minutes.

Add eggs, 1 at a time, beating thoroughly with a wooden spoon after each addition; then beat until dough is smooth. Spread into a greased 13- x 9-inch pan. Bake at 400° for 30 minutes or until golden and puffed. (Pastry will fall.) Cool completely in pan on a wire rack.

Beat cream cheese, pudding mix, and milk until smooth. Spread over pastry; cover and chill 20 minutes. Spread with whipped topping; drizzle with chocolate syrup before serving. Yield: 12 servings.

Alaska's Best
Alaska Telephone Pioneers
Anchorage, Alaska

Frozen Mocha Torte

Frosty slices of this frozen mocha marvel make summertime the season for serving.

1¼ cups chocolate wafer crumbs (about 25 wafers), divided
¼ cup sugar
¼ cup butter or margarine, melted
1 (8-ounce) package cream cheese, softened

1 (14-ounce) can sweetened condensed milk
⅔ cup chocolate syrup
2 tablespoons hot water
2 tablespoons instant coffee granules
1 cup whipping cream, whipped

Stir together 1 cup wafer crumbs, sugar, and butter; press mixture in bottom and 1 inch up sides of a 9-inch springform pan. Cover and freeze 8 hours or until firm.

Beat cream cheese at medium speed with an electric mixer until creamy. Gradually add condensed milk and chocolate syrup, beating 5 minutes or until smooth.

Combine water and coffee granules, stirring until granules dissolve. Add to cream cheese mixture, stirring well. Gently fold in whipped cream. Pour into prepared pan. Sprinkle with remaining ¼ cup chocolate wafer crumbs. Cover and freeze 8 hours or until firm. Let stand 15 minutes, and remove sides of pan before serving. Yield: 8 servings.   Wendy Avery

The Avery Family's Favorite Recipes
compiled by the Avery family to generate
contributions for Pittsfield Community Church
Wellington, Ohio

Lemon Ice Torte with Strawberry-Raspberry Sauce

If you have some of this luscious fruit sauce left over, cover it and store it in the refrigerator to serve with ice cream, cake, or pie.

3 cups slivered blanched almonds, toasted
½ cup sugar
5 tablespoons butter, softened
¼ teaspoon ground cinnamon
⅓ cup strawberry preserves
6 cups lemon sorbet, softened
Strawberry-Raspberry Sauce
Garnishes: fresh strawberries, fresh mint sprigs

Process almonds and sugar in a food processor 10 seconds or until almonds are finely chopped. Place almond mixture in a bowl; add butter and cinnamon, stirring well. Firmly press mixture in bottom and 2 inches up sides of a 9-inch springform pan; freeze 15 minutes. Bake at 350° for 20 minutes. Cool completely on a wire rack.

Melt preserves in a saucepan over low heat; spread over cooled crust. Cool completely.

Spread sorbet over crust. Freeze until firm. Serve with chilled Strawberry-Raspberry Sauce. Garnish, if desired. Yield: 12 servings.

Strawberry-Raspberry Sauce

1 cup sugar, divided
½ cup water
1 vanilla bean or ½ teaspoon vanilla extract
1 (20-ounce) package frozen unsweetened strawberries
1 (20-ounce) package frozen unsweetened raspberries

Combine ½ cup sugar and water in a saucepan; bring to a boil. Reduce heat, and simmer, stirring constantly, 2 minutes or until sugar dissolves. Scrape seeds from vanilla bean; add seeds and bean to sugar mixture. Stir in remaining ½ cup sugar; simmer, uncovered, 5 minutes. Add strawberries and raspberries; return to a boil. Reduce heat, and simmer, uncovered, 2 minutes. Discard vanilla bean. Cover sauce and chill. Yield: 5½ cups.

Cooking with Music: Celebrating the Tastes and Traditions of the
Boston Symphony Orchestra
Boston Symphony Association of Volunteers
Boston, Massachusetts

Eggs & Cheese

Killer Omelet with Garlic-Onion Potatoes and Bacon, page 156

Peach French Toast

Start–or end–your day with this peach-of-a-dish. Luscious peaches cushion thick slices of bread baked in an egg base. Remember to save the peach syrup to top the French toast; it really makes it memorable.

1 (29-ounce) can sliced peaches in heavy syrup	10 (1-inch-thick) French bread slices (about 8 ounces)
1 cup firmly packed light brown sugar	5 large eggs, lightly beaten
½ cup butter	1½ cups milk
2 tablespoons water	1 tablespoon vanilla extract

Drain peaches, reserving syrup; set peaches and syrup aside.

Combine brown sugar, butter, and water in a small saucepan; cook over medium heat 3 to 4 minutes or until sugar dissolves, stirring often. Pour butter mixture into a lightly greased 13- x 9-inch baking dish. Arrange peaches over butter mixture; top with bread slices. Whisk together eggs, milk, and vanilla. Pour milk mixture over bread. Cover and chill 8 hours.

Bake at 350° for 40 minutes. Meanwhile, place reserved syrup in a small saucepan; cook over low heat until warm. Serve toast with warm syrup. Yield: 10 servings.   Rhonda Husak and Jean Meyer

Savory Secrets
P.E.O. Chapter LR
St. Charles, Missouri

Baked Artichoke and Onion Frittata

A frittata is essentially a baked omelet that's cut into wedges rather than folded. This one incorporates artichoke hearts and two cheeses for a golden puffed egg dish delight.

¾ cup grated Parmesan cheese, divided
1 (9-ounce) package frozen artichoke hearts
1 medium onion, sliced vertically
1 tablespoon olive oil
1 tablespoon butter or margarine, melted
1 small garlic clove, minced

¼ teaspoon dried oregano
6 large eggs, lightly beaten
1 cup (4 ounces) shredded Monterey Jack cheese
½ cup milk
¼ teaspoon salt
⅛ teaspoon ground white pepper
⅛ teaspoon ground nutmeg

Grease bottom and sides of a 1½-quart quiche dish. Coat bottom and sides of dish with ¼ cup Parmesan cheese; set aside.

Cook artichoke hearts according to package directions just until tender; drain well, and coarsely chop. Cook onion in oil and butter in a skillet over medium heat until tender, stirring occasionally. Stir in artichokes, garlic, and oregano; remove from heat.

Combine ¼ cup Parmesan cheese, eggs, and remaining 5 ingredients; stir in artichoke mixture.

Pour into prepared dish. Bake at 350° for 20 minutes or until set. Sprinkle with remaining ¼ cup Parmesan cheese. Bake 5 more minutes or until frittata is puffed and golden. Let stand 10 minutes before serving. Yield: 6 servings.   Michelle Goldsmith

Cooking with Class
Forest Hills Elementary School PTO
Lake Oswego, Oregon

Killer Omelet with Garlic-Onion Potatoes and Bacon

If you prefer a spicier omelet, don't seed the jalapeño.

2 tablespoons olive oil
4 baking potatoes, unpeeled and cut into ½-inch cubes
1 teaspoon salt, divided
¾ teaspoon pepper, divided
½ medium onion, chopped
1 large garlic clove, minced
8 bacon slices
½ medium-size red bell pepper, chopped
½ medium-size green bell pepper, chopped

1 small jalapeño pepper, seeded and minced
2 medium tomatoes, peeled, seeded, and chopped
¼ cup (1 ounce) shredded sharp Cheddar cheese
¼ cup (1 ounce) shredded Swiss cheese
8 large eggs, lightly beaten
¼ cup whipping cream

Heat oil in a large nonstick skillet over medium-high heat until hot. Add potato; sprinkle with ¾ teaspoon salt and ½ teaspoon pepper. Toss with a spatula until potato is thoroughly coated with oil. Cover and cook 10 minutes, turning every 5 minutes with spatula. Add onion and garlic; toss until well blended. Cover and cook 5 minutes, turning once. Reduce heat to medium; uncover and cook 20 to 25 minutes or until potato is crisp and browned, turning with spatula every 5 minutes. Set aside, and keep warm.

While potato cooks, fry bacon in a large skillet until crisp; remove bacon, and drain on paper towels, reserving drippings in a small bowl. Set bacon aside; keep warm.

Heat 1 tablespoon reserved drippings in skillet over medium-high heat. Add peppers, and sauté 2 minutes. Stir in tomato; sauté 2 minutes. Cover and keep warm.

Combine cheeses; set aside.

Whisk together eggs, whipping cream, and remaining salt and pepper. Heat ½ teaspoon reserved drippings in an 8-inch nonstick omelet pan over medium heat until hot. Pour about ½ cup egg mixture into pan. As mixture starts to cook, gently lift edges of omelet with a spatula, and tilt pan so uncooked portion flows underneath.

Spoon about ½ cup reserved pepper mixture onto half of omelet; sprinkle with 2 tablespoons cheese mixture. Loosen omelet with a spatula; fold omelet in half. Gently slide omelet onto a serving platter.

Repeat procedure with remaining egg, pepper, and cheese mixtures, using ½ teaspoon drippings for each omelet. Serve omelets with potato and bacon. Yield: 4 omelets.   Straker Carryer

Note: To save time, cook 1 large omelet in a 10-inch nonstick skillet, using 2 teaspoons drippings. Cut into 4 wedges to serve.

The Heart of Pittsburgh
Sacred Heart Elementary School PTG
Pittsburgh, Pennsylvania

Fluffy Harvest Omelet

Serve a harvest blend of fresh zucchini and mushrooms in Italian-style tomato sauce alongside each serving of this cheesy baked omelet.

1 (15-ounce) can chunky
  Italian-style tomato sauce
1 cup chopped fresh zucchini
¾ cup sliced fresh mushrooms
6 large eggs, separated
¼ teaspoon salt
¼ cup half-and-half

¼ cup grated Parmesan cheese
¼ teaspoon pepper
2 tablespoons butter or
  margarine
1 cup (4 ounces) shredded
  mozzarella cheese

Combine first 3 ingredients in a saucepan; bring to a boil. Reduce heat; simmer, uncovered, 10 minutes or until zucchini is tender.

Beat egg whites at high speed with an electric mixer until foamy; add salt. Beat until stiff peaks form. Beat egg yolks in a large bowl until thick and pale. Add half-and-half, Parmesan cheese, and pepper; beat well. Gently fold egg white into egg yolk mixture.

Melt butter in an ovenproof 12-inch nonstick skillet over medium heat. Add egg mixture, and spread evenly in pan. Reduce heat to medium-low, and cook 8 minutes or until bottom is golden.

Bake at 350° for 10 minutes or until a knife inserted in center comes out clean. Loosen omelet with a spatula; sprinkle with mozzarella cheese. Fold omelet in half. Gently slide onto a serving plate. Serve with zucchini mixture. Yield: 4 servings.   Les and Helen Heath

North Country Cooking
51st National Square Dance Convention
Champlin, Minnesota

Pepper Jack Cheese and Herb Soufflé

Monterey Jack cheese with peppers lends a Southwest flair to this lighter-than-air soufflé, which can be used as a main dish for any meal of the day. For more kick, serve with a variety of flavored salsas.

2 (8-ounce) packages Monterey Jack cheese with peppers, cubed
1 (3-ounce) package cream cheese, cubed
1 cup cottage cheese
2 tablespoons butter or margarine, cut into pieces
8 large eggs, lightly beaten
1 cup milk
½ cup all-purpose flour
1 tablespoon baking powder
1 teaspoon chopped fresh oregano
1 teaspoon chopped fresh thyme
¼ teaspoon salt
¼ teaspoon pepper
Salsa

Combine first 4 ingredients in a bowl; stir well. Spoon mixture into a buttered 13- x 9-inch baking dish.

Whisk together eggs and next 7 ingredients in a large bowl. Pour over cheese mixture.

Bake at 350° for 35 to 40 minutes or until edges of soufflé are lightly browned. Let stand 10 minutes before serving. Serve with salsa. Yield: 8 servings.

Oh My Stars! Recipes That Shine
The Junior League of Roanoke Valley, Virginia

Roquefort Timbales

2 tablespoons unsalted butter, softened
2 ounces cream cheese, softened
3 ounces Roquefort cheese, softened
⅛ teaspoon ground white pepper
⅛ teaspoon ground red pepper
3 large eggs
¾ cup whipping cream, divided
2 tablespoons dry white wine
⅛ teaspoon salt
⅛ teaspoon ground white pepper
2 tablespoons chopped fresh chives
4 French bread slices, toasted

Process first 5 ingredients in a food processor 5 seconds or until smooth, stopping to scrape down sides.

Combine eggs and ¼ cup whipping cream; stir well. Add cheese mixture; stir well. Pour mixture through a wire-mesh strainer into a bowl. Pour mixture evenly into 4 lightly greased 6-ounce custard cups. Place custard cups in a 9-inch square pan; add hot water to pan to a depth of 1 inch. Bake, uncovered, at 325° for 30 minutes or until set. Remove from oven, and cool. Cover and chill 2 hours.

Bring wine to a boil in a small saucepan. Reduce heat, and simmer, uncovered, 5 minutes or until liquid is almost evaporated. Add remaining ½ cup whipping cream; return to a boil. Reduce heat, and simmer, uncovered, 5 minutes or until liquid is reduced by half. Stir in salt, pepper, and chives. Cover and chill sauce.

Arrange toast on 4 plates. Unmold timbales onto toast, and spread 1 tablespoon sauce on each serving. Yield: 4 servings.

A Thyme to Remember
Dallas County Medical Society Alliance
Dallas, Texas

Eggs Bel-Mar

¼ cup butter or margarine
¼ cup all-purpose flour
2 cups milk
1½ teaspoons salt
½ teaspoon pepper
1 (6-ounce) package Canadian bacon, chopped
1 (8-ounce) package sliced fresh mushrooms
¼ cup chopped green bell pepper
¼ cup chopped green onions
3 tablespoons butter or margarine, melted
1 tablespoon butter or margarine
18 large eggs, lightly beaten
1 cup soft breadcrumbs (homemade)
2 tablespoons butter or margarine, melted

Melt ¼ cup butter in a medium saucepan over medium-low heat; add flour, stirring until smooth. Cook 1 minute, stirring constantly. Gradually add milk; cook over medium heat, stirring constantly with a wire whisk, until thickened and bubbly. Stir in salt and pepper. Set aside.

Sauté bacon and next 3 ingredients in 3 tablespoons butter in a large skillet until vegetables are crisp-tender; drain and set aside.

Melt 1 tablespoon butter in skillet, tilting to coat bottom; add eggs. Cook without stirring until mixture begins to set on bottom. Draw a spatula across bottom of pan to form large curds. Continue until eggs are thickened but still moist (do not stir constantly). Remove from heat. Gently stir in white sauce and bacon mixture. Spoon egg mixture into a greased 13- x 9-inch baking dish.

Combine breadcrumbs and 2 tablespoons melted butter; sprinkle evenly over egg mixture.

Bake at 350° for 20 to 25 minutes or until thoroughly heated. Yield: 12 servings.

Note: To make ahead, prepare casserole as directed, but do not bake. Cover and chill up to 24 hours. Remove from refrigerator, and let stand 30 minutes. Bake as directed.

The Dining Car
The Service League of Denison, Texas

Breakfast Blue Cheese Egg Bake

Fresh asparagus happily accompanies baked eggs and blue cheese for a fabulous and classic combo.

12 large eggs
6 tablespoons butter or margarine
⅓ cup all-purpose flour
3 cups milk
½ cup (2 ounces) crumbled blue cheese

½ cup diced celery
¼ cup diced pimientos, drained
½ teaspoon salt
⅛ teaspoon pepper
1 cup crushed buttery crackers (about 20 crackers)

Place eggs (in shells) in a Dutch oven. Add enough water to measure at least 1 inch above eggs; bring to a boil. Cover, remove from heat, and let stand 15 minutes. Pour off water. Immediately run cold water over eggs, or place them in ice water until completely cooled.

To remove shell, gently tap egg all over, roll between hands to loosen egg shell; then hold egg under cold water while peeling off shell.

Slice eggs in half lengthwise. Arrange egg slices in a lightly greased 13- x 9-inch baking dish.

Melt butter in a medium saucepan over medium-low heat; add flour, stirring until smooth. Cook 1 minute, stirring constantly. Gradually add milk; cook over medium heat, stirring constantly with a wire whisk, until thickened. Stir in cheese and next 4 ingredients. Remove from heat. Pour over eggs. Bake at 375° for 30 minutes. Sprinkle with cracker crumbs. Bake 15 more minutes. Serve over toast or biscuits. Yield: 12 servings.   Barb Staskivige

Sharing Our Best
Hackensack American Legion Auxiliary Unit 202
Hackensack, Minnesota

Greek Egg Casserole

Spinach, feta, and oregano fete the flavors of the Greek isles.

12 large eggs, lightly beaten
1 (10-ounce) package frozen
   chopped spinach, thawed
   and drained
1 (8-ounce) package sliced
   fresh mushrooms
1 (8-ounce) package crumbled
   feta cheese
1 small onion, chopped

⅓ cup milk
1 teaspoon salt
1 teaspoon dried dillweed
1 teaspoon dried oregano
½ teaspoon pepper
1½ cups (6 ounces) shredded
   mozzarella cheese
2 tablespoons chopped fresh
   parsley

Combine first 10 ingredients in a large bowl; stir well. Pour into a greased 13- x 9-inch baking dish. Sprinkle with mozzarella cheese and parsley. Bake at 350° for 30 to 32 minutes or until almost set. Serve immediately. Yield: 6 to 8 servings.

A Taste of Washington State
Washington Bed & Breakfast Guild
Seattle, Washington

Shrimp Rarebit

Here's a seafood-inspired take on the popular British dish that consists of melted cheese, beer, and seasonings served over toast. If you're short on time, buy cooked and peeled shrimp (you'll need one pound purchased that way) to add to the rich, cheesy sauce.

6 cups water
2 pounds unpeeled, medium-size fresh shrimp
3 tablespoons butter or margarine
2 cups (8 ounces) shredded Swiss cheese
2 cups (8 ounces) shredded Cheddar cheese
½ cup heavy whipping cream

½ cup dry white wine
2 large eggs, lightly beaten
1 teaspoon dry mustard
¼ teaspoon Worcestershire sauce
¼ teaspoon salt
⅛ teaspoon freshly ground black pepper
12 bread slices, toasted and cut into triangles

Bring water to a boil; add shrimp, and cook 3 to 5 minutes or just until shrimp turn pink. Drain and rinse with cold water. Chill. Peel shrimp, and devein, if desired. Cut into bite-size pieces. Set aside.

Melt butter in a medium saucepan over medium heat; add Swiss and Cheddar cheeses, stirring until cheeses melt. Reduce heat to low; add whipping cream and next 6 ingredients to pan, and cook until smooth and thickened, stirring occasionally. Stir in shrimp. Serve over toast. Yield: 6 servings.

Shirley Mayer

The Western New York Federal Court Centennial Cookbook
U.S. District Court, Western District of New York
Buffalo, New York

Country Ham, Shiitake, and Leek Strata

Stratas are often a hostess's best friend because they're easy make-ahead dishes. Our strata recipe is no exception. Prepare it the day before, cover, and chill. Let it stand at room temperature 30 minutes before baking as directed.

5 cups leeks, cut crosswise into rounds (about 2½ pounds)
¼ cup unsalted butter or margarine, melted
8 ounces fresh shiitake mushrooms, stemmed and cut into ¼-inch strips
8 ounces country ham, cut into ¼-inch strips
12 large eggs, lightly beaten
5 cups whipping cream
1 teaspoon freshly grated nutmeg
½ teaspoon salt
½ teaspoon freshly ground black pepper
1½ cups (6 ounces) freshly grated Gruyère cheese
Garnish: minced fresh parsley

Sauté leeks in butter in a large skillet over medium-high heat until tender. Add mushrooms and ham, and cook 3 more minutes. Spread leek mixture into 2 greased 13- x 9-inch baking dishes.

Whisk together eggs and next 4 ingredients. Stir in 1 cup cheese. Pour egg mixture over leek mixture in dishes; sprinkle with remaining ½ cup cheese.

Bake at 375° for 25 minutes or until set. Let stand 10 minutes before serving. Garnish, if desired. Yield: 16 to 18 servings.

Yuletide on Hilton Head: A Heritage of Island Flavors
United Way of Beaufort County
Hilton Head Island, South Carolina

Goat Cheese, Artichoke, and Smoked Ham Strata

8 cups cubed sourdough bread (about 12 ounces)
2 cups milk
¼ cup olive oil
1½ cups whipping cream
5 large eggs, lightly beaten
1 tablespoon minced garlic
1½ teaspoons salt
¾ teaspoon pepper
½ teaspoon ground nutmeg
12 ounces goat cheese, crumbled
2 tablespoons chopped fresh sage
1 tablespoon chopped fresh thyme
1½ teaspoons herbes de Provence
12 ounces smoked ham, chopped
3 (6½-ounce) jars marinated artichoke hearts, drained
1 cup (4 ounces) shredded fontina cheese
1½ cups freshly grated Parmesan cheese

Place bread in a large bowl. Whisk together milk and oil; pour over bread, and stir gently. Let stand 10 minutes.

Whisk together whipping cream and next 5 ingredients; stir in goat cheese. Combine sage, thyme, and herbes de Provence in a bowl.

Layer half each of bread mixture, ham, artichoke hearts, cheeses, herb mixture, and whipping cream mixture in order listed in a greased 13- x 9-inch baking dish. Repeat layering procedure with remaining ingredients.

Bake at 350° for 1 hour or until set and golden around edges. Let stand 10 minutes before serving. Yield: 8 to 10 servings.

A Thyme to Remember
Dallas County Medical Society Alliance
Dallas, Texas

Spinach and Ham Strata

You'll love the texture of this colorful strata that incorporates all the basic food groups into one dish. Save any leftovers to reheat the next day, and add a crisp, green salad to complete the meal.

2 (10-ounce) packages frozen chopped spinach
2 tablespoons chopped onion
1 teaspoon butter or margarine, melted
½ teaspoon pepper
18 dry white bread slices, crusts trimmed

12 slices process American cheese
2 cups cubed honey-glazed ham
6 large eggs, lightly beaten
3 cups milk

Cook spinach according to package directions; drain well. Combine spinach, onion, butter, and pepper; stir well. Cut 6 slices of bread into triangles. Layer half each of remaining slices of bread, cheese, spinach mixture, and ham in a greased 13- x 9-inch baking dish. Repeat procedure with remaining half of ingredients.

Arrange bread triangles in 2 rows on top of ham mixture. Combine eggs and milk; pour over layers. Cover and chill 8 hours.

Bake at 325° for 1 hour. Let stand 10 minutes before serving. Yield: 12 servings.

Bay Tables
The Junior League of Mobile, Alabama

Torta Rustica

1 (17¼-ounce) package frozen puff pastry sheets, thawed and divided
2 (10-ounce) packages frozen chopped spinach, thawed and squeezed dry
2 cups (8 ounces) shredded mozzarella cheese
1 cup ricotta cheese
2 (4-ounce) packages crumbled feta cheese
¾ cup freshly shredded Parmesan cheese
4 large eggs
½ cup fine, dry breadcrumbs (store-bought)
½ cup chopped onion
1 (15-ounce) jar roasted sweet red peppers, drained and sliced
1 large egg, lightly beaten

Roll 1 pastry sheet into a 15-inch square on a lightly floured surface. Cut into a 15-inch circle, discarding excess pastry. Press into bottom and up sides of a lightly greased 8-inch springform pan, allowing pastry to overhang slightly.

Stir together spinach and next 7 ingredients. Spoon one-third of spinach mixture into prepared pan. Arrange half of sliced peppers on top of spinach mixture. Repeat with remaining spinach mixture and peppers, ending with spinach mixture.

Roll remaining pastry sheet slightly to remove creases. Cut into a 9-inch circle. Place on top of spinach mixture. Brush pastry with lightly beaten egg. Fold bottom pastry over top pastry, pressing lightly to seal. Brush again with egg. Place pan on a baking sheet. Bake at 425° for 1 hour and 5 minutes, shielding edges with aluminum foil after 40 minutes to prevent excessive browning. Let stand 20 minutes before serving. Yield: 10 servings.   Patty Schexnaider

Recipes and Recollections
The Hitchcock Heritage Society
Hitchcock, Texas

Tomato and Artichoke Focaccia

Chunks of tomatoes, mushrooms, and artichoke hearts stud this focaccia. Eat it as a satisfying snack, or serve it with soups or salads.

1 (10-ounce) package refrigerated pizza dough
1 (15-ounce) can pasta-style chunky tomatoes
1 (14-ounce) can quartered artichoke hearts
1 (7-ounce) can sliced mushrooms

1 tablespoon olive oil
1 tablespoon minced garlic
1 teaspoon dried basil
8 ounces feta cheese, crumbled
½ cup thinly sliced green bell pepper

Lightly coat a 13- x 9-inch pan with cooking spray. Unroll pizza dough, and press into bottom and 1 inch up sides of pan. Bake at 425° for 7 minutes.

Drain tomatoes in a wire-mesh strainer; press against sides of strainer with back of a spoon to squeeze out juice, discarding juice. Drain artichoke hearts and mushrooms, pressing between layers of paper towels to remove excess moisture.

Brush dough with olive oil; sprinkle with garlic and basil. Sprinkle tomatoes, artichoke hearts, mushrooms, cheese, and bell pepper over dough. Bake on bottom rack of oven at 425° for 18 minutes or until crust is browned. Cut into 8 rectangles. Serve immediately. Yield: 4 servings.

René Smith

From Our Homes to Yours
Baptist Homes of Western Pennsylvania
Pittsburgh, Pennsylvania

Fish & Shellfish

Paella, page 188

All King's Day Catfish

4 (6-ounce) catfish fillets
  (1 inch thick)
½ cup all-purpose flour
½ teaspoon salt, divided
¼ teaspoon ground red
  pepper, divided
¼ cup vegetable oil
6 tablespoons unsalted butter
  or margarine, divided

1 cup sliced fresh mushrooms
¼ cup chopped green onions
¼ cup chopped red bell pepper
¼ cup chopped purple bell
  pepper
1 teaspoon minced garlic
¼ cup chicken broth
3 tablespoons chopped fresh
  parsley

Dredge catfish fillets in flour; sprinkle fillets with ¼ teaspoon salt and ⅛ teaspoon ground red pepper.

Heat oil in a large skillet over medium-high heat. Add fillets, and sauté 4 to 5 minutes on each side or until fish flakes with a fork. Transfer fillets to a serving platter; keep warm.

Melt ¼ cup butter in a medium skillet over medium-high heat; add mushrooms and next 4 ingredients, and sauté 3 minutes. Add broth and remaining ¼ teaspoon salt, ⅛ teaspoon ground red pepper, and 2 tablespoons butter; cook until butter melts, stirring constantly. Spoon sauce over warm fish. Sprinkle with parsley. Yield: 4 servings.

Settings on the Dock of the Bay
ASSISTANCE LEAGUE® of the Bay Area
Houston, Texas

Grilled Grouper

¼ cup dry red wine
1 tablespoon minced onion
1 tablespoon lemon juice
2 teaspoons salt
1½ teaspoons grated Parmesan
  cheese
¾ teaspoon sugar
¾ teaspoon pepper

¾ teaspoon dry mustard
¾ teaspoon dried basil
¾ teaspoon dried oregano
½ cup olive oil
4 (8-ounce) grouper fillets
  (1½ inches thick)
Vegetable cooking spray

Process first 10 ingredients in a blender until smooth. Turn blender on high; gradually add oil in a slow, steady stream.

Place fillets in a large heavy-duty zip-top plastic bag. Pour marinade over fillets; seal bag, and turn to coat. Chill 15 minutes. Remove fillets from marinade, discarding marinade. Coat fillets with cooking spray.

Grill, covered with grill lid, over medium-high heat (350° to 400°) 7 minutes on each side or until fish flakes with a fork. Yield: 4 servings.

America Celebrates Columbus
The Junior League of Columbus, Ohio

Asian-Glazed Salmon

An exotic glaze of brown sugar, Dijon mustard, and soy sauce is brushed over salmon before broiling and spooned over the top before serving.

1 (1-pound) salmon fillet (1 inch thick)	2 tablespoons soy sauce
	1 tablespoon Dijon mustard
6 tablespoons firmly packed light brown sugar	3 tablespoons rice vinegar

Place salmon on a lightly greased rack in a broiler pan. Whisk together brown sugar, soy sauce, and mustard in a small bowl until smooth. Reserve 2 tablespoons glaze; brush remaining glaze over salmon.

Broil salmon 5½ inches from heat 10 to 15 minutes or until fish flakes with a fork.

Stir together reserved 2 tablespoons glaze and rice vinegar. Spoon over salmon. Serve immediately. Yield: 3 servings.

It's a Snap!
The Haven of Grace
St. Louis, Missouri

Pepper-Crusted Salmon Fillets

Coarsely ground black pepper is pressed gently into each piece of the marinated salmon before the fillets are seared to perfection in hot oil.

2 tablespoons soy sauce
1 teaspoon sugar
2 teaspoons fresh lemon juice
1 garlic clove, minced
1 (¾-pound) salmon fillet
   (1 inch thick), skinned and
   cut in half

2 teaspoons coarsely ground
   pepper
2 tablespoons olive oil

Combine first 4 ingredients in a large heavy-duty zip-top plastic bag. Add salmon; seal bag, and turn to coat. Chill 30 minutes.

Remove salmon from marinade, discarding marinade. Pat salmon dry with a paper towel. Sprinkle 1 teaspoon pepper on top of each fillet, and press gently.

Heat oil in a large nonstick skillet over medium-high heat until hot; add salmon, and cook 4 minutes on each side or until fish flakes with a fork. Yield: 2 servings.   Lois Folino

Note: This recipe can be doubled or tripled easily.

Sesquicentennially Delicious
Western Pennsylvania Hospital
Pittsburgh, Pennsylvania

Pargo Perle (Red Snapper Fingers)

3 tablespoons fresh lime juice
2 garlic cloves, minced
½ teaspoon salt
½ teaspoon olive oil
⅛ teaspoon ground nutmeg
1 pound (1-inch-thick) red
   snapper fillets, cut into strips

1 large egg
3 tablespoons water
½ cup all-purpose flour
¾ cup crushed saltine crackers
   (about 35 crackers)
½ cup olive oil, divided
Garnish: lime slices

Combine first 5 ingredients in a bowl. Add snapper strips, and toss to coat. Cover and chill 2 hours.

Whisk together egg and water. Dip strips in egg mixture; dredge in flour, and dip again in egg mixture. Coat with cracker crumbs.

Heat 2 tablespoons oil in a large skillet; add snapper strips, a few at a time, and cook 3 minutes on each side. Remove from skillet; set aside, and keep warm. Wipe skillet with a paper towel. Repeat procedure with remaining oil and snapper strips. Garnish, if desired. Yield: 3 to 4 servings.   Rosa M. Zaldo Hickey

De Nuestra Mesa: Our Food, Wine, and Tradition
New Hope Charities, Inc.
West Palm Beach, Florida

Red Snapper Puttanesca

Red snapper stars in this merry mélange of tomatoes, onion, capers, olives, and anchovies. Oregano and garlic join the festivities.

4 (6- to 8-ounce) red snapper fillets (1½ inches thick)
1 tablespoon fresh lemon juice
¼ teaspoon pepper
1 medium onion, chopped
2 teaspoons olive oil
3 garlic cloves, minced
3 large tomatoes, peeled and chopped
8 kalamata olives, pitted and sliced
¼ cup chopped fresh basil
2 tablespoons drained capers
2 tablespoons minced anchovies
1 tablespoon chopped fresh oregano
1 bay leaf
¼ cup chopped fresh parsley

Place fillets in a lightly greased 13- x 9-inch baking dish. Sprinkle with lemon juice and pepper; set aside.

Sauté onion in hot oil in a skillet over medium-high heat 4 minutes. Add garlic; sauté 1 minute. Add tomato and next 6 ingredients; bring to a boil. Reduce heat, and simmer, uncovered, 5 minutes, stirring constantly. Pour sauce over fillets. Sprinkle with parsley.

Bake, uncovered, at 350° for 30 minutes or until fish flakes with a fork. Discard bay leaf. Yield: 4 servings.

Settings on the Dock of the Bay
ASSISTANCE LEAGUE® of the Bay Area
Houston, Texas

Roasted Sea Bass Provençal

¼ cup undrained chopped
   dried tomatoes in oil
2 tablespoons drained capers
1 tablespoon minced fresh
   thyme
1 tablespoon chopped garlic

½ cup dry white wine
½ cup bottled clam juice
4 (6- to 7-ounce) sea bass fillets
   (2¼ inches thick)
¼ teaspoon salt
⅛ teaspoon pepper

Drain tomatoes, reserving 2 tablespoons oil. Place oil in a large ovenproof skillet; heat over medium-high heat until hot. Add tomatoes, capers, thyme, and garlic; sauté 1 minute. Add wine and clam juice; bring to a boil. Boil 3 minutes or until liquid is reduced to ¼ cup. Remove from heat.

Sprinkle fillets with salt and pepper. Place fillets in skillet; lightly spoon sauce over fillets.

Bake, uncovered, at 450° for 15 minutes or until fish flakes with a fork. Yield: 4 servings.

Cooks of the Green Door
The League of Catholic Women
Minneapolis, Minnesota

Grilled Swordfish with Cilantro Butter

Bunches of fresh cilantro and lots of freshly squeezed lemon juice comprise the unbeatable butter compound slathered over the grilled swordfish steaks.

2 bunches fresh cilantro
1 cup unsalted butter, softened
2½ tablespoons fresh lemon
   juice (about 2 medium
   lemons)

1 teaspoon salt, divided
¼ teaspoon pepper, divided
8 (8-ounce) swordfish steaks
   (1½ inches thick)
2 tablespoons olive oil

Wash cilantro; remove thick stems. Process cilantro, butter, lemon juice, ½ teaspoon salt, and ⅛ teaspoon pepper in a food processor 10 seconds, stopping to scrape down sides. Transfer mixture to a small bowl. Cover and chill 1 hour.

Coat steaks with olive oil; sprinkle with remaining ½ teaspoon salt and remaining ⅛ teaspoon pepper.

Grill, covered with grill lid, over medium-high heat (350° to 400°) 8 minutes on each side or until fish flakes with a fork. Top with cilantro butter. Yield: 8 servings.

Black Tie & Boots Optional
Colleyville Woman's Club
Colleyville, Texas

Grilled Tuna Steaks with Feta Cheese

Serve any extra lemony vinaigrette as a salad dressing or as a topping for a baked potato.

6 (1½-inch-thick) tuna steaks (about 1½ pounds)
Lemon-Herb Vinaigrette

1 (4-ounce) package crumbled feta cheese

Place tuna in a shallow dish. Brush with ¼ cup Lemon-Herb Vinaigrette. Cover and chill 1 hour.

Remove tuna from marinade, discarding marinade.

Coat food rack with cooking spray; place on grill over medium-high heat (350° to 400°). Place tuna on rack, and grill, covered with grill lid, 6 minutes on each side or until fish flakes with a fork.

Top tuna evenly with feta cheese. Drizzle remaining Lemon-Herb Vinaigrette over steaks. Yield: 6 servings.

Lemon-Herb Vinaigrette

1 cup olive oil
1 cup vegetable oil
⅓ cup red wine vinegar
3 tablespoons fresh lemon juice

2 tablespoons dried oregano
¾ teaspoon salt
¾ teaspoon minced garlic
⅛ teaspoon freshly ground pepper

Whisk together all ingredients in a small bowl. Yield: 2½ cups.

Pot Luck O' the Irish
Maud Gonne Division #32-LAOH
Pittsburgh, Pennsylvania

Crab Cakes with Cool Lime Sauce

Tender crab cakes take on terrific tang courtesy of fresh lemon and basil. A creamy sauce made with fresh lime offers camaraderie.

½ cup mayonnaise
¼ cup sour cream
2 teaspoons grated lime rind
1 tablespoon fresh lime juice
1 pound fresh crabmeat
1 large egg, lightly beaten
¼ cup mayonnaise
2 tablespoons chopped fresh basil

1 teaspoon grated lemon rind
1 tablespoon fresh lemon juice
1 tablespoon chopped shallots
1 cup soft breadcrumbs (homemade)
¼ teaspoon salt
¼ teaspoon pepper
4 tablespoons butter, melted

Combine first 4 ingredients in a small bowl, stirring well. Cover and chill.

Drain and flake crabmeat, removing any bits of shell; set crabmeat aside.

Combine egg and next 5 ingredients in a large bowl, and stir well. Gently fold in crabmeat, breadcrumbs, salt, and pepper (do not over-mix). Cover and chill 1 hour. Shape mixture into 8 (4-inch) patties.

Fry 4 patties in 2 tablespoons melted butter in a large skillet over medium heat 3 to 4 minutes on each side or until golden; drain and keep warm. Repeat procedure with remaining 2 tablespoons butter and patties. Serve crab cakes warm with chilled sauce. Yield: 4 servings.   Carol Ferlisi Sartain and Wendy Morgan Hagen

Beyond Cotton Country
The Junior League of Morgan County
Decatur, Alabama

Deviled Crab

1 large egg, lightly beaten
3 tablespoons minced green
  bell pepper
2 tablespoons mayonnaise
1 teaspoon dried parsley flakes
¾ teaspoon celery seeds
1½ teaspoons Worcestershire
  sauce
1 pound fresh lump crabmeat,
  drained

3 tablespoons butter or
  margarine
3 tablespoons all-purpose flour
1 cup milk
½ cup soft breadcrumbs
  (homemade)
2 tablespoons butter or
  margarine, melted
Paprika

Combine first 6 ingredients in a large bowl; gently stir in crabmeat. Set aside.

Melt 3 tablespoons butter in a heavy saucepan over low heat; whisk in flour until smooth. Cook 1 minute, whisking constantly. Gradually whisk in milk, and cook over medium heat, whisking constantly, until mixture is thickened and bubbly. Remove from heat; cool 5 minutes. Add to crabmeat mixture, and stir gently to combine.

Cover and chill 15 minutes.

Combine breadcrumbs and 2 tablespoons melted butter.

Divide crabmeat mixture among 6 lightly greased individual baking shells. Sprinkle evenly with breadcrumb mixture. Sprinkle with paprika. Bake, uncovered, at 350° for 30 to 32 minutes or until breadcrumbs are golden brown and mixture is thoroughly heated. Yield: 6 servings.

Mary Thayer

Dixon Fixins
Dixon Ambulatory Care Center
Westminster, Maryland

Crawfish and Crab Étouffée

This Cajun specialty cooks up in little more time than it takes to cook the rice to serve alongside. Start the rice as you sauté the veggies.

½ cup butter or margarine
2 cups chopped onion
1 cup chopped green bell pepper
½ cup chopped celery
2 garlic cloves, minced
1 (14½-ounce) can chicken broth, divided
⅓ cup cream sherry
1 (16-ounce) package crawfish tails without shells, rinsed and drained

1 pound fresh lump crabmeat, drained
1 tablespoon Creole seasoning
1 teaspoon garlic powder
½ teaspoon pepper
1 tablespoon cornstarch
3 cups hot cooked rice
½ cup chopped green onions

Melt butter in a large skillet over medium heat; add onion and next 3 ingredients, and sauté 10 minutes or until tender. Stir in 1½ cups broth and sherry; bring to a boil. Cover, reduce heat, and simmer 10 minutes.

Combine crawfish and next 4 ingredients; toss gently. Add crawfish mixture to skillet; bring to a boil. Cover, reduce heat, and simmer 5 minutes.

Combine cornstarch and remaining 2 tablespoons broth, stirring until smooth; add cornstarch mixture to skillet. Simmer until mixture is thickened, stirring constantly. Serve over rice. Sprinkle with green onions. Yield: 6 servings.

Secret Ingredients
The Junior League of Alexandria, Louisiana

Grilled Lobster Tails

Grilled lobster tails glory in a buttery drizzle of lemon and tarragon sauce.

6 tablespoons butter, melted	**⅛ teaspoon pepper**
2 tablespoons fresh lemon juice	**⅛ teaspoon dried tarragon**
½ teaspoon salt	**6 frozen lobster tails, thawed (about 1½ pounds)**

Stir together first 5 ingredients in a small bowl. Divide mixture in half; set aside.

Split lobster shells lengthwise, cutting through hard upper shells and meat to, but not through, bottom shell, using kitchen shears. Press shell halves apart to flatten exposed meat.

Brush meat with half of butter mixture. Place lobster, shell side down, on grill rack. Grill, covered with grill lid, over medium-high heat (350° to 400°) 6 minutes. Turn lobster, and grill 4 more minutes or until flesh is white and firm. Drizzle lobster with remaining half of sauce. Yield: 6 servings.   Cheri Standridge

Diamond Delights
Diamond Hill Elementary School
Abbeville, South Carolina

Mussels Steamed in White Wine

You'll need about half a bottle of your favorite white wine to star in this seafood dish. Chill the remainder of the bottle to serve alongside the mussels with a loaf of crusty French bread.

2 pounds raw mussels in shells
2 garlic cloves, minced
1 large shallot, minced
6 fresh thyme sprigs
2 bay leaves
½ teaspoon freshly ground
   pepper

2 tablespoons olive oil
1½ cups dry white wine
1 tablespoon chopped fresh
   Italian parsley
½ teaspoon salt
2 tablespoons butter or
   margarine

Scrub mussels with a brush; remove beards. Discard cracked or heavy mussels (they're filled with sand), or opened mussels that won't close when tapped.

Sauté garlic and next 4 ingredients in hot oil in a Dutch oven over medium heat 2 minutes. Add mussels; increase heat to high. Cover and cook 1 minute, shaking Dutch oven several times. Add wine; cover and cook 1 to 2 minutes or until mussels open, shaking pan several times.

Transfer mussels to a serving dish with a slotted spoon, discarding any unopened mussels. Cover and keep warm.

Pour remaining liquid in Dutch oven through a wire-mesh strainer into a skillet, discarding solids. Bring to a boil. Add parsley and salt; cook 2 minutes. Remove from heat; whisk in butter. Pour over mussels. Serve immediately. Yield: 2 to 3 servings.   Maureen O'Sullivan

Over the Bridge
Corpus Christi Women's Guild
East Sandwich, Massachusetts

Barbecued Shrimp

"Barbecue" here refers both to the tangy red sauce on the shrimp and its quick turn on the grill. Chopped fresh rosemary adds a new taste sensation to the sauce.

½ cup ketchup
¼ cup diced onion
2 tablespoons chopped fresh
   rosemary
1 tablespoon light brown sugar
1½ tablespoons dry mustard

½ teaspoon garlic powder
2 tablespoons white vinegar
1 teaspoon hot sauce
24 unpeeled, jumbo fresh
   shrimp (about 1¾ pounds)
Garnish: lemon wedges

Combine first 8 ingredients in a bowl. Let stand at room temperature 2 hours.

Soak 4 (8-inch) wooden skewers in water 30 minutes.

Peel shrimp, and devein, if desired. Pour ketchup mixture over shrimp; stir to coat. Thread 6 shrimp onto each skewer. (Thread tail and neck of shrimp onto skewers so shrimp will lie flat.)

Coat food rack with cooking spray; place on grill over medium-high heat (350° to 400°). Place skewers on rack; grill, covered with grill lid, 4 to 5 minutes on each side or until shrimp turn pink. Garnish, if desired. Yield: 4 servings.

A Century of Serving
The Junior Board of Christiana Care, Inc.
Wilmington, Delaware

Shrimp Fritters with Red Sauce

Crispy fried shrimp and rice fritters profit from a dip into a bowlful of homemade seafood sauce shot with horseradish and hot sauce. If you have any fritters left over, simply freeze them. To reheat, thaw them in the microwave and then bake in the oven until crisp.

1 pound unpeeled, medium-size fresh shrimp
2 cups cooked white rice
6 green onions, finely chopped
1 cup all-purpose flour
1 tablespoon baking powder
1 teaspoon salt
1 teaspoon sugar
½ teaspoon garlic powder
½ teaspoon ground red pepper
2 large eggs, lightly beaten
½ cup milk
Vegetable oil
Red Sauce

Peel shrimp, and devein, if desired. Chop shrimp; set aside.

Combine rice and next 7 ingredients in a medium bowl. Whisk together eggs and milk; add egg mixture to rice mixture, stirring just until moistened. Stir in shrimp.

Pour oil to a depth of 3 inches into a Dutch oven; heat to 360°. Carefully drop batter by rounded teaspoonfuls into hot oil; fry a few at a time 1 to 2 minutes or until golden, turning once. Drain on paper towels. Serve with Red Sauce. Yield: 12 servings.

Red Sauce

1 cup ketchup
1 tablespoon Worcestershire sauce
2 teaspoons lemon juice
1 teaspoon prepared horseradish
¼ teaspoon hot sauce

Combine all ingredients; stir well. Yield: 1 cup.   Kelly Galloway

Favorite Recipes Taste of Tradition
B.A. Ritter Senior Citizen Center
Nederland, Texas

Garlic Shrimp

Be sure to accompany this fresh shrimp dish with plenty of rice, pasta, or crusty bread to soak up every bit of the buttery wine sauce. It's too divine to miss a drop.

2 pounds unpeeled, medium-size fresh shrimp
Olive oil
¼ cup butter or margarine
1 medium onion, chopped
5 garlic cloves, minced
1 tablespoon chopped fresh basil
1 tablespoon finely chopped fresh rosemary

1 teaspoon freshly ground pepper
1 cup dry white wine
½ cup chopped fresh parsley
½ teaspoon salt
Grated Parmesan cheese to taste
Garnishes: chopped fresh parsley, lemon wedges

Peel shrimp, leaving tails on; devein, if desired. Butterfly shrimp by making a deep slit down the back of each from the large end to the tail, cutting to, but not through, inside curve of shrimp. Set aside.

Pour olive oil to a depth of ⅛ inch into a large skillet; add butter. Cook over medium heat until butter melts. Add onion and garlic, and sauté 5 minutes or until tender. Add shrimp, basil, rosemary, and pepper; cook 1 minute. Add wine, ½ cup parsley, and salt; cook 3 more minutes or until shrimp turn pink. Sprinkle with Parmesan cheese to taste. Garnish, if desired. Yield: 6 servings.   Ann Mehas

Flavor It Greek! A Celebration of Food, Faith and Family
Philoptochos Society of Holy Trinity Greek Orthodox Church
Portland, Oregon

Shrimp 'n' Grits

1 pound unpeeled, medium-
size fresh shrimp
6 bacon slices
1 (8-ounce) package sliced
fresh mushrooms
1 large garlic clove, minced
1 cup chopped green onions
2 tablespoons chopped fresh
parsley

1½ tablespoons fresh lemon
juice
½ teaspoon salt
¼ teaspoon freshly ground
pepper
Dash of hot sauce
Cheese Grits

Peel shrimp, and devein, if desired. Set aside.

Cook bacon in a large nonstick skillet until crisp; remove bacon, and drain on paper towels, reserving 2 tablespoons drippings in skillet. Crumble bacon, and set aside.

Heat drippings over medium-high heat until hot; add shrimp. Cook 1 minute, stirring often. Add mushrooms and garlic; cook 3 minutes or until shrimp turn pink. Stir in bacon, green onions, and next 5 ingredients. Serve over Cheese Grits. Yield: 4 servings.

Cheese Grits

3 cups water
2 tablespoons butter or
margarine
½ teaspoon salt
¾ cup quick-cooking grits
1 cup (4 ounces) shredded
sharp Cheddar cheese

1 tablespoon white wine
Worcestershire sauce
¼ teaspoon hot sauce
¼ teaspoon ground white
pepper
Dash of ground nutmeg

Bring first 3 ingredients to a boil in a saucepan; stir in grits. Return to a boil. Cover, reduce heat, and simmer 5 minutes, stirring occasionally. Remove from heat. Add cheese and remaining ingredients, stirring until cheese melts. Yield: 3½ cups.   Kim Brooks

Of Books and Cooks
Woman's Book Club
Harrison, Arkansas

Shrimp Provençal

Three cloves of garlic and a hefty helping of fresh basil help take you to the provence of France that made this shrimp dish famous.

2 pounds unpeeled, medium-
   size fresh shrimp
3 tablespoons olive oil
2 cups chopped red bell
   pepper
1 cup chopped onion
2 tablespoons chopped fresh
   thyme
3 garlic cloves, chopped

½ teaspoon fennel seeds
1 (14½-ounce) can diced
   tomatoes, undrained
¾ cup ripe olives
½ cup dry white wine
2 tablespoons tomato paste
½ cup chopped fresh basil
Hot cooked rice

Peel shrimp, and devein, if desired.

Heat oil in a large skillet over medium-high heat. Add shrimp, and cook 1 minute on each side. Transfer shrimp to a bowl; keep warm.

Add red bell pepper and next 4 ingredients to skillet. Cook 5 minutes or until onion is tender. Add tomatoes and next 3 ingredients; stir well. Reduce heat to medium-low, and simmer, uncovered, 10 minutes. Add shrimp, and simmer, uncovered, 3 minutes or until shrimp turn pink. Remove from heat; stir in basil. Serve over rice. Yield: 6 servings.

John McManus

Recipes from the Heart of Maine
Friends of the Millinocket Memorial Library
Millinocket, Maine

Blend of the Bayou

Celebrate the Bayou region with two of its own—fresh shrimp and lump crabmeat.

2 tablespoons butter or margarine
1 large onion, chopped
1 medium-size green bell pepper, chopped
2 celery ribs, chopped
1 pound peeled and deveined, medium-size fresh shrimp
1 (8-ounce) package cream cheese, softened
½ cup butter or margarine, softened
1 pound fresh lump crabmeat

2 cups hot cooked rice
1 (10¾-ounce) can cream of mushroom soup, undiluted
1 (4½-ounce) jar whole mushrooms, drained
1 tablespoon garlic salt
1 teaspoon hot sauce
½ teaspoon ground red pepper
1 cup round buttery cracker crumbs (about 20 crackers)
1 cup (4 ounces) shredded sharp Cheddar cheese

Melt 2 tablespoons butter in a Dutch oven over medium-high heat. Add onion, bell pepper, and celery; sauté 10 minutes. Add shrimp; sauté 2 minutes. Remove from heat. Add cream cheese and ½ cup butter, stirring until cream cheese and butter melt. Stir in crabmeat and next 6 ingredients. Spoon mixture into a lightly greased 13- x 9-inch baking dish.

Stir together cracker crumbs and cheese; sprinkle over shrimp mixture. Bake, uncovered, at 350° for 25 to 30 minutes or until bubbly. Yield: 8 to 10 servings.   Lois Marie (Dickie) Henckel Herman

Recipes and Recollections
The Hitchcock Heritage Society
Hitchcock, Texas

Miami Seafood Cakes with Jalapeño Tartar Sauce

½ pound unpeeled, medium-size fresh shrimp
½ pound lean whitefish fillets
½ cup diced onion
¼ cup diced celery
¼ cup diced green bell pepper
¼ cup mayonnaise
1 tablespoon butter or margarine, melted
1 large egg, lightly beaten
1 teaspoon Old Bay seasoning
2 teaspoons Worcestershire sauce
½ teaspoon paprika
¼ teaspoon salt
¼ teaspoon dried crushed red pepper
¼ teaspoon black pepper
½ pound fresh lump crabmeat, drained
3 cups soft breadcrumbs (homemade), divided
2 tablespoons butter or margarine, divided
2 tablespoons vegetable oil
Jalapeño Tartar Sauce

Peel shrimp, and devein, if desired. Arrange shrimp and fish in a steamer basket over boiling water. Cover and steam 10 minutes or until fish flakes with a fork. Cool. Chop shrimp and fish.

Combine onion and next 11 ingredients; stir in shrimp mixture, crabmeat, and 1 cup breadcrumbs. Shape mixture into 12 patties; coat with remaining 2 cups breadcrumbs. Cover and chill 1 hour.

Melt 1 tablespoon butter and add 1 tablespoon oil in a large skillet over medium heat; cook 6 patties 3 minutes on each side or until golden. Drain on paper towels. Repeat procedure with remaining butter, oil, and patties. Serve with Jalapeño Tartar Sauce. Yield: 6 servings.

Jalapeño Tartar Sauce

1 cup mayonnaise
1 jalapeño pepper, seeded and diced
2 tablespoons sweet pickle relish
1 tablespoon chopped fresh chives
1 tablespoon capers
¾ teaspoon dried dillweed

Stir together all ingredients; chill. Yield: 1⅓ cups.   Kris Major

Recipes from the Heart
Littleton Regional Hospital Helping Hands
Littleton, New Hampshire

Pasta Sauce, Florida Style

Spoon this shrimp-and-clam tomato sauce over mounds of your favorite hot cooked pasta.

1 pound unpeeled, medium-size fresh shrimp
1 onion, chopped
3 celery ribs, chopped
2 garlic cloves, minced
2 tablespoons olive oil
2 (14½-ounce) cans diced tomatoes, undrained
2 (8-ounce) bottles clam juice
2 (6-ounce) cans tomato paste
½ cup dry white wine
½ teaspoon salt
½ teaspoon dried oregano
¼ teaspoon dried thyme
¼ teaspoon dried basil
2 (6½-ounce) cans minced clams, drained
½ cup chopped fresh parsley

Peel shrimp, and devein, if desired. Set aside.

Sauté onion, celery, and garlic in hot oil in a Dutch oven over medium-high heat 5 minutes. Add tomatoes and next 7 ingredients; bring to a boil. Reduce heat, and simmer, uncovered, 1 hour, stirring occasionally. Stir in shrimp and clams; simmer, uncovered, 10 more minutes or until shrimp turn pink. Stir in parsley. Yield: 8 cups.

Gracious Gator Cooks
The Junior League of Gainesville, Florida

Paella

18 littleneck clams
18 raw mussels in shells
2 (32-ounce) containers chicken broth
½ teaspoon saffron threads
3 pounds chicken pieces
8 garlic cloves, halved
½ cup olive oil
1 cup diced cooked ham
1 medium onion, chopped
6 garlic cloves, minced
3 cups Arborio rice
⅓ cup chopped fresh parsley
½ cup dry white wine
1 tablespoon fresh lemon juice
1 teaspoon salt
1 teaspoon pepper
1 pound unpeeled, medium-size fresh shrimp
½ pound bay scallops
½ pound grouper or seabass fillets (about 1 inch thick), cut into 1-inch pieces
1½ cups frozen sweet green peas

Scrub clams thoroughly; discard opened, cracked, or heavy clams (they're filled with sand). Scrub mussels with a brush; remove beards. Discard cracked or heavy mussels or opened mussels that won't close when tapped. Set clams and mussels aside.

Bring chicken broth and saffron to a boil in a large saucepan; reduce heat, and simmer, uncovered, 15 minutes.

Brown chicken and 8 garlic cloves in hot oil in a large heavy-duty roasting pan or paella pan over medium heat; remove chicken and garlic from pan, discarding garlic and reserving drippings in pan. Set chicken aside.

Sauté ham, onion, and minced garlic in drippings 5 minutes or until tender. Add rice to ham mixture; sauté 5 minutes or until rice is golden. Add hot broth mixture, parsley, and next 4 ingredients; bring to a boil. Reduce heat to medium-low, and simmer, uncovered, 5 minutes. Add chicken to rice mixture; simmer, uncovered, 15 minutes. Press clams and mussels into rice mixture, hinge side down. Arrange shrimp, scallops, and grouper on top of rice mixture.

Cover with aluminum foil; simmer 20 to 25 minutes or until shells open and shrimp turn pink. Discard unopened clams and mussels. Sprinkle peas over rice mixture. Cover, remove from heat, and let stand 10 minutes or until liquid is absorbed and rice is tender. Yield: 10 servings.   Carolyn Deshon Rodriguez

Breakfast in Cairo, Dinner in Rome
International School of Minnesota Foundation
Eden Prairie, Minnesota

Seafood Thermidor

Celebrate your next special occasion with this dish. A lavish mix of fresh lobster tails, shrimp, and lump crabmeat is offered over rice to absorb its sumptuous cream sauce.

12 cups water
1 tablespoon Old Bay seasoning
5 (5-ounce) fresh lobster tails
3 pounds peeled and deveined, large fresh shrimp
¾ cup butter, divided
1½ pounds sliced fresh mushrooms
3 garlic cloves, minced
¾ cup all-purpose flour
2 cups chicken broth
2 cups half-and-half
1 cup heavy whipping cream
1 pound fresh lump crabmeat, drained
¼ cup dry sherry
2 tablespoons prepared mustard
1½ teaspoons salt
1 tablespoon lemon juice
½ teaspoon hot sauce
1 cup finely shredded Parmesan cheese
Hot cooked rice

Bring water and Old Bay seasoning to a boil in a large Dutch oven. Add lobster, and cook 5 minutes; cool. Remove and discard shells, and chop meat. Return water to a boil. Add shrimp, and cook 3 minutes or until shrimp turn pink. Drain and set aside.

Melt ¼ cup butter in a Dutch oven over medium-high heat; add mushrooms, and sauté 5 minutes. Pour mushroom mixture through a wire-mesh strainer, discarding liquid; set mushrooms aside.

Melt remaining ½ cup butter in Dutch oven over medium heat; add garlic, and sauté 1 minute. Add flour, and cook 3 minutes, stirring constantly.

Gradually stir in chicken broth, half-and-half, and heavy whipping cream; cook, stirring constantly, 7 minutes or until mixture is thickened and bubbly. Stir in reserved mushrooms, lobster, shrimp, crabmeat, and next 5 ingredients.

Spoon seafood mixture into a lightly greased 13- x 9-inch baking dish. Bake, uncovered, at 350° for 45 minutes. Sprinkle with Parmesan cheese. Bake, uncovered, 30 more minutes. Serve over rice. Yield: 12 servings.

Savoring the Seasons: Riverside
The Craven Regional Medical Center Foundation
New Bern, North Carolina

Meats

Rack of Lamb with Honey-Hazelnut Crust, page 202

Royal Rib-Eye Roast

¾ teaspoon fines herbes, divided
½ teaspoon salt
½ teaspoon lemon pepper
1 (4- to 4½-pound) boneless rib-eye roast
⅔ cup water
1 teaspoon beef bouillon granules
2 tablespoons chopped fresh parsley
Horseradish Mushrooms

Combine ½ teaspoon fines herbes, salt, and lemon pepper; rub over beef. Place beef, fat side up, on a rack in a shallow roasting pan; insert meat thermometer into thickest part of beef, making sure it does not touch fat.

Bake, uncovered, at 325° for 2½ to 3 hours or until thermometer registers 145° (medium-rare) or 160° (medium). Remove beef to a serving platter; cover and keep warm.

Add water to pan drippings; stir in bouillon granules and remaining ¼ teaspoon fines herbes. Bring mixture to a boil; reduce heat, and simmer, uncovered, 2 minutes. Pour mixture through a wire-mesh strainer into a small bowl, discarding solids.

To serve, place beef on a serving platter; sprinkle with parsley. Surround beef with Horseradish Mushrooms, and serve with sauce. Yield: 6 to 8 servings.

Horseradish Mushrooms

24 large fresh mushrooms
½ cup sour cream
2 tablespoons prepared horseradish
2 tablespoons Dijon mustard

Remove and discard stems from mushrooms.

Stir together sour cream, horseradish, and Dijon mustard. Spoon horseradish mixture evenly into mushroom caps. Place on a lightly greased 15- x 10-inch jellyroll pan. Bake, uncovered, at 325° for 15 minutes. Yield: 6 to 8 servings. Barbara Scott

Angels in the Kitchen
Grace Episcopal Church
Anderson, South Carolina

Sweet-and-Sour Brisket

Fork-tender brisket is sure to please the most finicky eater. The cranberry sauce, ketchup, and beer sauce make it memorable. If there's any of the sauce left over, try it with meatloaf.

1 (16-ounce) can whole-berry cranberry sauce
1 (12-ounce) bottle beer
½ cup ketchup
¼ cup all-purpose flour
2 tablespoons paprika
1 tablespoon kosher salt
2 teaspoons freshly ground pepper
1½ tablespoons minced garlic
1 (5- to 6-pound) boneless beef brisket, trimmed
¼ cup olive oil, divided
6 large onions, sliced (about 5¾ pounds)

Whisk together first 4 ingredients; set aside.

Combine paprika, salt, and pepper. Rub salt mixture and garlic over beef. Heat 2 tablespoons oil in a very large heavy-duty roasting pan or oven-proof skillet over medium heat until hot. Add beef; cook 8 to 10 minutes on each side or until browned. Remove beef from pan, and set aside.

Heat remaining 2 tablespoons oil in same roasting pan. Add onion, and cook over medium heat, stirring often, 12 minutes or until browned. Remove from heat. Place beef on top of onion; pour beer mixture over beef.

Bake, covered, at 400° for 3 hours. Let stand, covered, 30 minutes. To serve, slice beef diagonally across grain into thin slices. Yield: 8 to 10 servings.

The Kosher Palette
Joseph Kushner Hebrew Academy
Livingston, New Jersey

Blue Cheese Flank Steak

A buttery blend of blue cheese and chives is slathered over hot-off-the-grill flank steak.

½ cup olive oil
¼ cup lemon juice
1 tablespoon grated onion
1 garlic clove, minced
2 tablespoons chopped fresh
   parsley
1 teaspoon salt
1 teaspoon ground marjoram
1 teaspoon ground thyme

½ teaspoon hot sauce
¼ cup butter or margarine,
   softened
2 tablespoons chopped fresh
   chives
2 tablespoons crumbled blue
   cheese
1 (1½-pound) flank steak

Stir together first 9 ingredients; set marinade aside.

Stir together butter, chives, and blue cheese; set aside.

Make shallow cuts in steak diagonally across grain at 1-inch intervals. Place steak in a shallow dish or heavy-duty zip-top plastic bag. Pour marinade over steak; cover or seal. Marinate in refrigerator 4 hours, turning meat occasionally.

Remove steak from marinade, discarding marinade. Grill steak, covered with grill lid, over medium-high heat (350° to 400°) 7 to 8 minutes on each side or to desired degree of doneness.

To serve, spread blue cheese mixture over steak. Slice diagonally across grain into very thin slices. Yield: 4 servings.

Note: If desired, steak can be broiled 3 to 5 inches from heat for 5 minutes; turn steak. Broil 6 to 8 minutes more or to desired degree of doneness.

I'll Cook When Pigs Fly
The Junior League of Cincinnati, Ohio

Thai Beef Grill

Peanut butter, sweet onion, and dried crushed red pepper balance the tangy teriyaki sauce in this grilled sirloin special.

2 tablespoons lite teriyaki sauce

2 tablespoons creamy peanut butter

2 tablespoons water

¼ teaspoon dried crushed red pepper

2 (8-ounce) boneless top sirloin steaks (1 inch thick)

1 large sweet onion, cut into ½-inch slices

3 tablespoons lite teriyaki sauce

Stir together first 3 ingredients in a small bowl until smooth. Stir in red pepper; set sauce aside.

Brush both sides of steaks and onion slices with 3 tablespoons teriyaki sauce. Place steaks and onion slices on grill rack. Grill, covered with grill lid, over medium-high heat (350° to 400°) 4 minutes. Turn steak and onion; grill 5 more minutes or to desired degree of doneness, removing onion after 5 minutes.

Trim fat from steaks. Slice steak diagonally across grain into thick slices. Serve with grilled onions and sauce. Yield: 4 servings.

Vintage Virginia: A History of Good Taste
The Virginia Dietetic Association
Centreville, Virginia

Double-D Ranch Steaks with Jalapeño Pepper Sauce

A dry rub of garlic powder, chili powder, and oregano imparts its spicy essence to steaks. Serve this dish with lots of mashed potatoes. It's a must in order to soak up the sassy sauce made with pepper jelly.

¼ teaspoon salt
½ teaspoon coarsely ground pepper
½ teaspoon garlic powder
¼ teaspoon ground cumin
¼ teaspoon dried oregano
¾ teaspoon chili powder
4 (4-ounce) beef tenderloin steaks (about 1 inch thick)

1 teaspoon vegetable oil
½ cup reduced-sodium beef broth
¼ cup balsamic vinegar
2 tablespoons red jalapeño pepper jelly

Stir together first 6 ingredients. Rub chili powder mixture on both sides of steaks.

Heat oil in a large skillet over high heat until hot. Add steaks; reduce heat to medium, and cook 5 minutes on each side. Remove steaks from skillet; set aside, and keep warm. Wipe skillet with paper towels.

Add broth, vinegar, and jelly to skillet; bring to a boil. Reduce heat; simmer, uncovered, 4 minutes or until sauce is reduced to ½ cup. Spoon sauce over steaks. Yield: 4 servings. Sherry Blackmon

Walking with Christ
First Baptist Church
Mount Airy, North Carolina

Filet Mignon Bundles

Crisp and buttery sheets of phyllo pastry encase tenderloin steaks and mushrooms, creating beautiful bundles that are sure to impress your dinner guests.

6 (8-ounce) beef tenderloin steaks (about 1½ inches thick)
1 teaspoon salt
1 teaspoon freshly ground pepper
1 cup butter, melted and divided
2 tablespoons olive oil, divided

1 pound fresh mushrooms, chopped
¼ cup dry red wine
3 tablespoons chopped fresh chives
1 (16-ounce) package frozen phyllo pastry, thawed in refrigerator

Sprinkle steaks with salt and pepper. Heat 2 tablespoons butter and 1 tablespoon oil in a large nonstick skillet over medium-high heat until hot. Add steaks; cook 10 minutes, turning often, or until browned on all sides. Remove steaks from skillet; set aside, and keep warm.

Heat 6 tablespoons butter and remaining 1 tablespoon oil in skillet over high heat. Add mushrooms, and cook 4 minutes. Add wine, and cook 2 to 3 minutes or until liquid evaporates. Remove from heat; stir in chives.

Cut phyllo into 36 (13- x 9-inch) rectangles; cover phyllo with a slightly damp cloth. Layer 6 rectangles of phyllo, brushing each layer with remaining melted butter and placing every other phyllo rectangle perpendicular to the previous one. Spread ⅓ cup mushroom mixture in center of layered phyllo, and top with 1 steak. Lift corners of phyllo rectangles, and twist together. Place bundle on a lightly greased baking sheet; brush with butter. Repeat procedure with remaining phyllo, butter, mushroom mixture, and steaks. Bake at 400° for 18 to 20 minutes (medium) or to desired degree of doneness, shielding with aluminum foil after 15 minutes to prevent excessive browning. Yield: 6 servings.

Café Weller . . . Tastes to Remember
Apple Corps of the Weller Health Education Center
Easton, Pennsylvania

Meatball Sub Casserole

Meatball sub sandwich lovers stop here! This casserole is fit for a hungry family. Just add a generous tossed green salad to round out things.

1 **pound ground beef**
⅓ **cup chopped green onions**
¼ **cup fine, dry Italian-seasoned breadcrumbs (store-bought)**
3 **tablespoons freshly grated Parmesan cheese**
1 **(28-ounce) jar pasta sauce**
1 **cup water**
2 **garlic cloves, minced**

1 **(1-pound) loaf Italian bread, cut into ¾-inch slices**
1 **(8-ounce) package cream cheese, softened**
½ **cup mayonnaise**
1 **teaspoon dried Italian seasoning**
¼ **teaspoon pepper**
2 **cups (8 ounces) shredded mozzarella cheese, divided**

Combine first 4 ingredients in a large bowl; mix well. Shape mixture into 1-inch balls. Place on a rack in a shallow pan. Bake at 400° for 15 to 20 minutes or until no longer pink.

Meanwhile, combine pasta sauce, water, and garlic. Spread 1 cup sauce in an ungreased 13- x 9-inch baking dish. Line bottom with bread slices.

Combine cream cheese and next 3 ingredients in a small bowl. Spread cream cheese mixture over bread slices. Sprinkle with ½ cup mozzarella cheese. Top with meatballs. Pour remaining sauce mixture over meatballs; top with remaining 1½ cups mozzarella cheese. Bake, uncovered, at 350° for 20 to 22 minutes or until thoroughly heated. Yield: 6 to 8 servings.   Jacinda Schweitzer

Cooking with Class
Timber Lake Booster Club
Timber Lake, South Dakota

Sloppy Josés

Go south-of-the-border for a fresh take on a familiar favorite. Green chiles, salsa, refried beans, and beer turn the tables on this quick and easy pleaser. Toast the burger buns for extra flair.

¾ **pound ground chuck**
½ **(15-ounce) can refried beans (about 1 cup)**
½ **cup medium salsa**
1 **(4.5-ounce) can chopped green chiles, undrained**
1 **small onion, chopped (about ¾ cup)**
¼ **cup beer**
1 **garlic clove, minced**
½ **teaspoon chili powder**
6 **hamburger buns, split and toasted**

Cook beef in a large skillet, stirring until it crumbles and is no longer pink; drain well. Return beef to skillet; add beans and next 6 ingredients to skillet, stirring well. Bring to a boil; reduce heat, and simmer, uncovered, 10 to 15 minutes or until mixture reaches desired consistency.

To serve, spoon mixture onto bottoms of toasted buns. Cover with bun tops, and serve immediately. Yield: 6 servings.

Cooks of the Green Door
The League of Catholic Women
Minneapolis, Minnesota

Reuben Pie

The recognizable sandwich fixings of corned beef, cheese, sauerkraut, and Thousand Island dressing are nestled comfortably within a flaky pastry crust.

1 tablespoon caraway seeds
1 unbaked 9-inch pastry shell
½ pound thinly sliced deli
   corned beef, shredded
¼ cup Thousand Island
   dressing
1 tablespoon Dijon mustard
¾ cup chopped sauerkraut,
   drained

1½ cups (6 ounces) shredded
   Gruyère cheese
3 large eggs, lightly beaten
1 cup half-and-half
1 tablespoon grated onion
½ teaspoon salt
¼ teaspoon dry mustard
Garnish: kosher dill pickle
   spears

Press caraway seeds into pastry shell. Prick bottom and sides with a fork. Bake at 425° for 7 minutes. Remove pastry shell from oven, and reduce oven temperature to 350°.

Place beef in prepared shell. Stir together dressing and Dijon mustard; spread over beef. Top with sauerkraut; sprinkle with cheese. Combine eggs and next 4 ingredients; pour mixture evenly over cheese layer.

Bake, uncovered, at 350° for 40 minutes, shielding edges after 35 minutes to prevent excessive browning. Cool 5 minutes before serving. Garnish, if desired. Yield: 6 servings.   Jeanne Rigg

We're Cooking Up Something New:
50 Years of Music, History, and Food
Wichita Falls Symphony League
Wichita Falls, Texas

Veal Pecan with Brie Sauce

A delicate pecan breading cloaks these tender veal cutlets, and a creamy Brie and wine sauce caps the cutlets with flair enough for company.

1¼ pounds thinly sliced veal
    cutlets (about 12)
2 large eggs
¼ cup water
⅛ teaspoon salt
⅛ teaspoon ground white
    pepper

2 cups fine, dry breadcrumbs
    (store-bought)
1 cup finely chopped pecans
½ cup all-purpose flour
½ cup olive oil
Brie Sauce

Place veal between 2 sheets of heavy-duty plastic wrap; flatten to ⅛-inch thickness, using a meat mallet or rolling pin.

Whisk together eggs and next 3 ingredients in a shallow bowl. Stir together breadcrumbs and pecans in a shallow bowl. Dredge veal in flour, dip in egg mixture, and press both sides into breadcrumb mixture. Repeat procedure with remaining veal.

Heat 2 tablespoons oil in a large skillet over medium-high heat. Add veal, 4 pieces at a time, and cook 1 to 2 minutes on each side; place veal in an ungreased 13- x 9-inch baking dish. Wipe skillet. Repeat procedure with remaining oil and veal. Bake, uncovered, at 400° for 5 minutes. Serve with Brie Sauce. Yield: 4 to 6 servings.

Brie Sauce

10 ounces Brie
¼ cup half-and-half
¼ cup dry white wine
1 teaspoon cornstarch

¼ teaspoon salt
⅛ teaspoon ground white
    pepper

Slice rind from Brie, discarding rind. Chop Brie, and set aside.

Stir together half-and-half, wine, and cornstarch in a saucepan. Bring to a boil; reduce heat, and simmer, uncovered, 2 minutes, stirring constantly. Add cheese, salt, and pepper; stir until cheese melts and sauce is smooth. Yield: 1 cup.
    Paul Passafume

Sesquicentennially Delicious
Western Pennsylvania Hospital
Pittsburgh, Pennsylvania

Codellets de Veau

¼ cup thinly sliced onion
1 tablespoon butter, melted
2 pounds veal cutlets
¾ teaspoon salt
½ teaspoon pepper
1 cup soft, coarse breadcrumbs
  (homemade)

1 cup (4 ounces) shredded
  Swiss cheese
½ cup chopped fresh Italian
  parsley
1 cup dry white wine
¼ cup butter, melted

Sauté onion in 1 tablespoon melted butter in a skillet over medium heat until tender. Spread evenly in an ungreased 13- x 9-inch baking dish. Layer veal over onion. Sprinkle veal with salt and pepper. Top evenly with breadcrumbs, cheese, and parsley.

Pour wine around sides of dish. Drizzle with ¼ cup melted butter. Bake, uncovered, at 300° for 1 hour and 45 minutes to 2 hours or until top is crisp, basting occasionally. Yield: 6 to 8 servings.

More Enchanted Eating from the West Shore
Friends of the Symphony
Muskegon, Michigan

Rack of Lamb with Honey-Hazelnut Crust

Ask your butcher to "French" (trim the fat from) the rib bones of this elegant cut of lamb to save time. "Frenching" adds to the presentation.

¼ cup honey, divided
2 tablespoons Dijon mustard
3 (8-rib) lamb rib roasts (1½ to
  1¾ pounds each)
¼ teaspoon salt
¼ teaspoon freshly ground
  pepper

1 cup soft breadcrumbs
  (homemade)
1 cup ground hazelnuts
3 tablespoons minced fresh
  rosemary

Combine 1 tablespoon honey and Dijon mustard; spread over roasts. Sprinkle with salt and pepper. Combine breadcrumbs, hazelnuts, and rosemary; pat over roasts. Drizzle with remaining 3 tablespoons honey.

Place roasts in a lightly greased roasting pan, fat side up. Insert meat thermometer into thickest part, making sure it does not touch bone. Bake at 425° for 30 to 35 minutes or until thermometer registers 150°; shielding as necessary with aluminum foil to prevent overbrowning. Remove from oven; let stand 10 minutes. Yield: 6 to 8 servings.

Yuletide on Hilton Head: A Heritage of Island Flavors
United Way of Beaufort County
Hilton Head Island, South Carolina

Lamb Burgers with Yogurt-Dill Sauce

2 pounds ground lamb
½ cup minced onion
¼ cup chopped fresh mint or 1 tablespoon dried mint
2 tablespoons chopped fresh or 2 teaspoons dried oregano
1 large egg
1 large garlic clove, minced
1 teaspoon salt
¼ teaspoon pepper
4 (8-inch) pita bread rounds
2 tomatoes, seeded and chopped
1 onion, thinly sliced
1 green bell pepper, sliced
1 cucumber, peeled, seeded, and thinly sliced (optional)
Yogurt-Dill Sauce

Combine first 8 ingredients, mixing well. Shape into 8 patties. Grill, covered with grill lid, over medium-high heat (350° to 400°) about 5 minutes on each side or until done. Cut pita rounds in half, and place 1 patty in each pita. Top evenly with tomato, onion, bell pepper, and, if desired, cucumber. Top with Yogurt-Dill Sauce. Yield: 8 servings.

Yogurt-Dill Sauce

1 (8-ounce) container plain yogurt
1 tablespoon sugar
2 tablespoons minced onion
2 tablespoons chopped fresh mint
2 tablespoons chopped fresh dill or 2 teaspoons dried dillweed
¼ teaspoon salt
¼ teaspoon ground white pepper

Stir together all ingredients. Cover and chill 1 hour. Yield: 1 cup.

Always in Season
The Junior League of Salt Lake City, Utah

Cuban Roast Pork

Toasting and crushing cumin seeds and black peppercorns make this dish authentic and extraspecial. However, you can use the same amounts of ground cumin and black pepper called for if you're pressed for time.

1 (4-pound) boneless pork shoulder or Boston butt pork roast, trimmed
2 teaspoons cumin seeds
½ teaspoon black peppercorns
4 garlic cloves, minced
⅓ cup fresh orange juice
⅓ cup dry sherry
3 tablespoons fresh lemon juice
3 tablespoons fresh lime juice
2 tablespoons olive oil
2 teaspoons salt
1 teaspoon dried oregano

Tie roast at 2- to 3-inch intervals with heavy string; set aside.

Place a small skillet over medium-high heat until hot. Add cumin seeds and peppercorns; cook, stirring constantly, 2 minutes or until toasted. Crush mixture in a mortar and pestle or spice mill. Combine cumin mixture, garlic, and remaining 7 ingredients in a large heavy-duty zip-top plastic bag; add roast. Seal bag, and chill 8 hours, turning occasionally.

Place roast, fat side up, on a rack in a roasting pan; pour marinade over roast. Bake, uncovered, at 325° for 2 hours and 45 minutes or until a meat thermometer inserted into thickest part registers 160°, basting occasionally. Let stand 10 minutes; remove string, and slice. Yield: 8 to 10 servings.

John D. Morris

We're Cooking Up Something New:
50 Years of Music, History, and Food
Wichita Falls Symphony League
Wichita Falls, Texas

Pork Tenderloin with Fresh Rosemary Salsa

3 (1-pound) boneless pork
  tenderloins
1 tablespoon olive oil
3 garlic cloves, minced
1 tablespoon ground coriander
1 tablespoon coarsely ground
  pepper
½ teaspoon salt
Fresh Rosemary Salsa

Brush tenderloins with oil. Combine garlic and next 3 ingredients; stir well. Rub garlic mixture over tenderloins.

Grill tenderloins, without grill lid, over medium-high heat (350° to 400°) 3 to 4 minutes on each side or until browned. Remove from grill.

Place tenderloins in a lightly greased, preheated cast-iron skillet. Bake at 400° for 10 to 12 minutes or until a meat thermometer inserted into thickest part registers 160°. Let stand 5 minutes before slicing. Serve with Fresh Rosemary Salsa. Yield: 8 to 10 servings.

Fresh Rosemary Salsa

1½ cups chopped, seeded
  plum tomatoes
¼ cup finely chopped onion
¼ cup sliced ripe olives
1 garlic clove, minced
2 tablespoons olive oil
2 tablespoons red wine vinegar
2 tablespoons balsamic vinegar
1 tablespoon chopped fresh
  parsley
1 tablespoon chopped fresh
  rosemary
¼ teaspoon salt
¼ teaspoon pepper

Combine all ingredients; cover and chill 4 hours. Yield: 2 cups.

A Century of Serving
The Junior Board of Christiana Care, Inc.
Wilmington, Delaware

Potluck Spareribs

6 pounds boneless pork ribs
1½ cups ketchup
½ cup honey
½ cup white vinegar
⅓ cup soy sauce
¾ cup firmly packed light
   brown sugar

1½ teaspoons ground ginger
1 teaspoon salt
¾ teaspoon dry mustard
½ teaspoon garlic powder
¼ teaspoon pepper

Cut ribs into serving-size pieces; place on racks in 2 (13- x 9-inch) roasting pans. Cover and bake at 350° for 1 hour and 45 minutes. Drain ribs, and remove racks from pans; return meat to 1 pan.

Combine ketchup and remaining ingredients; pour over meat. Bake, uncovered, 1 hour, basting with sauce every 15 minutes. Yield: 8 to 10 servings.

Lisa Jewell Swanson

Fine Food from the Friends
Friends of the Superior Public Library, Inc.
Superior, Wisconsin

Pork Chops with Curried Apple and Onion Sauce

Serve these creamy apple- and onion-sauced pork loin chops with basmati rice for added nutlike aroma. Basmati is a long-grain rice with a delicate texture.

4 bone-in pork loin chops
   (about ¾ inch thick)
1 teaspoon dried thyme,
   divided
1 teaspoon dried marjoram,
   divided
¾ teaspoon salt, divided
¼ teaspoon pepper
1 tablespoon olive oil
1 large Granny Smith apple,
   peeled and chopped

½ sweet onion, chopped
6 garlic cloves, minced
¾ cup reduced-sodium chicken
   broth
½ cup dry white wine
¼ cup heavy whipping cream
2 tablespoons honey mustard
1 teaspoon curry powder

Sprinkle chops with ½ teaspoon thyme, ½ teaspoon marjoram, ½ teaspoon salt, and pepper. Heat oil in a large skillet over medium-high heat; add chops, and cook 5 minutes on each side or until done. Remove from skillet, reserving drippings in skillet. Set chops aside, and keep warm.

Add chopped apple, onion, and garlic to drippings in skillet; sauté over medium-high heat 2 minutes. Stir in broth and remaining 4 ingredients. Add remaining ½ teaspoon thyme, remaining ½ teaspoon marjoram, and remaining ¼ teaspoon salt. Cook 5 minutes or until slightly thickened, stirring often. Serve chops with sauce. Yield: 4 servings.

Oh My Stars! Recipes That Shine
The Junior League of Roanoke Valley, Virginia

Apple Cider Ham with Mustard

Apple cider and dried apples join forces with brown sugar, cider vinegar, and Dijon mustard to add sweet-and-sour interest to slices of ham.

1 (5- to 6-pound) smoked, fully
   cooked ham half
3 cups apple cider
1½ cups dried apples
¾ cup firmly packed light
   brown sugar

6 tablespoons apple cider
   vinegar
3 tablespoons Dijon mustard

Place ham, fat side up, in a shallow roasting pan. Bake, uncovered, at 325° for 2 hours or until a meat thermometer inserted into thickest part registers 140°.

Combine cider and apples in a medium saucepan; bring to a boil over medium-high heat. Reduce heat, and simmer, uncovered, 8 minutes or until liquid is reduced to 1½ cups.

Combine brown sugar, vinegar, and mustard. Stir into cider mixture, and simmer, uncovered, 6 minutes or until liquid is reduced to 2¼ cups, stirring occasionally. Slice ham, and serve with sauce. Yield: 12 servings.

Always in Season
The Junior League of Salt Lake City, Utah

Black Bean Cassoulet

1 pound smoked sausage, cut
  into ¼-inch-thick slices
1 medium onion, chopped
2 garlic cloves, minced
2 tablespoons olive oil
2 (15-ounce) cans black beans,
  undrained
¼ cup dry sherry

1 tablespoon lemon juice
1 tablespoon brown sugar
1 tablespoon ground cumin
2 teaspoons dried oregano
½ teaspoon salt
½ teaspoon pepper
⅛ teaspoon ground red pepper
3 cups hot cooked rice

Cook sausage in a Dutch oven over medium-high heat until browned; drain and set aside.

Sauté onion and garlic in hot oil in Dutch oven over medium-high heat 5 minutes. Add sausage, black beans, and next 8 ingredients; bring to a boil. Reduce heat, and simmer, uncovered, 20 minutes, stirring occasionally. Serve over rice. Yield: 5 servings.

Bay Tables
The Junior League of Mobile, Alabama

Crock-Pot™ Venison Roast

1½ cups vegetable oil
¾ cup soy sauce
½ cup red wine vinegar
⅓ cup lemon juice
¼ cup Worcestershire sauce
2 tablespoons dry mustard
1 tablespoon dried parsley
  flakes
1 tablespoon pepper
2 garlic cloves, minced
1 (4-pound) boneless venison
  roast
1 (14.5-ounce) can whole
  tomatoes, undrained and
  chopped

2 garlic cloves, minced
¼ cup lemon juice
2 tablespoons light brown
  sugar
1 tablespoon Worcestershire
  sauce
1 teaspoon prepared mustard
2 tablespoons all-purpose flour
1 tablespoon salt
1 tablespoon vegetable oil

Stir together first 9 ingredients in a large bowl. Add venison to marinade, turning to coat. Cover and chill 8 hours, turning occasionally.

Stir together tomatoes and next 5 ingredients in a medium bowl. Cover and chill.

Remove venison from marinade; discard marinade. Combine flour and salt; rub over roast. Brown roast in hot oil in a large skillet over medium-high heat. Place in a 4½-quart slow cooker. Pour tomato mixture over roast. Cover and cook on HIGH 1 hour; reduce setting to LOW, and cook 7 hours. Yield: 12 servings.   Elline Noben

North Country Cooking
51st National Square Dance Convention
Champlin, Minnesota

Fried Venison with Pan Gravy

2 pounds venison cube steak, thinly sliced	½ cup vegetable oil
½ cup all-purpose flour	3 tablespoons all-purpose flour
1 teaspoon salt	2¼ cups milk
¼ teaspoon pepper	1 teaspoon salt
	½ teaspoon pepper

Place venison between 2 sheets of heavy-duty plastic wrap; flatten to ¼-inch thickness, using a meat mallet or rolling pin. Cut into small pieces.

Combine ½ cup flour, 1 teaspoon salt, and ¼ teaspoon pepper in a shallow dish. Dredge venison in flour mixture. Heat 2 tablespoons oil in a large skillet over medium-high heat. Add one-fourth of venison, and cook 3 minutes on each side or until golden; set aside, and keep warm. Reserve pan drippings. Wipe skillet with paper towel. Repeat procedure with remaining oil and venison.

Stir together 3 tablespoons flour and ¼ cup reserved pan drippings in skillet. Cook over medium-high heat 1½ minutes, stirring constantly. Stir in milk. Bring to a boil; reduce heat, and simmer, uncovered 3 minutes, stirring constantly.

Pour gravy through a wire-mesh strainer into a bowl, discarding solids. Stir in 1 teaspoon salt and ½ teaspoon pepper. Serve venison with gravy. Yield: 6 servings.

The Dining Car
The Service League of Denison, Texas

Venison Rollemachen

You'll enjoy these venison rolls with mashed potatoes and the rich gravy made from reducing the pan drippings. When a recipe calls for a mixture to be reduced by half, simply place the handle of a wooden spoon in the mixture, and make a note of where the liquid leaves a mark on the spoon; then cook until a new mark of reduced liquid appears to be halfway up to the first mark.

2 pounds venison round steak
1½ cups diced onion
10 bacon slices
½ teaspoon garlic salt
½ teaspoon dried oregano
2 tablespoons vegetable oil

½ pound fresh morel
   mushrooms, drained
⅔ cup water
2 tablespoons all-purpose flour
¾ cup water

Cut venison into 5 pieces. Place between 2 sheets of heavy-duty plastic wrap; flatten to about ½-inch thickness, using a meat mallet or rolling pin. Divide onion over each piece of venison; top each with 2 bacon slices. Sprinkle with garlic salt and oregano. Roll up each piece of venison, jellyroll fashion; secure with heavy string.

Cook venison rolls in hot oil in a large Dutch oven over medium-high heat until browned on all sides. Add morels and ⅔ cup water, and cook 2 minutes. Cover and bake at 325° for 1½ hours or until venison is tender.

Remove venison rolls from Dutch oven; keep warm. Combine flour and ¾ cup water, whisking until smooth. Whisk flour mixture into mixture in Dutch oven; cook over medium heat until thickened, whisking constantly. Cook 5 more minutes or until mixture is reduced by half. Spoon over venison rolls. Yield: 5 servings.   Laurie Timm

The Cookbook Tour
Good Shepherd Lutheran Church
Plainview, Minnesota

Pasta, Rice & Grains

Pesto Fettuccine with Chicken and Vegetables, page 214

Capellini with Fresh Tomato and Basil Sauce

Delicate, thin strands of capellini flatter the simple nature of this plum tomato, basil, and caper sauce.

2 pounds plum tomatoes, seeded and chopped
1 cup chopped fresh basil
½ cup extra-virgin olive oil, divided
1 (3½-ounce) jar capers, drained

3 tablespoons sherry vinegar
1 teaspoon salt
½ teaspoon freshly ground pepper
16 ounces uncooked dried capellini

Stir together tomato, basil, ¼ cup olive oil, capers, and next 3 ingredients in a large bowl. Cover and chill 2 hours.

Cook capellini according to package directions; drain. Toss with remaining ¼ cup olive oil. Add pasta mixture to tomato mixture in bowl, and toss to coat. Let stand 5 minutes before serving. Yield: 8 servings.

Carol Radnor

Sharing Our Best
The Arrangement Hair Salon
Columbus, Ohio

Fusilli Tricolor with Olives, Basil, and Brie

Adding roasted chicken to this recipe turns it into a terrific entrée. It's a delightful mix of dried tomatoes, olives, Brie, and basil.

1 (7-ounce) jar dried tomatoes in oil, undrained
12 ounces Brie cheese
1 cup pitted ripe olives, halved
1 cup loosely packed fresh basil, thinly sliced
½ cup olive oil

2 garlic cloves, minced
1 teaspoon salt
1 teaspoon freshly ground pepper
16 ounces uncooked dried tricolored fusilli

Drain tomatoes, reserving ¼ cup oil. Cut tomatoes into ¼-inch strips.

Remove and discard rind from Brie; cube cheese.

Combine tomatoes, reserved oil, Brie, and next 6 ingredients in a large bowl. Cover and let stand at room temperature 2 hours.

Cook pasta according to package directions; drain well. Add hot pasta to Brie mixture, and toss well. Serve immediately. Yield: 10 to 12 servings.   Mary Lee Amato

Cookin' with Friends
National Presbyterian School Class of 2000
Washington, D.C.

Mexican Chicken Pasta

¼ cup pine nuts
3 tablespoons olive oil, divided
1 large onion, chopped
2 garlic cloves, minced
1½ teaspoons dried basil
1½ teaspoons dried oregano
¼ to ½ teaspoon dried crushed
   red pepper
2 small zucchini, thinly sliced
1 (8-ounce) package sliced
   fresh mushrooms

2 medium tomatoes, seeded
   and chopped
1 cup shredded cooked chicken
¾ cup freshly grated Parmesan
   cheese, divided
1 teaspoon salt
½ teaspoon black pepper
1 (9-ounce) package
   refrigerated fettuccine

Sauté pine nuts in 1 tablespoon hot olive oil in a large skillet over medium-high heat 1 minute. Remove pine nuts, and set aside.

Sauté onion and next 4 ingredients in remaining 2 tablespoons olive oil over medium-high heat 4 minutes. Add zucchini, mushrooms, and tomato; cook 3 minutes. Add chicken, ½ cup Parmesan cheese, salt, and black pepper; cook 1 minute.

Cook fettuccine according to package directions; drain and place on a large, deep serving platter. Spoon sauce over fettuccine; toss gently to coat. Sprinkle with remaining ¼ cup Parmesan cheese and pine nuts. Yield: 4 to 6 servings.

Savoring the Southwest Again
Roswell Symphony Guild
Roswell, New Mexico

Pesto Fettuccine with Chicken and Vegetables

Pick up a jar of your preferred brand of pesto to infuse this vegetable-packed chicken and pasta dish with the blessings of basil.

16 ounces uncooked dried fettuccine
2 tablespoons olive oil, divided
1 medium-size red bell pepper, thinly sliced
1 medium-size yellow bell pepper, thinly sliced
½ pound fresh asparagus, cut into 1-inch pieces
8 dried tomatoes in oil, drained and thinly sliced

1 pound skinned and boned chicken breast halves, cut into ½-inch strips
1 (7-ounce) jar pesto
6 tablespoons freshly grated Parmesan cheese
¾ teaspoon salt
½ teaspoon freshly ground pepper
Freshly grated Parmesan cheese

Cook fettuccine according to package directions; drain. Set aside, and keep warm.

Meanwhile, heat 1 tablespoon olive oil in a large skillet over medium heat. Add bell peppers and asparagus; cook 10 minutes, stirring occasionally. Transfer vegetables to a large bowl, and stir in dried tomatoes. Wipe skillet clean with paper towels. Heat remaining 1 tablespoon olive oil in skillet over medium-high heat; add chicken, and sauté 6 minutes or until done. Add chicken to vegetables in bowl. Add pasta. Stir in pesto, 6 tablespoons Parmesan cheese, salt, and pepper; toss well. Sprinkle with additional Parmesan cheese. Serve immediately. Yield: 6 servings.   Connie Smith

Menus & Memories
The University of Oklahoma Women's Association
Norman, Oklahoma

Maryland Crab Shells

This dish is a crab lover's delight. Jumbo pasta shells are stuffed with a succulent crab filling, then drizzled with a creamy Parmesan sauce and baked. The final touch is a sprinkling of zesty Old Bay seasoning.

40 uncooked jumbo pasta shells
3 tablespoons butter or margarine, divided
2 tablespoons chopped green bell pepper
1 tablespoon chopped purple onion
2½ cups milk, divided
1 teaspoon Old Bay seasoning, divided

1½ pounds fresh lump crabmeat, drained
1 cup mayonnaise
1 large egg, lightly beaten
½ teaspoon pepper
3 tablespoons all-purpose flour
1 cup freshly grated Parmesan cheese

Cook pasta shells according to package directions; drain and set aside.

Melt 1 tablespoon butter in a small skillet over medium heat. Add bell pepper and onion, and sauté 4 minutes.

Combine vegetables, ½ cup milk, ½ teaspoon Old Bay seasoning, crabmeat, and next 3 ingredients; stir gently. Spoon crabmeat mixture into pasta shells. Arrange filled pasta shells in 2 lightly greased 11- x 7-inch baking dishes.

Melt remaining 2 tablespoons butter in a small heavy saucepan over medium heat; whisk in flour until mixture is smooth. Cook 1 minute, whisking constantly. Gradually whisk in remaining 2 cups milk; cook over medium heat, whisking constantly, until mixture is thickened and bubbly. Remove from heat, and stir in Parmesan cheese. Drizzle sauce evenly over pasta shells; sprinkle with remaining ½ teaspoon Old Bay seasoning. Cover and bake at 350° for 20 minutes; uncover and bake 10 more minutes. Let stand 10 minutes before serving. Yield: 8 to 10 servings.

Barbara Wilson

Dixon Fixins
Dixon Ambulatory Care Center
Westminster, Maryland

Easy Lasagna

Yes, the lasagna noodles go into this recipe uncooked and the oven does the rest of the work to cook this pasta sauce and ground turkey lasagna to tender perfection.

1 pound ground turkey
4 cups pasta sauce (we tested with Prego)
½ cup water
1 teaspoon salt
½ teaspoon sugar
¼ teaspoon pepper
1 teaspoon dried Italian seasoning

8 ounces uncooked dried lasagna noodles
2 cups cottage cheese
1 (12-ounce) package shredded mozzarella cheese
½ cup grated Parmesan cheese

Brown turkey in a large skillet, stirring until it crumbles and is no longer pink. Add pasta sauce and next 5 ingredients. Bring to a boil; cover loosely, reduce heat, and simmer 10 minutes.

Layer 2 cups sauce mixture, half of uncooked lasagna noodles, 1 cup cottage cheese, and 1 cup mozzarella cheese in a lightly greased 13- x 9-inch baking dish. Repeat procedure with 2 cups sauce mixture, remaining lasagna noodles, remaining 1 cup cottage cheese, and 1 cup mozzarella cheese. Top with remaining 2 cups sauce and remaining mozzarella cheese. Sprinkle with Parmesan cheese. Cover with aluminum foil, and bake at 350° for 45 minutes. Uncover and bake 10 more minutes. Let stand 10 minutes before serving. Yield: 12 servings.

Business is Cookin' with FBLA
Lakeview Future Business Leaders of America
Columbus, Nebraska

Fresh Vegetable Lasagna

Instead of a spicy meat sauce, this sassy lasagna sports a white Alfredo sauce that cloaks the fresh vegetables in style.

8 uncooked dried lasagna noodles
2 pounds fresh spinach
½ cup butter or margarine
1 (8-ounce) package sliced fresh mushrooms
1 large onion, chopped
3 garlic cloves, minced
½ cup all-purpose flour
2½ cups milk
1 tablespoon chopped fresh basil

1½ teaspoons salt
1½ teaspoons dried oregano
¼ teaspoon pepper
2 large eggs, lightly beaten
½ cup freshly grated Parmesan cheese
1 (15-ounce) container ricotta cheese
2 ripe tomatoes, seeded and sliced
8 ounces thinly sliced mozzarella cheese

Cook noodles according to package directions; drain.

Remove stems from spinach; wash leaves thoroughly. Cook spinach in a small amount of boiling water 5 minutes or until tender. Drain; place on paper towels, and squeeze until very dry. Set aside.

Melt butter in a medium saucepan over medium heat. Add mushrooms, onion, and garlic, and sauté until tender. Stir in flour, and cook 1 minute, stirring constantly. Remove from heat; add milk, basil, salt, oregano, and pepper. Return to heat, and cook, stirring constantly, until mixture comes to a boil and thickens. Remove from heat. Gradually stir about one-fourth of sauce mixture into eggs; add egg mixture slowly to remaining sauce mixture, stirring constantly. Return to heat, and cook 1 minute, stirring constantly. Stir in Parmesan cheese.

Spread a thin layer of sauce in an ungreased 13- x 9-inch baking dish; layer with half of noodles, spinach, half of remaining sauce, ricotta cheese, half of tomato, and half of mozzarella. Top with remaining noodles, tomato, sauce, and mozzarella. Bake, covered, at 375° for 15 minutes; uncover and bake 30 more minutes. Let stand 15 minutes before serving. Yield: 8 servings.   Sharon St. Onge

Dixon Fixins
Dixon Ambulatory Care Center
Westminster, Maryland

Shrimp and Linguine with Sherry Cream Sauce

1 pound unpeeled, medium-size fresh shrimp
8 ounces uncooked dried linguine
3 tablespoons butter or margarine
1 tablespoon chopped garlic
2 teaspoons chopped shallot
1 cup whipping cream
6 tablespoons cream sherry
3 tablespoons chopped fresh parsley
½ teaspoon salt
¼ teaspoon freshly ground pepper
Garnishes: radicchio leaves, lemon slices, fresh parsley sprigs

Peel shrimp, and devein, if desired. Set aside.

Cook linguine according to package directions; drain well. Set aside, and keep warm.

Melt butter in a large skillet over medium-high heat; add shrimp, garlic, and shallot to skillet, and sauté 15 to 20 seconds. Stir in whipping cream and next 4 ingredients; cook 3 to 5 minutes or just until shrimp turn pink. Remove shrimp with a slotted spoon; set aside, and keep warm.

Bring whipping cream mixture to a boil; reduce heat, and simmer, uncovered, 5 minutes or until sauce thickens, stirring occasionally. Stir shrimp into sauce. Cook over medium heat just until thoroughly heated. Serve over linguine. Garnish, if desired. Yield: 2 servings.

Made in the Shade
The Junior League of Greater Fort Lauderdale, Florida

Baked Macaroni and Cheese

2 cups uncooked elbow macaroni (about 8 ounces)
1½ cups milk
½ cup (2 ounces) shredded mozzarella cheese
½ cup (2 ounces) shredded extra-sharp Cheddar cheese
½ cup (2 ounces) shredded Colby cheese
½ cup freshly shredded Parmesan cheese
3 slices process American cheese, chopped
¼ teaspoon salt
½ teaspoon pepper

Cook macaroni according to package directions, omitting salt and fat; drain well.

Combine macaroni, milk, and remaining ingredients, stirring well. Spoon mixture into a lightly greased 2-quart baking dish.

Bake, covered, at 400° for 15 minutes. Uncover and bake 15 to 20 more minutes or until thoroughly heated and lightly browned. Yield: 6 servings.   Mary Serfass and Sandy Haggard

Cookin' with Pride
4th Infantry Division
Ft. Hood, Texas

Night Nurse Noodle Bake

Angel hair pasta revels in a reassuring butter sauce of sour cream, cottage cheese, and Parmesan cheese.

6 ounces uncooked dried angel hair pasta
1 medium onion, sliced
⅓ cup butter or margarine, melted
1 (16-ounce) container sour cream

1 (8-ounce) container small-curd cottage cheese
⅛ teaspoon hot sauce
½ cup grated Parmesan cheese

Cook pasta according to package directions; drain and set aside.

Separate onion slices into rings; cook in melted butter in a large skillet over medium-high heat 3 minutes or until soft. Remove from heat. Stir in sour cream, cottage cheese, hot sauce, and pasta.

Spoon pasta mixture into a greased 13- x 9-inch baking dish. Sprinkle with Parmesan cheese.

Bake, uncovered, at 325° for 50 to 60 minutes or until bubbly and browned. Yield: 6 to 8 servings.

It's a Snap!
The Haven of Grace
St. Louis, Missouri

Orzo with Dilled Lemon Sauce

16 ounces uncooked orzo
½ cup chopped green onions
3 tablespoons chopped fresh dill
3 tablespoons fresh lemon juice
1 tablespoon Dijon mustard
½ teaspoon salt
¾ teaspoon freshly ground pepper
1 cup warm chicken broth
¼ cup olive oil
2 (14-ounce) cans artichoke heart quarters, rinsed and drained
1 cup kalamata olives, pitted and halved
1 cup crumbled feta cheese
Bibb or Boston lettuce leaves (optional)

Cook orzo according to package directions; drain well. Place in a large bowl, and set aside.

Process green onions and next 5 ingredients in a blender or food processor 45 seconds. Add warm chicken broth; process 20 seconds, stopping to scrape down sides. Turn blender or food processor on high; gradually add oil in a slow, steady stream.

Pour sauce over orzo; toss well. Add artichokes, olives, and feta cheese; toss well. Serve at room temperature, or cover and chill. Serve on lettuce leaves, if desired. Yield: 8 to 10 servings.

Bay Tables
The Junior League of Mobile, Alabama

Vodka Rigatoni

A splash of vodka impeccably complements this prosciutto and creamy tomato pasta sauce.

16 ounces uncooked rigatoni
1 tablespoon olive oil
¼ pound thinly sliced prosciutto
1 garlic clove, minced
1 (16-ounce) can crushed tomatoes
¼ teaspoon freshly ground black pepper
¼ teaspoon dried crushed red pepper
⅔ cup vodka
1 cup heavy whipping cream
3 tablespoons grated Parmesan cheese

Cook pasta according to package directions; drain and keep warm.

Heat oil in a large skillet over medium-high heat. Add prosciutto and garlic, and sauté 1 minute. Add tomatoes, black pepper, and red pepper. Bring to a boil; reduce heat, and simmer, uncovered, 20 minutes. Stir in vodka; simmer, uncovered, 3 minutes. Stir in heavy whipping cream and Parmesan cheese; simmer, uncovered, 15 minutes. Serve immediately over rigatoni. Yield: 8 servings.

A Century of Serving
The Junior Board of Christiana Care, Inc.
Wilmington, Delaware

Million Dollar Spaghetti Casserole

The hearty spaghetti combo of Italian sausage and ground beef makes this casserole model potluck cuisine. It easily feeds 10 to 12 people.

16 ounces uncooked dried angel hair pasta	1 (8-ounce) package cream cheese, softened
1 pound Italian sausage	¼ cup sour cream
1 pound ground beef	⅓ cup chopped green onions
1 medium onion, chopped	¼ cup chopped green bell pepper
1 (26-ounce) jar pasta sauce	
1 cup small-curd cottage cheese	¼ cup grated Parmesan cheese

Cook pasta according to package directions; drain and keep warm.

Remove and discard casings from sausage. Cook sausage, ground beef, and onion in a large skillet over medium-high heat, stirring until meats crumble and are no longer pink; drain well. Reserve ½ cup pasta sauce. Stir remaining pasta sauce into meat mixture.

Spread about ½ cup meat sauce in a greased 13- x 9-inch baking dish. Layer half of cooked pasta. Spoon 2¾ cups meat sauce over pasta. Combine cottage cheese and next 4 ingredients; stir well. Spoon over meat sauce layer. Top with remaining half of pasta and remaining meat sauce. Drizzle with reserved ½ cup pasta sauce. Sprinkle with Parmesan cheese. Bake, uncovered, at 350° for 35 minutes. Yield: 10 to 12 servings.   Boden Family

Cookin' with Friends
National Presbyterian School Class of 2000
Washington, D.C.

Tortellini with Feta Cheese, Tomato, and Basil

1 (9-ounce) package
   refrigerated cheese-filled
   tortellini
2 cups thinly sliced leeks
¼ cup olive oil
½ cup chicken broth
2 tablespoons lemon juice

2 large tomatoes, peeled,
   seeded, and chopped
5 ounces feta cheese, crumbled
½ cup loosely packed, thinly
   sliced fresh basil
¼ teaspoon salt
½ cup grated Parmesan cheese

Cook tortellini according to package directions; drain. Keep warm.

Sauté leeks in hot oil in a large skillet over medium-high heat 5 minutes or until tender. Add chicken broth and lemon juice. Bring to a boil; reduce heat, and simmer, uncovered, 5 minutes or until liquid is almost evaporated.

Add tortellini, tomato, and next 3 ingredients; toss well. Cook over medium heat until thoroughly heated. Sprinkle with Parmesan cheese. Serve immediately. Yield: 4 servings.

More Enchanted Eating from the West Shore
Friends of the Symphony
Muskegon, Michigan

Ziti and Portobellos

Meaty-textured portobello mushrooms lend a beefy taste, which adds to the satisfaction of this meatless main dish.

4 large portobello mushrooms
   (about 2 pounds)
¼ cup olive oil, divided
2 tablespoons butter or
   margarine, divided
3 medium onions, cut in half
   lengthwise and thinly sliced
16 ounces uncooked ziti

2 (3-ounce) packages goat
   cheese, crumbled
⅓ cup chopped Italian parsley
3 tablespoons freshly grated
   Parmesan cheese
2 teaspoons salt
1 teaspoon freshly ground
   pepper

Remove and discard stems and gills from mushrooms; cut mushrooms in half. Cut crosswise into ¼-inch-thick slices; set aside.

Heat 1 tablespoon oil and 1 tablespoon butter in a large skillet over medium heat until hot. Add onion, and cook, stirring often, 20 minutes or until golden. Transfer to a large serving bowl; keep warm. Heat 2 tablespoons oil and remaining 1 tablespoon butter in skillet over medium heat. Add mushrooms, and cook, stirring often, 6 to 8 minutes or until mushrooms are tender and liquid is absorbed. Add to onion; keep warm.

Cook pasta according to package directions; drain and add to onion mixture. Stir in remaining 1 tablespoon oil; stir in goat cheese and remaining ingredients. Serve immediately. Yield: 6 servings.

Cooks of the Green Door
The League of Catholic Women
Minneapolis, Minnesota

Onion Risotto with Feta Cheese

2 tablespoons olive oil
2 cups chopped sweet onion
2 garlic cloves, chopped
1½ cups uncooked Arborio rice
4 cups warm vegetable broth
½ cup crumbled feta cheese, divided
⅓ cup chopped fresh Italian parsley
¼ cup freshly grated Parmesan cheese
¼ teaspoon salt
¼ teaspoon freshly ground pepper

Heat oil in a large saucepan over medium heat; add onion and garlic, and sauté 2 minutes. Stir in rice. Add ½ cup warm broth, stirring constantly, until liquid is absorbed. Repeat procedure with remaining broth, ½ cup at a time. (Total cooking time is about 30 minutes.)

Remove pan from heat, and stir in ¼ cup feta cheese, parsley, and remaining 3 ingredients. Sprinkle with remaining ¼ cup feta cheese. Yield: 5 servings.   Vicki Nield

We're Cooking Up Something New: 50 Years of Music, History, and Food
Wichita Falls Symphony League
Wichita Falls, Texas

Malaysian Brown Basmati Rice

This creamy risotto-like rice rendition is steeped in the exotic flavor notes of curry, cumin, and coconut. It has the personality to partner well with roasted chicken, pork, or lamb.

1 tablespoon butter or margarine
½ cup finely chopped onion
¼ cup chopped shallot
1 garlic clove, minced
1¼ cups uncooked brown basmati rice
½ cup currants
2 teaspoons curry powder
1 teaspoon ground cumin
¼ teaspoon salt
¼ teaspoon ground red pepper
¼ teaspoon freshly ground black pepper
2 cups chicken broth
1 (14-ounce) can coconut milk
2 large bay leaves
1 tablespoon butter or margarine
¼ cup sliced almonds
¼ cup shredded unsweetened coconut

Melt 1 tablespoon butter in a 4-quart ovenproof saucepan over medium heat; add onion and shallot, and sauté until tender. Add garlic, and sauté 30 seconds. Stir in rice and next 6 ingredients. Stir in chicken broth, coconut milk, and bay leaves. Bring to a boil, stirring often. Remove from heat. Cover and bake at 350° for 1 hour and 10 minutes or until liquid is absorbed and rice is tender.

Remove from oven; let stand 5 minutes. Discard bay leaves.

Melt 1 tablespoon butter in a small skillet over medium heat. Add almonds and coconut, and sauté until lightly browned. Stir into rice mixture. Yield: 4 servings.

Bravo! Recipes, Legends & Lore
University Musical Society
Ann Arbor, Michigan

Pecan Pilaf

½ cup butter or margarine, divided
1 cup chopped pecans
½ cup chopped onion
2 cups uncooked long-grain rice
4 cups chicken broth
1 teaspoon salt
¼ teaspoon dried thyme
⅛ teaspoon pepper
2 tablespoons chopped fresh parsley

Melt 3 tablespoons butter in a large skillet over medium heat. Add pecans; sauté 10 minutes or until lightly browned. Remove pecans from skillet; set aside.

Melt remaining 5 tablespoons butter in skillet over medium heat; add onion, and cook until tender, stirring occasionally. Stir in rice and next 4 ingredients. Bring mixture to a boil; cover, reduce heat, and simmer 20 minutes or until liquid is absorbed and rice is tender. Remove skillet from heat; stir in reserved pecans and parsley. Yield: 8 to 10 servings. Steve Stockton

Look Who Came to Dinner
The Junior Auxiliary of Amory, Mississippi

Wild Rice, Mushrooms, and Asparagus

1 (6-ounce) package long-grain and wild rice mix (we tested with Uncle Ben's)	1 tablespoon all-purpose flour
	¾ cup milk
	¼ teaspoon salt
½ cup chopped pecans	⅛ teaspoon pepper
1 (4.5-ounce) jar sliced mushrooms, undrained	1 (3-ounce) package cream cheese, softened
1 tablespoon butter or margarine	1 pound fresh asparagus

Cook rice mix according to package directions; stir in pecans. Set aside, and keep warm.

Drain mushrooms, reserving liquid. Set mushrooms and liquid aside.

Melt butter in a large skillet over low heat; whisk in flour until smooth. Cook 1 minute, whisking constantly. Gradually whisk in reserved mushroom liquid, milk, salt, and pepper; cook over medium heat, whisking constantly, 3 minutes or until mixture is thickened and bubbly. Add cream cheese, whisking until blended. Stir in mushrooms. Set aside, and keep warm.

Snap off tough ends of asparagus; place in a large skillet, and add cold water to cover. Bring to a boil; cook 1 minute. Drain. To serve, place rice mix on a serving platter; top with asparagus and sauce. Yield: 6 servings. Mrs. C. Y. Workman Jr. (Frances Stone)

Tapestry: A Weaving of Food, Culture and Tradition
The Junior Welfare League of Rock Hill, South Carolina

Grits Soufflé with Caramelized Onions

Don't let the title of this exotic side dish make you think it's difficult to make. Our Test Kitchens' records note that it's easy to make, and it received our highest rating.

4 cups milk
1 cup uncooked
   quick-cooking grits
3 cups (12 ounces) shredded
   smoked Gouda or Cheddar
   cheese

½ cup butter or margarine, cut
   into small pieces
½ teaspoon salt
⅛ teaspoon ground red pepper
3 large eggs, lightly beaten
Caramelized Onions

Bring milk to a simmer in a 4-quart saucepan; add grits, stirring constantly. Reduce heat to medium, and cook, stirring constantly, 4 to 5 minutes or until mixture is thickened and bubbly. Add cheese and next 3 ingredients, stirring until cheese melts. Quickly whisk in eggs. Pour into a buttered 2½-quart soufflé dish or baking dish. Bake, uncovered, at 350° for 55 minutes or until puffed and golden brown.

To serve, spoon grits onto serving plates; top with Caramelized Onions. Serve immediately. Yield: 8 to 10 servings.

Caramelized Onions

¼ cup olive oil
5 large Texas sweet onions,
   Vidalia onions, or other
   sweet onions, thinly sliced
   (about 10 cups)

2 tablespoons sugar

Heat oil in a large skillet over high heat until hot; add onion, and cook over high heat 15 minutes, stirring often. Sprinkle with sugar; reduce heat to medium high, and cook 10 minutes or until golden. Yield: 2 cups.

Settings on the Dock of the Bay
ASSISTANCE LEAGUE® of the Bay Area
Houston, Texas

Pies & Pastries

Chocolate Turtle Tart, page 236

Crunchy Caramel Apple Pie

A mix of oats, butter, and pecans forms the crispy crumb topping for tart slices of Granny Smith apple.

½ cup sugar
3 tablespoons all-purpose flour
1 teaspoon ground cinnamon
⅛ teaspoon salt
6 cups peeled, thinly sliced Granny Smith apples (about 7 small apples)
1 unbaked 9-inch pastry shell

1 cup firmly packed light brown sugar
½ cup uncooked regular oats
½ cup all-purpose flour
½ cup butter or margarine
½ cup chopped pecans
⅓ cup caramel topping

Combine first 4 ingredients in a large bowl; stir well. Add apple slices, and toss until coated. Spoon apple mixture into pastry shell; set aside.

Combine brown sugar, oats, and ½ cup flour; cut in butter with a pastry blender until crumbly. Stir in pecans. Sprinkle crumb topping over apple mixture. Bake at 375° for 55 minutes, shielding edges with aluminum foil after 25 minutes to prevent excessive browning. Drizzle warm pie with caramel topping. Serve pie warm with ice cream. Yield: 1 (9-inch) pie.

Marne Bickel

Cooking with Class
Timber Lake Booster Club
Timber Lake, South Dakota

Cranberry Streusel Pie

½ (15-ounce) package refrigerated piecrusts
2 cups fresh or frozen cranberries, thawed
1 cup chopped pecans
¼ cup sugar
¼ cup firmly packed brown sugar

½ teaspoon ground cinnamon
¼ cup butter or margarine, melted
⅓ cup sugar
3 tablespoons all-purpose flour
1 large egg, lightly beaten

Fit piecrust into a 9-inch pieplate according to package directions; fold edges under, and crimp. Set aside.

Combine cranberries and next 4 ingredients; spoon into piecrust. Whisk together melted butter, ⅓ cup sugar, flour, and egg; pour over cranberry mixture.

Bake at 400° for 20 minutes, shielding edges with aluminum foil to prevent excessive browning, if necessary. Reduce oven temperature to 350°, and bake 30 minutes. Yield: 1 (9-inch) pie.

Everything But the Entrée
The Junior League of Parkersburg, West Virginia

Amish Lemon Pie

Simplicity shines with the subtle lemon nature of this homespun pie. Hot milk, eggs, and sugar form the foundation.

1 unbaked 9-inch pastry shell	1½ cups hot milk
1 cup sugar	2½ teaspoons grated lemon
2 tablespoons butter or	rind
margarine, softened	2 tablespoons fresh lemon
3 large eggs, separated	juice
3 tablespoons all-purpose flour	Whipped cream (optional)
½ teaspoon salt	

Prick bottom and sides of pastry shell with a fork; bake at 450° for 9 minutes. Set aside.

Meanwhile, beat sugar and butter at medium speed with an electric mixer until creamy; add egg yolks, beating well. Gradually add flour and salt, beating well. Gradually stir in milk, lemon rind, and juice.

Beat egg whites at high speed until stiff peaks form; gently fold into lemon mixture. Pour lemon mixture into prepared shell. Bake at 350° for 30 to 35 minutes or until almost set, shielding edges with aluminum foil to prevent excessive browning. Cool completely on a wire rack. Serve with whipped cream, if desired. Yield: 1 (9-inch) pie.

Historically Heavenly Home Cooking
Corry Area Historical Society
Corry, Pennsylvania

Muscadine Pie

Muscadines are purple grapes found in the southeastern part of the country. They have a thick skin that can be removed more easily when the grapes are very ripe. Their strong, musky taste is distinctive. Slices of this sublime pie balance nicely with scoops of vanilla ice cream.

1¼ cups sugar
¼ cup all-purpose flour
3½ pounds very ripe muscadines (about 11 cups)
1 tablespoon fresh lemon juice

1 (15-ounce) package refrigerated piecrusts
2 tablespoons butter or margarine

Stir together sugar and flour; set aside.

Remove stems and skins from muscadines; set skins aside. Discard stems.

Cook muscadine pulp in a large saucepan over medium heat 10 minutes or until seeds loosen, stirring occasionally. Press mixture through a food mill or wire-mesh strainer into a bowl, discarding seeds. Return pulp and juice to saucepan; stir in reserved skins. Cook over low heat 25 minutes or until skins are tender. Remove from heat; stir in sugar mixture and lemon juice. Cool slightly.

Fit 1 piecrust into a 9-inch deep-dish pieplate according to package directions; pour muscadine mixture into piecrust, and dot with butter. Unfold remaining piecrust, and press out fold lines; place on top of pie. Fold edges under, and crimp. Cut slits in top for steam to escape.

Bake at 425° for 5 minutes. Reduce oven temperature to 375°; bake 35 to 40 minutes or until crust is browned, shielding edges with aluminum foil to prevent excessive browning, if necessary. Yield: 1 (9-inch) deep-dish pie.

Flavors of the Gardens
Callaway Gardens
Pine Mountain, Georgia

Peach-Raspberry Pie

Take advantage of summer's bounty with this fruit-laden pie that showcases succulent peaches and plump raspberries. A scoop of vanilla ice cream deliciously tops off a slice.

2 cups peeled, sliced fresh
  peaches
2 cups fresh raspberries
1 cup sugar
½ cup all-purpose flour

1 (15-ounce) package
  refrigerated piecrusts
1 tablespoon fresh lemon juice
1 tablespoon butter or
  margarine

Combine first 4 ingredients in a large bowl, stirring gently. Set aside.

Roll 1 piecrust to ⅛-inch thickness on a lightly floured surface. Fit into a 9-inch pieplate. Spoon peach mixture into pastry shell. Sprinkle with lemon juice, and dot with butter.

Roll remaining piecrust to ⅛-inch thickness on a lightly floured surface; place over filling. Trim off excess pastry along edges. Fold edges under, and crimp. Cut slits in top for steam to escape.

Cover edges with aluminum foil to prevent excessive browning. Bake at 425° for 10 minutes; reduce oven temperature to 375°, and bake 30 to 32 minutes or until browned. Cool completely on a wire rack. Yield: 1 (9-inch) pie.   Joyce Flesher

A Peach Flavored Past
Altrusa International, Inc., of Palisade, Colorado

Raisin-Nut Pie

3 large eggs
1 cup sugar
½ teaspoon ground cinnamon
¼ teaspoon ground nutmeg
½ cup milk
6 tablespoons butter or
   margarine, melted

1 cup raisins
¾ cup coarsely chopped
   walnuts
1 unbaked 9-inch pastry shell

Whisk together first 4 ingredients in a medium bowl. Add milk and butter, whisking well. Stir in raisins and walnuts. Pour mixture into pastry shell.

Bake at 400° for 10 minutes; reduce oven temperature to 350°, and bake 30 minutes, shielding edges with aluminum foil after 15 minutes to prevent excessive browning, if necessary. (Center of pie will not be completely set, but will firm up as it cools.) Cool completely on a wire rack. Yield: 1 (9-inch) pie.   Gladys Moshier

Good Food, Served Right
Traditional Arts in Upstate New York
Canton, New York

White Chocolate Magnolia Pecan Pie

Here's a helpful hint that we discovered: Placing a baking sheet under this pie before baking ensures that the crust will be crisp.

2 large eggs
2 cups chopped pecans
4 (1-ounce) white chocolate
   baking squares, melted
   (we tested with Baker's)
1 (14-ounce) can sweetened
   condensed milk
⅓ cup butter or margarine,
   melted

3 tablespoons milk
1 tablespoon white crème de
   cacao (optional)
2 teaspoons vanilla extract
½ teaspoon salt
1 unbaked 9-inch pastry shell
Garnish: pecan halves

Combine first 9 ingredients in a large mixing bowl; beat at medium speed with an electric mixer until blended. Pour filling into pastry shell. Garnish, if desired.

Place pie on a baking sheet. Bake at 400° for 12 minutes. Reduce oven temperature to 325°, and bake 35 minutes or until set. Cool on a wire rack. Yield: 1 (9-inch) pie.   Tracy Roberts

Southern Elegance: A Second Course
The Junior League of Gaston County
Gastonia, North Carolina

Heavenly Pie

A divine meringue crust embraces a tart lemony filling that's topped with fluffy whipped cream. One bite and you'll agree that heavenly only begins to describe this pie.

4 large eggs, separated	2 cups heavy whipping cream,
¼ teaspoon cream of tartar	whipped
1½ cups sugar, divided	Additional grated lemon rind
1 tablespoon grated lemon rind	(optional)
¼ cup fresh lemon juice	

Beat egg whites and cream of tartar at high speed with an electric mixer until foamy. Add 1 cup sugar, 1 tablespoon at a time, beating until stiff peaks form and sugar dissolves (2 to 4 minutes).

Spread meringue in bottom and up sides of a lightly greased 9-inch pieplate. Make a large indentation in center of meringue. Bake at 275° for 1 hour. Remove from oven, and cool on a wire rack.

Lightly beat egg yolks. Combine egg yolks, remaining ½ cup sugar, 1 tablespoon lemon rind, and lemon juice in a medium saucepan. Cook over medium heat, stirring constantly, 8 to 10 minutes or until mixture is thickened. Remove from heat, and cool.

Fold half of whipped cream into lemon mixture. Spoon filling into meringue shell. Top with remaining whipped cream. Sprinkle with additional lemon rind, if desired. Chill pie at least 3 hours. Yield: 1 (9-inch) pie.   Diane Winer

. . . And It Was Very Good
Temple Emeth
Teaneck, New Jersey

Pumpkin Praline No-Bake Pie

Here's an easy-to-make, no-bake pumpkin pie that's nicely spiced.

¼ cup butter or margarine
1 cup chopped pecans
½ cup sugar
1 (3.4-ounce) package vanilla instant pudding mix
1 cup canned, mashed pumpkin
⅔ cup milk
½ cup firmly packed light brown sugar
¼ teaspoon ground nutmeg
¼ teaspoon ground ginger
¼ teaspoon ground cinnamon
1 (8-ounce) container frozen whipped topping, thawed and divided
1 baked 9-inch pastry shell

Melt butter in a large skillet over medium heat; add pecans and ½ cup sugar. Cook mixture 12 to 15 minutes or until golden brown, stirring often. Spoon onto wax paper; cool and crumble into pieces. Set praline pieces aside.

Stir together pudding mix and next 6 ingredients. Fold in 1 cup whipped topping.

Sprinkle half of reserved praline pieces in pastry shell. Pour pumpkin mixture into pastry shell, and chill 1 hour. Spread remaining 2½ cups whipped topping over filling. Sprinkle with remaining half of praline pieces. Yield: 1 (9-inch) pie.   Sharri Hackbarth

The Cookbook Tour
Good Shepherd Lutheran Church
Plainview, Minnesota

Rich's Fat Pie

Gather the kids for this pleasing pie. It stars ice cream, hot fudge and caramel toppings, plus marshmallow creme in a graham cracker crust.

1 (6-ounce) graham cracker crust
⅔ cup hot fudge topping, divided
2 cups vanilla ice cream, softened and divided
⅓ cup caramel topping
½ cup marshmallow creme
1½ cups frozen whipped topping, thawed
¼ cup chopped walnuts, toasted

Freeze crust ½ hour.

Heat ⅓ cup hot fudge topping in a microwave-safe bowl at HIGH 20 seconds. Spoon fudge topping into crust, and spread evenly. Working quickly, spread 1 cup ice cream over hot fudge layer; freeze until firm.

Spoon caramel topping over ice cream layer, and spread evenly.

Heat marshmallow creme in a microwave-safe bowl at HIGH 10 seconds. Drizzle marshmallow creme over caramel layer. Spread remaining 1 cup ice cream over marshmallow layer. Freeze at least 3 hours or until firm.

Heat remaining ⅓ cup fudge topping as directed. Spoon remaining ⅓ cup fudge topping over ice cream layer; spread evenly. Spread whipped topping over hot fudge layer. Sprinkle with nuts. Cover and freeze at least 8 hours or overnight. Remove from freezer; let stand 10 minutes before serving. Yield: 1 (9-inch) pie. Jean Garard

Sharing Our Best
Hackensack American Legion Auxiliary Unit 202
Hackensack, Minnesota

Grasshopper Delight Frozen Pie

30 cream-filled chocolate
   sandwich cookies
⅓ cup butter or margarine,
   melted
½ gallon mint chocolate chip
   ice cream, softened

1 (8-ounce) container frozen
   whipped topping, thawed
½ cup sifted powdered sugar
½ teaspoon vanilla extract

Process cookies in a food processor or blender until ground; add butter, and process until blended. Reserve ½ cup crumb mixture. Firmly press remaining crumb mixture in an ungreased 13- x 9-inch pan. Chill 30 minutes.

Spoon ice cream over crust; cover and freeze 1 hour. Stir together whipped topping, powdered sugar, and vanilla; spread over ice cream layer. Sprinkle remaining ½ cup crumb mixture over whipped topping mixture. Cover and freeze 8 hours. Remove from freezer; let stand 10 minutes before serving. Yield: 12 servings. Sue Lowe

Favorite Recipes
Friends of Memorial Hospital
Weiser, Idaho

Chocolate Turtle Tart

Serve lavish wedges of this grand tart sumptuously bathed in Warm Caramel Sauce.

1¾ cups pecans	12 (1-ounce) semisweet
⅓ cup sugar	chocolate squares, chopped
¼ cup unsalted butter, melted	½ cup finely chopped pecans
1½ cups whipping cream	Warm Caramel Sauce

Process 1¾ cups pecans and sugar in a food processor until finely ground; add melted butter, and process until combined. Press mixture firmly in bottom and up sides of a 9-inch tart pan with removable bottom.

Bake at 350° for 20 to 23 minutes or until golden brown; cool completely in pan on a wire rack.

Bring whipping cream to a simmer in a medium saucepan; reduce heat to low, and add chocolate, whisking until smooth. Remove from heat; cool.

Pour chocolate mixture into prepared crust; chill 30 minutes. Sprinkle ½ cup finely chopped pecans around edges. Chill 3 hours or until firm.

Loosen tart pan sides, and remove. Serve tart with Warm Caramel Sauce. Yield: 1 (9-inch) tart.

Warm Caramel Sauce

½ cup unsalted butter	1 cup whipping cream
1 cup sugar	

Melt butter in a saucepan over medium heat; add sugar, and cook 8 minutes or until deep golden brown, stirring occasionally. Whisk in whipping cream until smooth; cool. Yield: 1⅔ cups.

Creating a Stir
The Fayette County Medical Auxiliary
Lexington, Kentucky

Apple Custard Tart

This puddinglike dessert makes a perfect ending to a feast on a brisk fall evening. Accompany it with a mug of warm apple cider.

1 unbaked 9-inch pastry shell
1½ cups sour cream
1 (14-ounce) can sweetened
　condensed milk
¼ cup frozen apple juice
　concentrate, thawed
1 large egg

1½ teaspoons vanilla extract
¼ teaspoon ground cinnamon
2 Rome apples, peeled and
　thinly sliced (about 2 cups)
1 tablespoon butter or
　margarine, melted
Apple-Cinnamon Glaze

Bake pastry shell at 375° for 15 minutes.

Beat sour cream and next 5 ingredients at medium speed with an electric mixer until smooth. Pour mixture into prepared pastry shell. Bake at 375° for 30 minutes or until set. Cool.

Cook apple in butter in a skillet over medium heat, stirring gently, until crisp-tender. Arrange apple slices on tart; drizzle with Apple-Cinnamon Glaze. Yield: 1 (9-inch) tart.

Apple-Cinnamon Glaze

¼ cup frozen apple juice
　concentrate, thawed

1 teaspoon cornstarch
¼ teaspoon ground cinnamon

Combine all ingredients in a small saucepan; stir well. Cook over low heat, stirring constantly, until mixture thickens. Yield: ¼ cup.

Favorite Recipes Taste of Tradition
B.A. Ritter Senior Citizen Center
Nederland, Texas

Berry Tart with Mascarpone Cream

Strawberries, raspberries, blueberries, and blackberries atop a buttery cheese filling make this tart a red, white, and blue wonder. It's destined to become a Fourth of July tradition.

Sweet Pastry Dough
1 cup mascarpone cheese
⅓ cup whipping cream
¼ cup sugar
1½ cups small strawberries, quartered
1 cup fresh raspberries

1 cup fresh blueberries
1 cup fresh blackberries
2 tablespoons orange marmalade
2 tablespoons blackberry or crème de cassis liqueur

Roll pastry for Sweet Pastry Dough into an 11-inch circle on a lightly floured surface. Fit pastry into a 9-inch tart pan with removable bottom; trim off excess pastry along edges. Prick bottom and sides of pastry with a fork; chill 30 minutes.

Line pastry with aluminum foil, and fill with pie weights or dried beans. Bake at 375° for 20 minutes. Remove weights and foil; bake 10 more minutes. Cool completely on a wire rack.

Beat mascarpone cheese, whipping cream, and sugar at medium speed with an electric mixer until stiff peaks form. Spoon into prepared crust.

Combine strawberries and next 3 ingredients in a medium bowl; toss gently.

Combine marmalade and liqueur in a small saucepan. Bring to a boil; reduce heat, and simmer 5 minutes or until reduced to 3 tablespoons. Pour over berry mixture, and toss gently. Spoon berry mixture over cheese mixture. Yield: 1 (9-inch) tart.

Sweet Pastry Dough

1⅓ cups all-purpose flour
½ cup unsalted butter, cut into pieces
2 tablespoons sugar

¼ teaspoon salt
1 egg yolk, lightly beaten
2½ tablespoons ice water

Combine first 4 ingredients with a pastry blender until crumbly. Combine egg yolk and water. Sprinkle yolk mixture, 1 tablespoon at a time, evenly over surface; stir with a fork until dry ingredients are moistened. Shape into a ball.

Gently press pastry into a 6-inch circle on a sheet of plastic wrap; cover dough with plastic wrap, and chill 1 hour. Yield: enough pastry for 1 (9-inch) tart.

A Sunsational Encore
The Junior League of Greater Orlando, Florida

Mango Tarts

A rum-kissed mango jelly glaze glistens atop these golden tarts. They showcase a double nut-coconut crust, lime custard filling, and ripe mango topping.

2 cups macadamia nuts	1 cup sugar
1½ cups pistachios	¾ cup fresh lime juice
1½ cups flaked coconut	½ cup butter or margarine, cut
½ cup firmly packed light	into pieces
brown sugar	3 mangoes, sliced into wedges
3 egg whites	¼ cup mango or guava jelly
10 egg yolks	1 tablespoon dark rum

Combine first 4 ingredients in a large bowl. Process nut mixture in batches in a food processor until ground. Beat egg whites until soft peaks form. Fold into nut mixture. Let stand 5 minutes.

Lightly grease bottom and sides of 12 (4-inch) tart pans with removable bottoms or 8 (4½-inch) tart pans with removable bottoms; press nut mixture into bottom and up sides of pans. Place tart pans on a baking sheet. Bake at 350° for 17 minutes or until lightly browned. Cool completely on a wire rack.

Stir together egg yolks, sugar, and lime juice in top of a double boiler; bring water to a boil. Reduce heat to medium; cook, stirring constantly, about 20 minutes or until mixture is thickened. Remove from heat, and gradually whisk in butter. Fill each tart with custard, and top with mango slices.

Melt jelly in a small saucepan over medium heat; stir in rum. Brush mango slices with warm jelly mixture. Cover and chill 1 hour. Yield: 12 (4-inch) tarts or 8 (4½-inch) tarts.

Bravo! Recipes, Legends & Lore
University Musical Society
Ann Arbor, Michigan

Strawberry Pizza

*Fruit pizza goes deep-dish with this thick cream cheese-filled version.
Add your favorite berry to change up the toppings.*

1½ cups self-rising flour
⅓ cup firmly packed light
  brown sugar
¾ cup butter or margarine, cut
  into small pieces
⅓ cup chopped pecans

1 (8-ounce) package cream
  cheese, softened
2 cups sifted powdered sugar
1 (8-ounce) container frozen
  whipped topping, thawed
1 quart strawberries, sliced

Stir together flour and brown sugar. Cut in butter with a pastry
blender until crumbly. Stir in pecans. Knead dough slightly to form a
smooth ball. Roll out into a 12-inch circle on a 14-inch pizza pan. Bake
at 300° for 30 to 35 minutes or until edges are brown. Cool completely
on a wire rack.

Beat cream cheese at medium speed with an electric mixer until
creamy. Add powdered sugar; beat until smooth. Fold in whipped topping. Spread cream cheese mixture over pastry. Arrange strawberries
over cream cheese mixture. Yield: 16 servings.   Sharon St. Onge

Dixon Fixins
Dixon Ambulatory Care Center
Westminster, Maryland

Best-Ever Blueberry Cobbler

3 cups fresh blueberries
⅓ cup orange juice
3 tablespoons sugar
½ cup butter, softened
½ cup sugar

1 large egg
½ teaspoon vanilla extract
⅔ cup all-purpose flour
¼ teaspoon baking powder
Pinch of salt

Toss together first 3 ingredients in a medium bowl; spoon into a
lightly greased 8-inch baking dish.

Beat butter and ½ cup sugar at medium speed with an electric
mixer until creamy. Add egg and vanilla, beating well.

Combine flour, baking powder, and salt; gradually add to butter
mixture, mixing at low speed just until blended. Drop batter by tablespoonfuls over berry mixture.

Bake at 375° for 35 minutes or until crust is lightly browned and filling is bubbly. Serve warm with whipped cream or vanilla ice cream. Yield: 6 servings.

What Can I Bring?
The Junior League of Northern Virginia
McLean, Virginia

Pear Dumplings

A homemade dough caresses sweet pears in this traditional dumpling recipe. Don't limit yourself to just blueberry syrup–try a warm caramel or chocolate topping.

1½ cups all-purpose flour
½ teaspoon salt
½ cup shortening or butter
4 to 5 tablespoons ice water
2 small pears, peeled, cored, and halved vertically (we tested with Bartlett)

1 egg white, lightly beaten
2 tablespoons sugar
Blueberry syrup

Combine flour and salt in a bowl. Cut in shortening with a pastry blender until crumbly. Sprinkle ice water, 1 tablespoon at a time, evenly over surface; stir with a fork until dry ingredients are moistened. Shape into a ball. Roll pastry to ⅛-inch thickness on a lightly floured surface. Cut pastry into quarters.

Place 1 pear half, core side down, on each pastry quarter. Brush edges with egg white. Bring sides up, smoothing dough until it covers pear half completely; pinch to seal. Place on an ungreased baking sheet. Brush with egg white; sprinkle with sugar. Bake at 400° for 30 minutes or until golden.

To serve, pour a small amount of blueberry syrup onto individual plates. Top each with a dumpling. Yield: 4 servings.

Dining by Design: Stylish Recipes, Savory Settings
The Junior League of Pasadena, California

Apple Orchard Snowballs

This recipe is similar to a dumpling, but with a twist. Instead of placing the apples on the dough and sealing, the apples are wrapped with the dough and then sealed. Good things do come in small packages!

4 teaspoons light brown sugar
1 teaspoon ground cinnamon
1 (8-ounce) package refrigerated crescent dinner rolls
4 small Golden Delicious or Granny Smith apples, peeled and cored

Butter or margarine
½ cup sifted powdered sugar
2 to 3 teaspoons milk

Stir together brown sugar and cinnamon in a small bowl; set aside.

Unroll dough; divide into 4 sections, and firmly pinch perforations on each section. Roll into 4 (10- x 6½-inch) rectangles on a lightly floured work surface. Wrap 1 rectangle of dough around outside edge of each apple, extending dough 1 inch on top and bottom of apple, pinching side seam to seal. Bring bottom edges of dough together, and seal; turn apples upright. Sprinkle each apple with 1¼ teaspoons cinnamon mixture; dot with butter. Bring top edges of dough together, and seal. Place apples on an ungreased baking sheet.

Bake at 350° for 35 minutes or until pastry is golden and apples are tender.

Combine powdered sugar and milk, stirring until smooth; drizzle over hot apples. Serve warm with vanilla ice cream or whipped cream, if desired. Yield: 4 servings.   Melinda Jones

Sharing Recipes from Green Road Baptist Church
Green Road Baptist Church
Green Road, Kentucky

Poultry

Glazed Cornish Hens with Curried Rice, page 258

Apricot and Currant Chicken

Try this eye-catching dish during the holidays. A glistening glaze of orange marmalade, dried apricots, and apple juice makes the chicken quarters shine.

2 (2½- to 3-pound) whole
   chickens, quartered
1½ teaspoons salt
1 teaspoon pepper
1 teaspoon ground ginger
1½ cups orange marmalade
½ cup apple juice

⅓ cup fresh orange juice
1 (6-ounce) package dried
   apricots
1 cup currants
¼ cup firmly packed light
   brown sugar

Place chicken in a large shallow roasting pan. Combine salt, pepper, and ginger, and sprinkle over chicken. Brush chicken with marmalade; pour juices over chicken. Bake, uncovered, at 400° for 20 minutes.

Sprinkle apricots, currants, and sugar over chicken. Bake, uncovered, 15 to 20 more minutes or until a meat thermometer inserted into thigh registers 180°, basting occasionally with pan juices. Yield: 8 servings.
                                      Baila Bender

Look What's Cooking . . .
Temple Sinai Sisterhood
Cranston, Rhode Island

Bruce's Bluegrass Barbecued Chicken

Horseradish and chili powder create an out-of-the-ordinary experience for the barbecue sauce aficionado.

¾ cup Worcestershire sauce
½ cup water
½ cup apple cider vinegar
½ cup butter or margarine
½ (8-ounce) jar horseradish
   mustard

2 teaspoons salt
1 teaspoon chili powder
1 (3-pound) whole chicken,
   cut up

Combine first 7 ingredients in a medium saucepan; bring to a boil, stirring occasionally. Remove from heat, and cool.

Place chicken pieces in an ungreased 13- x 9-inch dish. Pour marinade over chicken. Cover and chill 8 hours.

Remove chicken from marinade, discarding marinade.

Grill, covered with grill lid, over medium heat (300° to 350°) about 10 minutes on each side or until done. Yield: 3 to 4 servings.

Creating a Stir
The Fayette County Medical Auxiliary
Lexington, Kentucky

Crispy Lemon Fried Chicken

2 (2½- to 3-pound) whole chickens, cut up, or 5 pounds chicken pieces
1 tablespoon salt
¼ cup fresh lemon juice (about 1 large lemon)
½ teaspoon salt
1 cup all-purpose flour
1 teaspoon paprika
⅛ teaspoon pepper
Vegetable oil

Place chicken in a large bowl; add 1 tablespoon salt, lemon juice, and enough water to cover chicken. Cover and chill at least 8 hours. Remove chicken from liquid, discarding liquid.

Combine ½ teaspoon salt, flour, paprika, and pepper in a large heavy-duty zip-top plastic bag. Add chicken, a few pieces at a time, and shake to coat.

Pour oil to depth of ½ inch into a large skillet or chicken fryer; heat to 360°. Add chicken, in batches, and brown on both sides. Remove chicken; set aside. Repeat procedure with remaining chicken. Return chicken to skillet; cover, reduce heat, and cook 20 minutes or until done, turning once. Uncover; cook 8 more minutes or until chicken is crisp. Drain on paper towels. Yield: 8 servings.   Erma Neve

Christian Women's Fellowship
Oak Grove Christian Church
Shellsburg, Iowa

Jack and Lin's Jamaican Jerk Chicken

Seed the habanero chile pepper in this jerk mixture to turn down the heat level of the blend. This not-too-hot mix also works well with roast pork, beef brisket, and game birds.

6 green onions, sliced
2 shallots, minced
2 garlic cloves, minced
½ cup fresh orange juice
½ cup rice vinegar
¼ cup red wine vinegar
¼ cup soy sauce
¼ cup olive oil
1 tablespoon dark brown sugar
1 tablespoon fresh thyme
1 tablespoon minced fresh
   ginger

1 tablespoon seeded, minced
   habanero chile pepper
1½ teaspoons ground allspice
1 teaspoon kosher salt
1 teaspoon freshly ground
   black pepper
¾ teaspoon ground cinnamon
½ teaspoon ground red pepper
¼ teaspoon ground nutmeg
8 chicken leg-thigh
   combinations (about
   5 pounds)

Process all ingredients except chicken in a blender 2 to 3 minutes or until smooth. Place chicken in large heavy-duty zip-top plastic bags. Pour marinade over chicken; seal bags, and chill 8 hours, turning bags occasionally.

Remove chicken from marinade, reserving marinade. Bring marinade to a boil in a small saucepan; remove from heat, and set aside.

Place chicken on a lightly greased rack in a broiler pan. Bake, uncovered, at 350° for 45 minutes, turning and basting occasionally.

Coat food rack with cooking spray; place rack on grill over medium-high heat (350° to 400°). Place chicken on rack, and grill 30 minutes or until done, turning and basting occasionally with reserved marinade. Yield: 8 servings.   Jack and Lin Reeves

Cooking with Class
Forest Hills Elementary School PTO
Lake Oswego, Oregon

Indonesian Fried Chicken

This chicken is fried twice to make sure it's crispy. The generous amount of accompanying Dipping Sauce can be halved, or use any leftovers for chicken-finger dipping.

2 green onions, finely chopped
2 garlic cloves, minced
3 tablespoons soy sauce
2 tablespoons dry sherry
1 tablespoon grated fresh ginger
2 teaspoons dark sesame oil
1 teaspoon sugar
1 teaspoon salt
2 teaspoons black pepper
½ teaspoon dried crushed red pepper
¼ teaspoon ground cinnamon
¼ teaspoon ground cloves
2½ pounds chicken thighs
Vegetable oil
1 large egg, lightly beaten
1 cup cornstarch
Dipping Sauce

Combine first 12 ingredients in a shallow dish or large heavy-duty zip-top plastic bag; add chicken. Cover or seal, and chill 8 hours, turning occasionally.

Pour oil to a depth of 3 inches into a Dutch oven; heat to 375°. Drain chicken; dip chicken in egg, and dredge in cornstarch, coating chicken well. Fry chicken, in batches, in hot oil 12 minutes. Drain on paper towels; let stand 5 minutes. Return chicken to skillet, and fry 5 more minutes or until golden and crisp. Serve with Dipping Sauce. Yield: 4 servings.

Dipping Sauce

1 cup firmly packed light brown sugar
1 cup water
1 cup soy sauce
¼ cup molasses
1 teaspoon grated fresh ginger
½ teaspoon ground coriander
½ teaspoon pepper

Combine all ingredients in a large saucepan. Bring mixture to a simmer over medium heat, and simmer, uncovered, 5 minutes. Yield: 3 cups.

Bing Santos

Flavors of the Tenderloin
Sidewalk Clean-Up, Recycling & Urban Beautification (SCRUB)
San Francisco, California

Chicken with Chutney

Sweet and tart fruit combined with mango chutney pleases the palate as well as the eye. Use any leftovers for an exotic chicken salad.

8 bone-in chicken breast halves, skinned
4 chicken legs, skinned
1 teaspoon salt
1 teaspoon pepper
¼ cup olive oil
1 large onion, chopped
1 Granny Smith apple, peeled and chopped
½ cup raisins
1½ cups mango chutney
1 cup chicken broth

Sprinkle chicken with salt and pepper.

Brown chicken, in batches, on both sides in hot oil in a large skillet.

Place chicken in a large greased roasting pan. Sprinkle onion, apple, and raisins around chicken. Spoon chutney over chicken. Pour broth over mixture.

Bake, covered, at 350° for 1 hour. Uncover and bake 30 more minutes or until done. Yield: 10 servings.   Georgia Weir

NPT's Community Cookbook
Neighborhood Pride Team
Portland, Oregon

Chicken Breasts in Phyllo

You won't need much more than a crisp green salad to round out the meal for your guests when you serve this hearty entrée.

2 tablespoons butter or margarine
1 medium onion, minced
1 (8-ounce) package sliced fresh mushrooms
2 garlic cloves, minced
2 tablespoons chopped fresh parsley
½ teaspoon salt, divided
1 tablespoon all-purpose flour
¼ cup dry white wine

4 skinned and boned chicken breast halves
1 tablespoon olive oil
16 (14- x 18-inch) sheets frozen phyllo pastry, thawed in refrigerator
¾ cup butter or margarine, melted
¼ cup fine, dry breadcrumbs (store-bought)
8 ounces feta cheese, crumbled

Melt 2 tablespoons butter in a large skillet over medium heat; add onion, mushrooms, and garlic, and sauté 5 minutes or until tender. Add parsley and ¼ teaspoon salt. Stir in flour. Add wine, and cook, stirring constantly, 3 to 4 minutes or until mixture is thickened. Remove mushroom mixture from pan, and set aside.

Sprinkle chicken with remaining ¼ teaspoon salt. Heat olive oil in skillet until hot; add chicken, and cook 4 minutes on each side. Remove from skillet, and set aside.

Place 1 sheet of phyllo on a clean work surface (keep remaining sheets covered with a damp towel). Brush phyllo with melted butter; top with another sheet of phyllo. Brush with butter, and sprinkle with 1 tablespoon breadcrumbs. Top with 2 more layers of phyllo brushed with butter. Place a chicken breast half on the lower half of the phyllo; top with one-fourth of mushroom mixture and one-fourth of cheese. Fold phyllo over chicken, starting from the bottom. Fold sides in, and roll up packet. Place seam side down on an ungreased baking sheet. Brush entire packet with melted butter. Repeat procedure with remaining phyllo, melted butter, breadcrumbs, chicken, mushroom mixture, and cheese. Bake at 375° for 30 to 35 minutes or until golden brown. Yield: 4 servings.   Nancy Fasilis

Flavor It Greek! A Celebration of Food, Faith and Family
Philoptochos Society of Holy Trinity Greek Orthodox Church
Portland, Oregon

Chicken Stuffed with Spinach and Feta Cheese

10 (6-ounce) skinned and boned chicken breast halves
½ (10-ounce) package frozen chopped spinach, thawed
1½ cups small-curd cottage cheese
8 ounces feta cheese, crumbled
1¼ cups Italian-seasoned breadcrumbs (store-bought), divided

2 large eggs, lightly beaten
¼ cup freshly grated Parmesan cheese
1 teaspoon dried oregano
½ teaspoon garlic powder
½ teaspoon pepper
¼ teaspoon ground nutmeg
6 tablespoons butter or margarine, melted

Place chicken between 2 sheets of heavy-duty plastic wrap, and flatten to ¼-inch thickness, using a meat mallet or rolling pin.

Drain spinach well, pressing between layers of paper towels to remove excess moisture. Stir together spinach, cottage cheese, feta cheese, and ¾ cup breadcrumbs in a large bowl. Stir in eggs and next 5 ingredients.

Spoon about ⅓ cup spinach mixture in center of each chicken breast, fold 2 sides to center of chicken. Fold remaining 2 sides to center of chicken, securing with wooden picks, if necessary. Brush chicken with melted butter; sprinkle with remaining ½ cup breadcrumbs. Place chicken on a foil-lined, lightly greased large jellyroll pan. Cover and chill 1 hour or up to 4 hours. Bake, uncovered, at 325° for 52 minutes or until done. Yield: 10 servings.

Vintage Virginia: A History of Good Taste
The Virginia Dietetic Association
Centreville, Virginia

Creamy Gorgonzola Chicken

Elegance reigns with a rich sauce made of heavy whipping cream, dry white wine, and Gorgonzola cheese.

2 tablespoons olive oil
6 skinned and boned chicken breast halves
½ cup chopped green onions
1 garlic clove, minced
3 tablespoons butter or margarine, melted
¼ cup all-purpose flour
¼ teaspoon pepper

1 cup chicken broth
¾ cup heavy whipping cream
1 tablespoon dry white wine
2 teaspoons Worcestershire sauce
¼ cup crumbled Gorgonzola cheese
Garnish: fresh parsley sprigs or fresh chives

Heat oil in a large skillet over medium-high heat until hot; add chicken, and cook 5 minutes on each side or until chicken is done. Remove chicken from skillet; set aside, and keep warm.

Cook green onions and garlic in butter in skillet over medium-high heat 3 minutes or just until onion is tender; whisk in flour and pepper. Cook 1 minute, whisking constantly. Gradually whisk in chicken broth. Stir in cream, wine, and Worcestershire sauce. Cook over medium heat, whisking constantly, until mixture is thickened and bubbly. Stir in cheese. Drizzle sauce over chicken. Garnish, if desired. Yield: 6 servings.

Splendor in the Bluegrass
The Junior League of Louisville, Kentucky

Green Chile Chicken

Serve these southwestern-spiced chicken breasts topped with Monterey Jack cheese over rice to capture all their green chile goodness.

4 (4.5-ounce) cans chopped
   green chiles, undrained, or
   1 (16-ounce) package frozen
   chopped green chiles, thawed
2 medium onions, chopped
   (about 2 cups)
5 garlic cloves, minced

1½ teaspoons ground cumin
1 teaspoon chili powder
1 teaspoon dried oregano
8 skinned and boned chicken
   breast halves
2 cups (8 ounces) shredded
   Monterey Jack cheese

Stir together first 6 ingredients in a medium bowl. Place chicken in a lightly greased 13- x 9-inch baking dish; pour green chile mixture over chicken. Bake, uncovered, at 375° for 40 minutes. Sprinkle chicken with cheese, and bake 5 more minutes or until cheese melts. Yield: 8 servings.

Seasons of Santa Fe
Kitchen Angels
Santa Fe, New Mexico

Grilled Pesto-Prosciutto Chicken with Basil Cream

8 skinned and boned chicken
  breast halves
½ cup pesto
8 (1-ounce) slices prosciutto or
  cooked ham

¼ cup olive oil
2 garlic cloves, minced
¼ teaspoon salt
¼ teaspoon pepper
Basil Cream

Place each chicken breast half between 2 sheets of plastic wrap; flatten to ¼-inch thickness, using a meat mallet or rolling pin. Spread 1 tablespoon pesto over each chicken breast. Place 1 slice prosciutto over pesto. Roll up crosswise; secure with a wooden pick. Place in an ungreased 13- x 9-inch pan. Combine oil, garlic, salt, and pepper. Pour over chicken; cover and chill 2 hours.

Grill, covered with grill lid, over medium-high heat (350° to 400°) 15 to 20 minutes or until done, turning occasionally. Serve with Basil Cream. Yield: 8 servings.

Basil Cream

⅓ cup dry white wine
3 shallots, chopped
1½ cups whipping cream
1 (14½-ounce) can diced
  tomatoes, drained and finely
  chopped

¼ cup minced fresh basil
½ teaspoon salt
¼ teaspoon freshly ground
  pepper

Combine wine and shallots in a saucepan; bring to a boil, and cook 2 minutes or until liquid is reduced to about ¼ cup. Add whipping cream; return to a boil, and simmer 8 to 10 minutes or until reduced to about 1 cup. Stir in tomatoes and remaining ingredients; cook just until thoroughly heated. Yield: 2 cups.   Mary Roberge

The Heart of Pittsburgh
Sacred Heart Elementary School PTG
Pittsburgh, Pennsylvania

Cajun Chicken Strips

Strips seasoned with red and black pepper, garlic, and poultry seasoning make perfect morsels to toss into salads, sandwiches, or quesadillas.

1 tablespoon all-purpose flour
1 teaspoon poultry seasoning
¾ teaspoon garlic salt
½ teaspoon paprika
¼ teaspoon black pepper

⅛ teaspoon ground red pepper
1½ pounds skinned and boned chicken breast halves, cut into ½-inch strips
¼ cup butter or margarine

Combine first 6 ingredients in a large heavy-duty zip-top plastic bag. Place half of chicken in bag. Seal and shake to coat chicken completely. Repeat procedure with remaining half of chicken.

Melt 2 tablespoons butter in a large skillet over medium-high heat. Add half of chicken; cook 8 to 10 minutes or until done, turning occasionally. Set aside, and keep warm. Repeat procedure with remaining butter and chicken. Yield: 4 to 6 servings.   Ethel Sweet

Christian Women's Fellowship
Oak Grove Christian Church
Shellsburg, Iowa

Cashew Chicken Stir-Fry

2 cups chicken broth, divided
¼ cup cornstarch
3 tablespoons soy sauce
½ teaspoon ground ginger
1 pound skinned and boned chicken breast halves, cut into ½-inch strips
2 garlic cloves, minced

½ cup julienne-sliced carrot
½ cup thinly sliced celery
3 cups broccoli florets
1 cup fresh or frozen snow pea pods, thawed
1½ cups salted cashews
Hot cooked rice

Place 3 tablespoons chicken broth in a large skillet; set aside.

Combine remaining chicken broth, cornstarch, soy sauce, and ginger, stirring until smooth. Set aside.

Heat chicken broth in skillet over medium heat until hot. Add chicken, and stir-fry 4 minutes or until chicken is no longer pink. Remove chicken from skillet; set aside, and keep warm. Add garlic, carrot, and celery to skillet; stir-fry 3 minutes. Add broccoli and snow peas; stir-fry 5 minutes or until crisp-tender. Add chicken. Stir chicken broth mixture, and add to mixture in skillet; stir-fry 2 minutes. Stir in cashews. Serve over rice. Yield: 4 servings. Joyce Ogle

Lake Waccamaw United Methodist Church Cookbook
Lake Waccamaw United Methodist Church
Lake Waccamaw, North Carolina

Chicken and Black Bean Enchiladas

3 bacon slices
¾ pound skinned and boned chicken breast halves, cut into short, thin strips
2 garlic cloves, minced
2 cups picante sauce, divided
1 (15-ounce) can black beans, undrained
1 red bell pepper, chopped
1 teaspoon ground cumin
¼ teaspoon salt
½ cup sliced green onions
10 (8-inch) flour tortillas
1½ cups (6 ounces) shredded Monterey Jack cheese, divided
Shredded lettuce
Chopped tomato
Chopped avocado
Sour cream

Cook bacon in a skillet until crisp; remove bacon, and drain on paper towels, reserving 1 tablespoon drippings in skillet. Crumble bacon, and set aside.

Heat drippings in skillet over medium heat until hot; add chicken and garlic, and sauté 3 minutes. Stir in ½ cup picante sauce, beans, and next 3 ingredients. Simmer 7 to 10 minutes or until slightly thickened, stirring occasionally. Stir in bacon and green onions.

Spoon about ¼ cup chicken mixture in center of each tortilla; sprinkle each with about 1 tablespoon cheese. Roll up tortillas, and place seam side down in a lightly greased 13- x 9-inch baking dish. Spoon remaining 1½ cups picante sauce over enchiladas.

Bake, covered, at 350° for 15 minutes. Sprinkle remaining cheese over enchiladas; bake, covered, 5 more minutes or until cheese melts. Top enchiladas with lettuce, tomato, avocado, and sour cream. Yield: 5 servings.

Chautauqua Celebrations
Wythe Arts Council, Ltd.
Wytheville, Virginia

Marinated Chicken Pizza

A gutsy marinade for the chicken provides plenty of flavor for this gourmet pizza.

2 tablespoons pine nuts
½ cup sliced green onions, divided
2 tablespoons olive oil, divided
2 garlic cloves, minced
2 tablespoons reduced-sodium soy sauce
2 tablespoons rice vinegar
½ teaspoon dried crushed red pepper
½ teaspoon black pepper
3 skinned and boned chicken breast halves, cut into ½-inch pieces
1 tablespoon cornstarch
1 (16-ounce) Italian bread shell
½ cup (2 ounces) shredded mozzarella cheese
½ cup (2 ounces) shredded Monterey Jack cheese

Bake pine nuts in a shallow pan at 350°, stirring occasionally, 5 minutes or until toasted. Set aside.

Combine ¼ cup green onions, 1 tablespoon oil, garlic, and next 4 ingredients in a large bowl; add chicken, stirring to coat. Cover and let stand at room temperature 30 minutes. Remove chicken from marinade, reserving marinade.

Cook chicken in remaining 1 tablespoon hot oil in a large skillet over medium heat 3 minutes or until done, stirring often.

Stir cornstarch into reserved marinade; add to skillet. Cook, stirring constantly, until mixture is thickened and bubbly. Spoon mixture onto bread shell. Sprinkle with cheeses.

Bake at 400° for 12 minutes. Sprinkle with remaining ¼ cup green onions and reserved pine nuts, and bake 2 more minutes. Yield: 4 to 6 servings.

Lighthouse Secrets: A Collection of Recipes from the Nation's Oldest City
The Junior Service League of St. Augustine, Florida

Chicken Pot Pie with Cornbread Crust

Loads of thick cornbread house tender morsels of chicken and a mix of vegetables. It's definitely warming winter fare.

4 cups water, divided
½ cup peeled, cubed baking
    potato
½ cup cubed carrot
1 medium onion, chopped
3 tablespoons olive oil
¼ cup all-purpose flour
2 cups chicken broth
2 cups chopped cooked
    chicken
½ cup frozen sweet green peas
½ teaspoon salt

⅛ teaspoon freshly ground
    pepper
¼ teaspoon hot sauce
⅓ cup yellow cornmeal
⅓ cup all-purpose flour
1 tablespoon sugar
1½ teaspoons baking powder
¼ teaspoon salt
1 large egg, lightly beaten
⅓ cup milk
2 tablespoons canola oil

Bring 2 cups water to a boil in a small saucepan. Add potato; cook 5 minutes or until tender. Drain and set aside. Bring 2 cups water to a boil in a small saucepan. Add carrot; cook 7 minutes or until tender. Drain and set aside.

Sauté onion in hot olive oil in a large saucepan over medium-high heat 4 minutes or until tender. Add flour; cook 1 minute, stirring constantly. Gradually whisk in broth; cook over medium heat, whisking constantly, until mixture is thickened and bubbly. Remove from heat; stir in reserved potato, carrot, chicken, and next 4 ingredients. Spoon mixture into a lightly greased 11- x 7-inch baking dish.

Stir together cornmeal and next 4 ingredients in a medium bowl. Add egg, milk, and canola oil, stirring until smooth. Spoon cornmeal mixture over chicken mixture. Bake, uncovered, at 400° for 17 minutes. Serve immediately. Yield: 4 to 6 servings.   Wanda Hogge

St. Andrew's Cooks Again
Presbyterian Women of St. Andrew
Beaumont, Texas

Glazed Cornish Hens with Curried Rice

½ cup butter or margarine
1 cup chopped onion
10 cups soft breadcrumbs
   (homemade)
2 garlic cloves, minced
1 cup slivered blanched
   almonds, toasted
¼ cup chopped celery
⅓ cup dry white wine
2 teaspoons salt
⅛ teaspoon pepper

½ teaspoon dried rosemary
12 (1½-pound) Cornish hens
½ cup butter or margarine,
   melted
1 (12-ounce) jar apricot
   preserves
¼ cup lemon juice
3 (7-ounce) packages curried
   rice mix
¼ cup chutney

Melt ½ cup butter in a large skillet over medium heat; add onion, and sauté until tender. Combine onion, breadcrumbs, and next 7 ingredients in a large bowl. Remove and discard giblets and neck, and rinse hens with cold water; pat dry. Stuff hens lightly with breadcrumb mixture, and close cavities, securing with wooden picks. Tie ends of legs with string; lift wing tips up and over back, and tuck under bird.

Place in 2 large ungreased roasting pans; brush hens with ½ cup melted butter. Bake, uncovered, at 450° for 40 minutes, basting with butter every 10 minutes. Rotate pans after 20 minutes, moving pan on top rack to bottom rack, and pan on bottom rack to top rack.

Heat preserves in a small saucepan over low heat until melted. Stir in lemon juice. Brush hens with preserve mixture. Bake 20 more minutes or until juices run clear and a meat thermometer inserted into thigh registers 180°, rotating pans after 10 minutes.

Meanwhile, prepare rice mix according to package directions. Stir in chutney. Serve hens with rice mixture. Yield: 12 servings.

The Guild Collection: Recipes from Art Lovers
The Guild, The Museum of Fine Arts, Houston, Texas

Lemon-Rosemary Turkey

Fresh rosemary, sage, and lemon infuse turkey with potent flavor—inside and out.

1 (10- to 12-pound) turkey
8 garlic cloves
2 large lemons, halved
3 fresh rosemary sprigs
3 fresh sage sprigs
Vegetable cooking spray

1 tablespoon salt
2 teaspoons pepper
¼ cup finely chopped fresh rosemary
¼ cup finely chopped fresh sage

Remove and discard giblets and neck, and rinse turkey with cold water; pat dry. Loosen skin from turkey breast without totally detaching it; place garlic under skin. Squeeze 2 lemon halves inside turkey, and place in cavity. Squeeze remaining lemon halves over outside of turkey. Place rosemary and sage sprigs in cavity. Tie ends of legs together with string; lift wing tips up and over back, and tuck under bird. Coat turkey with cooking spray. Sprinkle turkey with salt and pepper. Rub chopped rosemary and sage on outside of turkey.

Place turkey, breast side up, on a lightly greased rack in a broiler pan. Bake, uncovered, at 325° for 1 hour and 30 minutes. Cover loosely with aluminum foil; bake 2½ to 3 more hours or until a meat thermometer inserted into meaty part of thigh registers 180°. Remove turkey from pan; cover and let stand 15 minutes before carving. Yield: 8 servings.

Meet Us in the Kitchen
The Junior League of St. Louis, Missouri

Ginger-Glazed Garlic Turkey

Fresh ginger adds a pleasingly pungent flavor to the sweet glaze for turkey legs and thighs. The economical turkey pieces are more readily available around the holiday season.

1 cup apple juice
½ cup firmly packed light
   brown sugar
3 tablespoons freshly grated
   ginger
2¼ pounds turkey legs or
   thighs

12 garlic cloves, peeled
1 teaspoon salt
2 teaspoons cracked pepper
2 tablespoons olive oil

Combine apple juice, sugar, and ginger in a small saucepan. Bring to a boil; reduce heat, and simmer, uncovered, 5 minutes or until ginger mixture is reduced by half. Set aside.

Cut slits in turkey pieces; stuff each slit with a garlic clove. Sprinkle turkey with salt and pepper; drizzle evenly with oil. Place turkey on an ungreased baking sheet. Bake at 350° for 1½ hours, brushing with ginger mixture 5 times during last 30 minutes of baking time. Yield: 3 to 4 servings.   G. E. William Jr.

A Dab of This and a Dab of That
Bethlehem Baptist Church Senior Missionary
Ninety Six, South Carolina

Turkey Tetrazzini

¼ cup finely chopped onion
2 tablespoons butter or
   margarine, melted
3¾ teaspoons all-purpose flour
½ teaspoon salt
⅛ teaspoon pepper
¼ teaspoon dried parsley
   flakes
½ cup chicken broth
½ cup milk

½ cup evaporated milk
1 (4-ounce) can sliced
   mushrooms, drained
7 ounces uncooked dried
   spaghetti
2½ to 3 cups chopped cooked
   turkey
1 cup (4 ounces) shredded
   sharp Cheddar cheese

Sauté onion in melted butter in a skillet until golden. Stir in flour and next 3 ingredients. Cook 1 minute, stirring constantly. Gradually whisk in chicken broth, milk, and evaporated milk; cook over medium heat, stirring constantly, until mixture is thickened and bubbly. Stir in mushrooms.

Cook spaghetti according to package directions; drain well. Combine spaghetti and half of sauce; toss well. Add remaining sauce and turkey; toss well.

Spoon mixture into a greased 11- x 7-inch baking dish. Bake, covered, at 350° for 30 minutes. Uncover, sprinkle with Cheddar cheese, and bake 5 more minutes or until cheese melts. Serve immediately. Yield: 6 servings.

Specialties of the Haus
TCM International, Inc.
Indianapolis, Indiana

Cheese-Stuffed Turkey Burgers

Salsa and Monterey Jack cheese with peppers are blended into the turkey burgers, giving them a light pink hue that looks almost like salmon burgers, plus gusto in every bite.

3 **pounds ground turkey**	¾ **teaspoon black pepper**
1 **(16-ounce) jar thick and chunky salsa**	12 **hamburger buns, toasted**
1 **cup diced Monterey Jack cheese with peppers**	12 **slices tomato**
1 **jalapeño pepper, seeded and minced**	12 **lettuce leaves**
	Additional salsa

Combine first 5 ingredients in a large bowl, mixing well. Shape mixture into 12 patties. Grill, covered with grill lid, over medium heat (300° to 350°) 15 minutes or until done, turning once. Place burgers on bottom halves of buns; top each burger with a tomato slice, lettuce leaf, and additional salsa. Cover burgers with tops of buns. Yield: 12 servings.   Billie Jo Petersen

Business is Cookin' with FBLA
Lakeview Future Business Leaders of America
Columbus, Nebraska

Duck with Cherry Sauce

Sweet dark cherries and cherry jam make up the fragrant and fruity sauce to spoon atop the slices of rich, dark duck.

1 (5-pound) duck, dressed
1 teaspoon salt
¼ teaspoon pepper
1 (16.5-ounce) can pitted dark
    sweet cherries, undrained

2 tablespoons cherry jam
2 teaspoons cornstarch
Garnish: fresh parsley sprigs

Rinse duck under cold water, and pat dry with paper towels. Sprinkle cavities and skin with salt and pepper. Prick skin with a meat fork. Tie ends of legs together with string; lift wing tips up and over back, and tuck under bird.

Place duck, breast side up, on a lightly greased rack in a broiler pan. Bake, uncovered, at 325° for 3 hours or until a meat thermometer inserted into thigh registers 180°. Transfer duck to a serving platter; cover and let stand 10 minutes.

Combine cherries, jam, and cornstarch in a small saucepan, stirring mixture well. Bring to a boil over medium heat; reduce heat, and simmer 2 minutes. Serve duckling with sauce. Garnish, if desired. Yield: 4 servings.

Historically Heavenly Home Cooking
Corry Area Historical Society
Corry, Pennsylvania

Salads

Grilled Vegetable Salad with Greens, page 269

Tangy Congealed Asparagus

Chopped water chestnuts and fresh asparagus lend lots of crunch to this tangy-sweet salad.

2 pounds fresh asparagus
2 envelopes unflavored gelatin
½ cup cold water
1 cup water
¾ cup sugar
½ cup white vinegar
1 (8-ounce) can sliced water chestnuts, drained and coarsely chopped
1 cup chopped celery
1 (2-ounce) jar diced pimiento, drained
1 small onion, chopped
2 tablespoons lemon juice
1 teaspoon salt

Snap off tough ends of asparagus. Cook asparagus in boiling water to cover 10 seconds; drain and plunge into ice water to stop the cooking process. Drain asparagus well, and coarsely chop. Set aside.

Sprinkle gelatin over ½ cup cold water in a bowl; stir and let stand 1 minute.

Combine 1 cup water, sugar, and vinegar in a medium saucepan; bring to a boil. Add gelatin mixture, and stir until gelatin dissolves. Remove from heat. Cover and chill until consistency of unbeaten egg white.

Combine reserved asparagus, water chestnuts, and remaining 5 ingredients. Fold into gelatin mixture. Pour mixture into a lightly oiled 5-cup mold. Cover and chill until firm. Unmold onto a serving plate. Yield: 6 servings.

Simply Divine
Second-Ponce de Leon Baptist Church
Atlanta, Georgia

Tantalizing Fruit Salad

¼ cup sugar
1½ teaspoons grated lime rind
¼ cup fresh lime juice
2 tablespoons fresh lemon
   juice
1 tablespoon orange liqueur

4½ cups cantaloupe balls
2 cups honeydew melon balls
1 cup quartered fresh
   strawberries
1 cup black or red seedless
   grapes

Stir together first 5 ingredients in a large bowl. Add cantaloupe and remaining ingredients; toss gently. Cover and chill 1 hour, stirring often. Yield: 8 servings.   Linda Lowder

We're Cooking Up Something New:
50 Years of Music, History, and Food
Wichita Falls Symphony League
Wichita Falls, Texas

Orange and Avocado Salad

3 oranges, peeled and sliced
2 avocados, sliced
1 small purple onion, sliced

Green Leaf lettuce leaves
Creamy Chile Dressing

Arrange orange, avocado, and onion on a bed of lettuce. Serve with Creamy Chile Dressing. Yield: 6 servings.

Creamy Chile Dressing

1 (4.5-ounce) can chopped
   green chiles, undrained
2 tablespoons egg substitute
2 tablespoons red wine vinegar

1 teaspoon salt
¼ teaspoon pepper
¾ cup vegetable oil

Process first 5 ingredients in a blender until blended. With blender running, add oil in a slow, steady stream until thickened. Yield: 1½ cups.   Doris Whinery

Menus & Memories
The University of Oklahoma Women's Association
Norman, Oklahoma

Artichoke and Mandarin Orange Salad

To preserve maximum crispness, toss the salad with the dressing right before serving, and then sprinkle with bodacious blue cheese.

½ teaspoon dry mustard
¼ teaspoon sugar
¼ teaspoon paprika
½ cup red wine vinegar
2 teaspoons water
½ cup olive oil
2 garlic cloves, sliced
1 head Red Leaf lettuce, torn
1 head Bibb lettuce, torn

1 (14-ounce) can artichoke hearts, drained and quartered
1 (11-ounce) can mandarin oranges, drained
⅛ teaspoon salt
¼ teaspoon freshly ground pepper
½ cup crumbled blue cheese

Combine first 3 ingredients in a small bowl. Whisk in vinegar and water. Slowly add oil, whisking constantly. Add garlic. Cover and chill.

Combine lettuces, artichoke hearts, and oranges in a large salad bowl. Sprinkle with salt and pepper. Remove garlic from dressing. Toss salad with desired amount of dressing, and sprinkle with blue cheese. Serve immediately. Yield: 8 to 10 servings.

Always in Season
The Junior League of Salt Lake City, Utah

Strawberry-Mango Mesclun Salad

Nestled like treasures among gourmet mixed salad greens are morsels of strawberries, mango, cranberries, and almonds.

¾ cup canola or vegetable oil
½ cup sugar
⅓ cup balsamic vinegar
1 teaspoon salt
8 cups mesclun or gourmet mixed salad greens
8 ounces fresh strawberries, quartered

1 large mango, cubed
1 cup sweetened dried cranberries
½ cup thinly sliced onion
1 cup slivered almonds, toasted

Whisk together first 4 ingredients in a small bowl; set aside.
Combine greens and next 4 ingredients in a large bowl, tossing

gently. Add desired amount of dressing, and toss gently to coat. Sprinkle with almonds. Yield: 6 to 8 servings.

The Kosher Palette
Joseph Kushner Hebrew Academy
Livingston, New Jersey

White Bean-Asparagus Salad

1 pound fresh asparagus, cut into 1½-inch pieces

2 (15-ounce) cans navy or cannellini beans, rinsed and drained

1 red bell pepper, diced

½ purple onion, diced (about ¾ cup)

⅓ cup thinly sliced fresh basil leaves

½ cup balsamic vinegar

2 tablespoons Dijon mustard

½ teaspoon salt

½ teaspoon pepper

½ cup olive oil

Cook asparagus in a small amount of boiling water until crisp-tender; drain. Plunge into ice water to stop the cooking process, and drain well.

Combine asparagus, beans, and next 3 ingredients in a large bowl.

Whisk together vinegar and next 3 ingredients; slowly whisk in oil. Add ⅔ cup dressing mixture to vegetable mixture; toss gently. Cover and chill 2 hours. Yield: 6 servings.   Mary Ann Giordano

Note: Save remaining dressing to use on another salad.

On Course
Women Associates of the Buffalo Power Squadron
Lancaster, New York

Two Shades of Red Salad

Beets and tomatoes provide two shades of red to this exceptional salad, while feta cheese and cilantro lend lively tang.

1 pound beets
1¼ cups seeded, coarsely
   chopped tomato
½ medium-size purple onion,
   minced
¼ cup chopped fresh Italian
   parsley
¼ cup chopped fresh cilantro

1 garlic clove, minced
½ cup fresh lemon juice
2 tablespoons extra-virgin olive
   oil
½ teaspoon salt
¼ teaspoon freshly ground
   black pepper
½ cup crumbled feta cheese

Leave roots and 1 inch of stem on beets; discard greens. Scrub beets with a vegetable brush. Wrap beets tightly in aluminum foil; bake at 400° for 1 hour or until tender. Cool completely. Trim off roots and stems; rub off skins. Dice beets.

Place beets, tomato, and next 4 ingredients in a small bowl; toss well. Whisk together lemon juice and next 3 ingredients in a large bowl. Drizzle over beet mixture, and toss gently. Sprinkle with feta cheese. Yield: 8 servings.

Seasons of Santa Fe
Kitchen Angels
Santa Fe, New Mexico

Grilled Vegetable Salad with Greens

Grilled veggies placed atop salad greens gently wilt the greens and taste terrific with the homemade vinaigrette that blends the flavors.

3 small zucchini, halved lengthwise and cut into 1-inch chunks
3 small yellow squash, halved lengthwise and cut into 1-inch chunks
1 small eggplant, halved lengthwise and cut into 1-inch chunks
1 large purple onion, sliced into ¼-inch-thick slices
2 large red bell peppers, sliced into ½-inch pieces
¾ cup olive oil
¼ cup balsamic vinegar
½ teaspoon salt
½ teaspoon pepper
8 cups mixed salad greens
2 tablespoons chopped fresh basil
2 tablespoons chopped fresh chives
1 tablespoon dried marjoram
½ cup crumbled feta cheese
¼ cup freshly grated Parmesan cheese
½ cup pitted ripe olives, halved
3 plum tomatoes, sliced

Place vegetables in a large shallow dish. Whisk together olive oil and vinegar; pour over vegetables. Sprinkle with salt and pepper. Remove vegetables with a slotted spoon, and place in a large grill basket coated with cooking spray. Set remaining oil mixture aside.

Place grill basket on grill rack. Grill, covered with grill lid, over medium-high heat (350° to 400°) 20 to 25 minutes or until vegetables are crisp-tender, turning once.

Place salad greens on a large serving platter; top with grilled vegetables. Combine basil, chives, and marjoram; sprinkle over salad. Top with cheeses, olives, and tomato. Serve with reserved oil mixture. Yield: 8 to 10 servings.

Shirley W. Bolton

Olivet Heritage Cookbook
Olivet Presbyterian Church
Charlottesville, Virginia

Romaine Salad with Blue Cheese, Chili-Toasted Pecans, and Pears

½ cup sour cream
½ cup buttermilk
¼ cup half-and-half
¼ cup fresh orange juice
1 tablespoon minced fresh mint
2 teaspoons minced fresh basil
½ small shallot, minced
¼ teaspoon salt
¼ teaspoon ground red pepper
4 ounces blue cheese, crumbled
2 ounces goat cheese, crumbled
1 head Romaine lettuce, torn
2 Bartlett pears, cut into thin wedges
3 tablespoons fresh lemon juice
Chili-Toasted Pecans
¼ teaspoon freshly ground pepper

Combine first 9 ingredients in a bowl; stir well. Add cheeses; stir well. Place lettuce in a large bowl; add cheese mixture, and toss gently. Combine pears and lemon juice; toss to coat. Arrange pears over salad. Sprinkle with Chili-Toasted Pecans and freshly ground pepper. Yield: 4 to 6 servings.

Chili-Toasted Pecans

2 tablespoons vegetable oil
2 teaspoons coffee liqueur
1 cup pecan halves
1 tablespoon chili powder
¼ teaspoon ground red pepper
2 teaspoons sugar

Combine vegetable oil and liqueur. Add pecan halves, and toss to coat. Stir in chili powder, red pepper, and sugar. Spread on an ungreased baking sheet. Bake at 300° for 25 minutes or until toasted, stirring often. Cool in pan on a wire rack. Yield: 1 cup.

From Black Tie to Blackeyed Peas: Savannah's Savory Secrets
St. Joseph's Foundation of Savannah, Inc.
Savannah, Georgia

Walnut-Gorgonzola Salad

Crumbles of creamy, pungent Gorgonzola and sugared walnuts grace gourmet salad greens.

1 cup walnut pieces	⅓ cup olive oil
2 tablespoons butter or margarine, melted	¼ cup balsamic vinegar
1 tablespoon sugar	¼ teaspoon salt
1 pound gourmet mixed salad greens	¼ teaspoon pepper
	1 cup crumbled Gorgonzola cheese

Sauté walnuts in melted butter in a large skillet over medium-high heat 5 minutes. Sprinkle with sugar, and sauté 1 to 2 more minutes or until walnuts are crisp. Drain on paper towels; cool completely.

Toss salad greens with olive oil. Drizzle balsamic vinegar over salad greens; sprinkle with salt and pepper.

Toss salad mixture with walnuts and Gorgonzola cheese. Yield: 8 servings.

Flavors of Hawaii
Child and Family Service Guild
Honolulu, Hawaii

Uptown Bluegrass Salad

Artichoke hearts, avocado, bacon, and Parmesan cheese add class to this salad. It's bathed in a spicy brown mustard dressing.

1 pound bacon, cooked and crumbled
2 heads Romaine lettuce, torn
1 (14-ounce) can artichoke hearts, drained and chopped
1 large avocado, cut into bite-size pieces
6 ounces freshly grated Parmesan cheese
Spicy Mustard Dressing

Combine first 5 ingredients in a large bowl. Add Spicy Mustard Dressing, and toss gently to coat. Serve immediately. Yield: 10 to 12 servings.

Spicy Mustard Dressing

⅓ cup chopped onion
3 tablespoons cider vinegar
2 teaspoons spicy brown mustard
½ teaspoon sugar
½ teaspoon salt
¼ teaspoon freshly ground pepper
¾ cup olive oil

Process first 6 ingredients in a food processor until pureed. With processor running, slowly pour olive oil through food chute, processing until blended. Yield: 1 cup.

Note: This dressing can be mixed by hand if you don't have a food processor. Mince the onion, and whisk with remaining ingredients.

Creating a Stir
The Fayette County Medical Auxiliary
Lexington, Kentucky

Napa Cabbage and Pear Slaw

½ cup plain yogurt
¼ cup mayonnaise
¼ teaspoon freshly ground black pepper
¼ to ½ teaspoon salt
3 firm ripe Bosc pears

2 tablespoons fresh lime juice
5 cups very thinly sliced Napa cabbage
1 cup julienne-sliced carrot
½ cup thinly sliced purple onion

Stir together first 4 ingredients; set aside.

Peel pears, if desired; cut in half, and remove core. Cut pears into thin slices. Toss with lime juice in a large bowl. Add cabbage, carrot, and yogurt mixture; toss gently to coat. Sprinkle with sliced onion. Yield: 10 servings.

Tom Mierzwinski

Flavors of the Tenderloin
Sidewalk Clean-Up, Recycling & Urban Beautification (SCRUB)
San Francisco, California

Piquant Coleslaw

½ small cabbage, finely shredded
2 large carrots, shredded
2 green onions, thinly sliced
½ red bell pepper, finely chopped
2 tablespoons sweet pickle relish

½ cup mayonnaise
2 tablespoons red wine or cider vinegar
1 tablespoon fresh lemon juice
½ teaspoon salt
½ teaspoon Worcestershire sauce

Toss together first 5 ingredients in a large bowl.

Stir together mayonnaise and remaining 4 ingredients. Drizzle dressing over vegetables; toss to coat. Cover and chill at least 1 hour. Yield: 6 servings.

Joyce O'Reilly

Rave Reviews
Ogunquit Playhouse
Ogunquit, Maine

Potato Salad with Goat Cheese and Roasted Red Peppers

3 pounds red potatoes, peeled and cut into ¼-inch-thick slices
3 large red bell peppers
⅓ cup olive oil
½ cup thinly sliced green onions
⅓ cup chopped fresh basil
2 teaspoons salt
1 teaspoon freshly ground pepper
⅓ cup chopped dried tomatoes in oil, drained
8 bacon slices, cooked and crumbled
6 ounces goat cheese, crumbled

Cook potatoes in boiling, salted water to cover 15 minutes or until tender; drain well. Cool slightly.

Cut peppers in half crosswise; discard seeds and membranes. Place peppers, skin side up, on an ungreased baking sheet; flatten with palm of hand.

Broil peppers 3 inches from heat 15 minutes or until charred. Place peppers in a heavy-duty zip-top plastic bag; seal and let stand 10 minutes to loosen skins. Peel peppers, and discard skins; cut into ½-inch pieces.

Combine warm potato, olive oil, and next 4 ingredients in a large bowl; toss gently. Add reserved peppers, tomatoes, and bacon; toss gently. Sprinkle with goat cheese, and serve immediately. Yield: 10 to 12 servings.

Meet Us in the Kitchen
The Junior League of St. Louis, Missouri

Black Bean and Orzo Salad

1½ cups uncooked orzo
1 (15-ounce) can black beans, rinsed and drained
1 red bell pepper, chopped
½ cup chopped fresh parsley
½ cup chopped fresh basil
¼ cup chopped purple onion
¼ cup red wine vinegar
3 tablespoons water
2 tablespoons balsamic vinegar
1 tablespoon olive oil
2 garlic cloves, minced
1 teaspoon pepper
¾ teaspoon salt
½ teaspoon sugar

Cook orzo according to package directions; drain. Rinse with cold water; drain well.

Combine orzo, beans, and next 4 ingredients in a large bowl; toss well. Combine wine vinegar and remaining 7 ingredients; pour over orzo mixture, and toss well. Cover and chill. Yield: 8 to 10 servings.

A Sunsational Encore
The Junior League of Greater Orlando, Florida

Bulghur Salad

Fresh lemon juice, olive oil, and garlic classically compliment this Middle Eastern-style wheat salad.

1½ cups uncooked bulghur
    wheat
1½ cups frozen whole kernel
    corn, thawed
1 medium tomato, seeded and
    chopped
1 small zucchini, halved and
    thinly sliced
¼ cup quartered, thinly sliced
    purple onion

3 tablespoons finely chopped
    fresh basil
¼ cup olive oil
¼ cup fresh lemon juice
2 garlic cloves, pressed
½ teaspoon salt
¼ teaspoon freshly ground
    pepper
Lettuce leaves

Place bulghur in a large bowl; cover with boiling water, and let stand 30 minutes or until water is absorbed. Drain well in a wire-mesh strainer or small colander. Press excess water from bulghur, using a fork. (This will prevent salad from becoming soggy.)

Combine bulghur, corn, and next 4 ingredients in bowl; toss gently. Whisk together olive oil and next 4 ingredients in a small bowl. Pour dressing over salad, and toss gently. Cover and let stand 30 minutes. Serve at room temperature on lettuce-lined salad plates. Yield: 8 servings.

Emily Steinberg

. . . And It Was Very Good
Temple Emeth
Teaneck, New Jersey

Greek Pasta Salad

3 quarts water
1 teaspoon salt
1¼ cups uncooked orzo
2 cups thinly sliced cucumber
1 (15-ounce) can garbanzo
    beans, rinsed and drained
¾ cup chopped tomato
½ cup chopped green bell
    pepper
½ cup chopped purple onion
¼ cup chopped fresh parsley
¼ cup chopped ripe olives,
    drained
¼ cup olive oil
¼ cup fresh lemon juice
¼ teaspoon salt
½ cup crumbled feta cheese

Combine water and 1 teaspoon salt in a Dutch oven; bring to a boil. Add orzo, and cook according to package directions. Drain; rinse with cold water, and drain well.

Combine orzo, cucumber, and next 9 ingredients in a large bowl; toss well. Cover and chill 1 hour. Sprinkle with feta cheese. Yield: 8 servings.

Sharing Our Best
The Arrangement Hair Salon
Columbus, Ohio

Island Chicken Salad

This main-dish salad boasts bright colors and a taste of the tropics with mango chutney, curry, and ginger. Papayas and macadamia nuts complete the pretty picture.

3 pounds skinned and boned
    chicken breast halves
1 cup mayonnaise
½ cup sour cream
¼ cup mango chutney
1 tablespoon curry powder
1 tablespoon ground ginger
1 teaspoon salt
1 cup thinly sliced celery
¼ cup thinly sliced green
    onions
3 papayas, sliced
¼ cup chopped macadamia
    nuts

Place chicken on a greased baking sheet. Bake at 350° for 25 to 35 minutes or until done; cool completely. Cut chicken into cubes.

Combine mayonnaise and next 5 ingredients in a bowl. Add chicken, celery, and green onions; toss well. Cover and chill 8 to 10 hours.

Divide papaya slices evenly among 6 salad plates; top each with 1¼ cups chicken salad; sprinkle with macadamia nuts. Yield: 6 servings.

Flavors of Hawaii
Child and Family Service Guild
Honolulu, Hawaii

Wild Rice and Chicken Salad

Water chestnuts and salty cashews add a distinct crunch to this easy-to-assemble salad. Serve on a bed of mixed baby greens for a dressed-up look.

1 (6-ounce) package wild rice
3 cups cubed cooked chicken
  breast (about 6 breast halves)
2 (5-ounce) cans sliced water
  chestnuts, drained
¼ cup chopped green onions
¼ cup fresh lemon juice
¼ cup olive oil
3 tablespoons mayonnaise
½ teaspoon salt
¼ teaspoon pepper
1 cup seedless green grapes,
  sliced
¾ cup salted cashews

Cook rice according to package directions. Spoon onto a large baking sheet; chill 30 minutes.

Stir together rice, chicken, and next 7 ingredients in a large bowl, stirring well. Cover and chill 3 hours. Add grapes and cashews; toss well. Yield: 6 to 8 servings.   Mary Alice Carpenter

Spice It Up!
Baton Rouge Branch of American Association of University Women
Baton Rouge, Louisiana

Apple-Potato Salad

Potato salad takes a tempting turn when made with buttery Yukon gold potatoes, Granny Smith apples, and ham. Bold blue cheese and dillweed add depth.

3 pounds Yukon gold potatoes, peeled
2 Granny Smith apples, peeled and chopped
2 tablespoons fresh lemon juice
1 cup (4 ounces) crumbled blue cheese
¾ cup mayonnaise
¾ cup sour cream
1 teaspoon salt
½ teaspoon dried dillweed
⅛ teaspoon pepper
3 cups cooked ham, cut into thin strips

Cook potatoes in boiling water to cover 25 minutes or just until tender. Drain well, and cool slightly. Cube potatoes, and place in a large bowl.

Toss apple and lemon juice in a small bowl; set aside.

Stir together blue cheese and next 5 ingredients in a small bowl.

Add apple mixture, dressing, and ham to potato, and toss gently. Cover and chill. Yield: 12 servings.

Historically Heavenly Home Cooking
Corry Area Historical Society
Corry, Pennsylvania

Melon and Prosciutto Salad with Grilled Scallops

A delightful dressing created with pesto and jalapeño pepper perks up this scallop, melon, and arugula salad.

2 teaspoons pesto
1 tablespoon white wine vinegar
¼ cup olive oil
1 jalapeño pepper, seeded and minced
2 teaspoons chopped fresh parsley
1 teaspoon chopped fresh chives
⅛ teaspoon salt
¼ teaspoon freshly ground black pepper

1 large avocado, chopped
3 tablespoons fresh lemon juice
8 cups loosely packed torn fresh arugula
1 medium cantaloupe, cubed
3 ounces prosciutto, cut into thin strips
2 teaspoons olive oil
1 pound bay scallops or sea scallops, halved

Combine pesto and vinegar in a small bowl. Gradually add ¼ cup olive oil, whisking until blended. Stir in jalapeño pepper and next 4 ingredients. Set aside.

Combine avocado and lemon juice in a large bowl; toss gently. Add arugula, cantaloupe, and prosciutto, and toss gently. Set aside.

Heat 2 teaspoons olive oil in a large nonstick skillet over medium-high heat; add scallops, and sauté 1 to 2 minutes on each side or until done. Remove scallops, and add to salad. Whisk reserved dressing, and pour over salad; toss gently to coat. Serve immediately. Yield: 4 servings.

John Williams

Cooking with Music: Celebrating the Tastes and Traditions of the Boston Symphony Orchestra
Boston Symphony Association of Volunteers
Boston, Massachusetts

Creamy Basil Dressing

Fragrant fresh basil stars in this balsamic vinegar and tarragon merger.

2 cups firmly packed chopped
  fresh basil
¼ cup olive oil
1 cup mayonnaise
¼ cup chopped fresh parsley
3 tablespoons balsamic vinegar

2 large garlic cloves
¼ teaspoon dried tarragon
½ teaspoon dry mustard
3 green onions, chopped
½ teaspoon freshly ground
  pepper

Process all ingredients in a food processor until smooth, stopping to scrape down sides. Yield: 2 cups.

The Guild Collection: Recipes from Art Lovers
The Guild, The Museum of Fine Arts, Houston, Texas

Honey-Bourbon Salad Dressing

Pair this tasty topper with a fresh fruit or spinach salad. The Dijon mustard, honey, and bourbon blend beyond compare.

6 tablespoons olive oil
⅓ cup honey
¼ cup vegetable oil
¼ cup bourbon

2 tablespoons Dijon mustard
¼ cup red wine vinegar
⅛ teaspoon ground white
  pepper

Whisk together all ingredients in a small bowl. Cover and chill. Whisk just before serving. Yield: 1½ cups.　　　　　Lois Mateus

Look Who's Cooking in Louisville
Pitt Academy
Louisville, Kentucky

Sauces & Condiments

Peach Marmalade, page 290

Caramel Dip for Apples

¾ cup firmly packed light
   brown sugar
¼ cup sugar

1 (8-ounce) package cream
   cheese, softened

Combine all ingredients in a mixing bowl. Beat at medium speed with an electric mixer until smooth. Cover and chill. Serve with apple slices. Yield: 1½ cups.

Cynthia Baker

Angels in the Kitchen
Grace Episcopal Church
Anderson, South Carolina

Blueberry Sauce

Imagine plump blueberries and just the right amount of tangy lemon juice and rind to create this fresh sauce, and you'll envision why it's the perfect partner for fluffy buttermilk pancakes or scoops of creamy vanilla ice cream.

3 cups fresh blueberries
1 cup cold water
⅔ cup sugar
2 tablespoons cornstarch

¼ teaspoon grated lemon rind
1½ tablespoons fresh lemon
   juice

Combine first 4 ingredients in a medium saucepan; cook over medium heat, stirring constantly. Bring to a boil, and boil 1 minute, stirring constantly.

Remove from heat, and stir in lemon rind and lemon juice. Serve sauce warm over pancakes or waffles, or serve chilled over ice cream, angel food cake, or cheesecake. Yield: 3 cups.

Doris M. Cook

Savor the Flavor: Delightfully Vegetarian
Portland Adventist Community Services
Portland, Oregon

Chili Dog Sauce

Be prepared to see big smiles on your children's faces when you top hot dogs with this yummy sauce. Create even more excitement by crowning them again with a creamy coleslaw or Cheddar cheese sauce.

2 pounds ground beef
1 medium onion, minced
4 garlic cloves, minced
3 tablespoons chili powder
1 tablespoon ground cumin

2 cups tomato juice
1 tablespoon pepper
1 teaspoon salt
1 teaspoon ground ginger

Cook ground beef and onion in a Dutch oven over medium-high heat, stirring until meat crumbles and is no longer pink; drain well.

Add garlic, chili powder, and cumin; cook 3 minutes, stirring constantly. Add tomato juice and remaining ingredients; bring to a boil. Reduce heat, and simmer, uncovered, 30 minutes or until thickened. Serve warm over hot dogs in buns. Yield: 5 cups.   Judy Pinkoski

Fine Food from the Friends
Friends of the Superior Public Library, Inc.
Superior, Wisconsin

Green Peppercorn Cream Sauce

6 tablespoons butter or
  margarine
2 tablespoons minced shallots
1 tablespoon all-purpose flour
1 cup heavy whipping cream
¼ cup brandy

1 tablespoon green
  peppercorns, drained
¼ teaspoon salt
⅛ teaspoon pepper

Melt butter in a large skillet over medium heat; add shallots, and sauté 2 minutes. Stir in flour. Stir in cream, and cook until slightly thickened (do not boil). Stir in brandy, and cook 2 minutes. Stir in peppercorns, salt, and pepper. Serve warm over chicken, pork, or veal. Yield: 1½ cups.

Lighthouse Secrets: A Collection of Recipes from the Nation's Oldest City
The Junior Service League of St. Augustine, Florida

Sweet Asian Lamb Marinade

3 garlic cloves, minced
1 teaspoon chopped fresh mint
¼ teaspoon pepper

1 tablespoon lemon juice
2 tablespoons honey
¼ cup soy sauce

Combine all ingredients in a small bowl, and stir mixture well. Yield: 1 cup.   Whitney Wilson Ferguson

Note: To marinate lamb, place in a large heavy-duty zip-top plastic bag or shallow dish; pour marinade over lamb. Seal securely, or cover and marinate in refrigerator at least 8 hours.

Beyond Cotton Country
The Junior League of Morgan County
Decatur, Alabama

Taco Seasoning Mix

Making your own seasoning mix enables you to eliminate the additives and high sodium content of packaged varieties.

2 teaspoons dried minced
   onion
1 teaspoon salt
1 teaspoon chili powder
½ teaspoon cornstarch
½ teaspoon instant minced
   garlic

½ teaspoon dried crushed red
   pepper
½ teaspoon ground cumin
¼ teaspoon dried oregano

Stir together all ingredients. Store in an airtight container up to 1 month. Yield: 2 tablespoons.   Jane Sholes

Note: To use for tacos, cook 1 pound ground beef in a large skillet, stirring until it crumbles and is no longer pink; drain. Stir in Taco Seasoning Mix and ½ cup water. Cook over medium heat 5 minutes or until liquid evaporates. Spoon meat mixture into taco shells.

Inman Pioneer Day Cookbook
Inman Community Improvement Council
Inman, Nebraska

Fresh Fruit Salsa

This salsa doubles as a sauce and a condiment. Serve it as a salsa over grilled fish, chicken, or pork. It also works as a condiment spooned over cream cheese and served with cinnamon-flavored crisps or crackers. For the best texture and prettiest appearance, chop the ingredients by hand.

1 medium-size orange, peeled, sectioned, and finely chopped
2 large kiwifruit, peeled and finely chopped
1 ripe peach, peeled and finely chopped
½ cup finely chopped fresh pineapple
¼ cup thinly sliced green onions
¼ cup finely chopped green bell pepper
1 jalapeño pepper, seeded and finely chopped
1 tablespoon fresh lime juice
1 cup fresh strawberries, quartered

Combine first 8 ingredients in a large bowl; toss gently. Cover and chill at least 8 hours. Add strawberries to salsa, and toss gently just before serving. Yield: 2½ cups.

Flavors of Hawaii
Child and Family Service Guild
Honolulu, Hawaii

Flavored Butters

These sweet-flavored butters are yummy on toast, biscuits, or pancakes. Enjoy the savory ones atop fish, poultry, or vegetables.

Almond-Peach Butter

½ **cup butter, softened**   ½ **teaspoon almond extract**
⅓ **cup peach preserves**   ½ **teaspoon powdered sugar**

Combine all ingredients in a small bowl. Stir with a wooden spoon until blended. Cover and chill at least 8 hours. Let stand at room temperature 30 minutes before serving. Yield: ¾ cup.

Honey-Orange Butter

½ **cup butter, softened**   2 **tablespoons orange**
¼ **cup honey**   **marmalade**

Combine all ingredients in a small bowl. Stir with a wooden spoon until blended. Cover and chill at least 8 hours. Let stand at room temperature 30 minutes before serving. Yield: ¾ cup.

Cinnamon-Maple Butter

½ **cup butter, softened**   ½ **teaspoon ground cinnamon**
2 **tablespoons maple syrup**

Combine all ingredients in a small bowl. Stir with a wooden spoon, or beat at medium speed with an electric mixer until blended. Cover and chill at least 8 hours. Let stand at room temperature 30 minutes before serving. Yield: ¾ cup.

Strawberry Butter

½ **cup butter, softened**   ½ **teaspoon fresh lemon juice**
⅓ **cup strawberry preserves**   ½ **teaspoon powdered sugar**

Combine all ingredients in a small bowl. Stir with a wooden spoon, or beat at medium speed with an electric mixer until blended. Cover and chill at least 8 hours. Let stand at room temperature 30 minutes before serving. Yield: ¾ cup.

Fines Herbes Butter

1 cup butter, softened
2 tablespoons minced fresh
  tarragon
2 tablespoons minced fresh
  chives

2 tablespoons minced fresh
  parsley
½ teaspoon ground white
  pepper

Combine all ingredients in a small bowl. Stir with a wooden spoon, or beat at medium speed with an electric mixer until blended. Cover and chill at least 8 hours. Let stand at room temperature 30 minutes before serving. Yield: 1 cup.

Dill Butter

1 cup butter, softened
2 tablespoons minced fresh
  dill
3 tablespoons fresh lemon
  juice

1 teaspoon dried dillweed
½ teaspoon ground white
  pepper
¼ teaspoon salt

Combine all ingredients in a small bowl. Stir with a wooden spoon, or beat at medium speed with an electric mixer until blended. Cover and chill at least 8 hours. Let stand at room temperature 30 minutes before serving. Yield: 1 cup.

Chive Butter

1 cup butter, softened
½ cup minced fresh chives
2 tablespoons fresh lemon
  juice

¼ teaspoon salt

Combine all ingredients in a small bowl. Stir with a wooden spoon, or beat at medium speed with an electric mixer until blended. Cover and chill at least 8 hours. Let stand at room temperature 30 minutes before serving. Yield: 1¼ cups.

Favorite Recipes Taste of Tradition
B.A. Ritter Senior Citizen Center
Nederland, Texas

Italian Relish

Grilled beef or tuna steaks stand out when accompanied with this intense relish. To create a simple appetizer instead, spread it over toasted French baguette slices.

8 ounces kalamata olives, pitted
8 ounces green olives, pitted
1 large red bell pepper, cut into 8 pieces
⅔ cup chopped dried tomatoes in oil, undrained
⅓ cup olive oil
3 garlic cloves, finely minced

2 tablespoons chopped fresh Italian parsley
1 tablespoon chopped fresh oregano or 1 teaspoon dried oregano
2 tablespoons red wine vinegar
1 tablespoon balsamic vinegar
½ teaspoon freshly ground pepper

Process first 4 ingredients in a food processor until coarsely chopped. Combine olive oil and remaining 6 ingredients in a medium saucepan. Add olive mixture, and bring to a boil, stirring often. Remove from heat; cool 10 minutes. Chill. Store in an airtight container in refrigerator up to 1 week. Yield: 4 cups.

America Celebrates Columbus
The Junior League of Columbus, Ohio

Beet Pickles

1 cup sugar
1 cup water
1 cup apple cider vinegar

2 (15-ounce) cans whole beets, drained and halved
¼ teaspoon ground cloves

Combine first 3 ingredients in a medium saucepan; stir well. Bring to a boil; reduce heat, and simmer, uncovered, 15 minutes. Add beets and cloves, and simmer, uncovered, 15 minutes. Cover and chill. Yield: 3½ cups.

Marian Sundell

Our Favorite Recipes
Lutheran Church of the Good Shepherd
Billings, Montana

Orange-Cream Cheese Spread

2 (8-ounce) packages cream
   cheese, softened
½ cup sifted powdered sugar
2 tablespoons grated orange
   rind

2 tablespoons frozen orange
   juice concentrate, thawed
2 tablespoons orange liqueur

Combine all ingredients in a mixing bowl; beat at medium speed with an electric mixer until smooth. Cover and chill 8 hours. Serve with fruit, scones, breakfast breads, or biscuits. Yield: 2¼ cups.

A Taste of Washington State
Washington Bed & Breakfast Guild
Seattle, Washington

Easy Rhubarb Jam

5 cups diced fresh rhubarb
3 cups sugar
1 cup chopped fresh
   strawberries

1 (3-ounce) package strawberry
   gelatin

Process rhubarb and sugar in a food processor 10 seconds, stopping to scrape down sides.

Transfer rhubarb mixture to a large saucepan; bring to a boil. Reduce heat, and simmer 10 minutes, stirring constantly. Add strawberries; simmer 5 minutes, stirring constantly. Remove from heat. Stir in gelatin; let stand 5 minutes, stirring often.

Pour hot jam into hot, sterilized jars, filling to ¼ inch from top; wipe jar rims. Cover at once with metal lids, and screw on bands; cool. Store in refrigerator. Yield: 6 half-pints.

Marilyn Herbold

North Country Cooking
51st National Square Dance Convention
Champlin, Minnesota

Peach Marmalade

This golden marmalade lets you enjoy the essence of summer peaches year-round. You'll need 4½ cups of the cooked fruit mixture to jell correctly with the pectin. If you have a little fruit mixture left over, sweeten it and spoon it over pancakes or ice cream.

1 orange
2 lemons
1 cup water
2 pounds fresh ripe peaches, peeled (6 medium)

7 cups sugar
1 (3-ounce) package liquid pectin

Cut orange and lemons into quarters; remove seeds and center pith. Process orange and lemon quarters in a food processor until ground; transfer to a Dutch oven. Add water, and bring to a boil. Cover, reduce heat, and simmer 20 minutes.

Cut peaches into quarters, removing pits; add peaches to food processor, and pulse 5 times or until chopped. Add peaches to citrus mixture. Measure 4½ cups of fruit mixture to use for marmalade. Reserve any leftover fruit mixture for other uses. Stir sugar into 4½ cups fruit mixture; bring to a rolling boil.

Add liquid pectin to peach mixture; return to a boil, and boil 1 minute, stirring constantly. Remove from heat, and skim off foam with a metal spoon.

Pour hot marmalade into hot, sterilized jars, filling to ¼ inch from the top; wipe jar rims. Cover jars at once with metal lids, and screw on bands. Process the jars in boiling-water bath for 5 minutes. Yield: 9 half-pints.

Celeste Sweet

Good Food, Served Right
Traditional Arts in Upstate New York
Canton, New York

Soups & Stews

Seafood Gumbo, page 305

Chilled Cantaloupe Soup

4 small ripe cantaloupes,
   chilled (about 3 pounds each)
1½ cups apple juice
⅔ cup sugar
½ cup dry sherry
1 tablespoon fresh lemon juice
¾ teaspoon ground ginger
¾ teaspoon vanilla extract
Garnishes: fresh mint sprigs,
   whipped cream, fresh lime
   slices

Cut cantaloupes in half crosswise; remove and discard seeds. Scoop out melon with a spoon to equal 18 cups, reserving shells; cover and chill shells.

Process melon, in batches, in a blender until smooth. Pour into a large serving bowl. Stir in apple juice and next 5 ingredients. Cover and chill 1 hour, stirring occasionally. Serve soup in reserved shells or soup bowls. Garnish, if desired. Yield: 16 cups.

Tucson Treasures: Recipes & Reflections
Tucson Medical Center Auxiliary
Tucson, Arizona

Cream of Artichoke Soup

4 (14-ounce) cans artichoke
   hearts, drained
2 (10¾-ounce) cans cream of
   mushroom soup, undiluted
2 cups half-and-half
2 cups chicken broth
½ cup dry white wine
1 teaspoon salt
1 teaspoon pepper

Process artichoke hearts, in batches, in a food processor until smooth, stopping to scrape down sides.

Combine mushroom soup, half-and-half, and chicken broth in a Dutch oven, stirring until smooth. Add artichoke puree, wine, salt, and pepper; cook over medium heat, stirring constantly, until thoroughly heated. Yield: 11 cups.   Donna deHoll

Angels in the Kitchen
Grace Episcopal Church
Anderson, South Carolina

Tortellini Bean Soup

Cheese-filled tortellini, frozen spinach, and prosciutto star in this easy soup. Serve bowlfuls with lots of crusty bread and a green salad to make a meal.

¼ pound prosciutto, finely
  chopped
1 medium onion, chopped
2 large garlic cloves, minced
2 tablespoons olive oil
6 cups chicken broth
1 (28-ounce) can diced
  tomatoes, undrained
2 (9-ounce) packages
  refrigerated cheese-filled
  tortellini

1 (16-ounce) can kidney beans,
  rinsed and drained
¼ teaspoon dried basil
¼ teaspoon dried oregano
¼ teaspoon pepper
1 (10-ounce) package frozen
  chopped spinach, thawed
  and well drained
¼ cup freshly grated Romano
  cheese

Sauté first 3 ingredients in hot olive oil in a Dutch oven over medium heat 5 to 7 minutes or until onion is tender.

Stir in broth and next 6 ingredients. Bring to a boil; reduce heat, and simmer, uncovered, 5 minutes. Stir in spinach, and cook until thoroughly heated.

To serve, ladle soup into individual bowls. Sprinkle each serving with cheese. Yield: 13 cups.

Twice Treasured Recipes
The Bargain Box, Inc.
Hilton Head Island, South Carolina

Butternut Squash Soup

This delicate beauty of a squash soup boasts aromatic rosemary and toasted walnuts.

1 small onion, chopped
1 fresh rosemary sprig
1 tablespoon minced garlic
2 tablespoons unsalted butter or margarine, melted
1 large butternut squash, peeled and cut into chunks
4 cups chicken broth
1 cup heavy whipping cream
1 teaspoon salt
½ teaspoon ground white pepper
½ teaspoon pepper sauce
½ cup chopped walnuts, toasted

Sauté onion, rosemary, and garlic in butter in a Dutch oven over low heat 5 minutes or until onion is tender. Add squash and next 5 ingredients. Cover, reduce heat, and simmer 1 hour or until squash is very tender. Discard rosemary sprig. Process mixture, in batches, in a blender until smooth.

To serve, ladle soup into individual bowls. Sprinkle each serving with toasted walnuts. Yield: 8 cups.   Stacy Coon

Homemade with Love
Swanton-Missisquoi Valley Lions Club
Highgate Center, Vermont

Golden Cream Soup

3 cups peeled, chopped baking potato
1 cup water
½ cup sliced carrot
½ cup sliced celery
¼ cup chopped onion
1 chicken bouillon cube
1 teaspoon dried parsley flakes
½ teaspoon salt
⅛ teaspoon pepper
1½ cups milk
2 tablespoons all-purpose flour
⅓ pound pasteurized prepared cheese product, cubed

Combine first 9 ingredients in a large saucepan; bring to a boil over medium-high heat. Cover, reduce heat, and simmer 5 minutes or until vegetables are tender.

Gradually add milk to flour in a small bowl, whisking until smooth. Add milk mixture to pan; cook, stirring constantly, 9 minutes or until thickened. Add cheese cubes, stirring until cheese melts. Serve immediately. Yield: 6 cups.   Terry Lisowski

On Course
Women Associates of the Buffalo Power Squadron
Lancaster, New York

Parsnip Soup

Fresh parsley and celery lend green goodness and a gentle hue to this creamy parsnip soup.

¼ cup butter or margarine
1 pound parsnips, peeled and thinly sliced
1 cup chopped celery
4 cups chicken broth, divided
¼ cup chopped fresh parsley
3 tablespoons all-purpose flour

⅛ teaspoon ground white pepper
½ teaspoon salt
Sour cream
Freshly grated Parmesan cheese

Melt butter in a large saucepan over medium heat; add parsnips and celery. Cover and cook 10 to 15 minutes or until parsnips are tender, stirring occasionally.

Process cooked vegetables, 1 cup chicken broth, parsley, flour, and pepper in a blender until smooth. Add 1 cup chicken broth, and process until blended. Return pureed mixture to pan; stir in remaining 2 cups chicken broth. Cook over medium heat until thoroughly heated, stirring often. Stir in salt.

To serve, ladle soup into individual bowls. Top each serving with a dollop of sour cream, and sprinkle with cheese. Yield: 5½ cups.

More Enchanted Eating from the West Shore
Friends of the Symphony
Muskegon, Michigan

Potato Soup

The toppings make this soup incredible. Crumbled bacon, shredded Cheddar cheese, and chopped green onions load this warming soup with flavor.

6 large baking potatoes, peeled and cubed (about 4½ pounds)
1¼ cups chopped onion
2 celery ribs, chopped
2 carrots, sliced
1 (8-ounce) package cream cheese, softened
½ cup butter or margarine, softened
1 (10¾-ounce) can cream of chicken soup, undiluted
2 cups milk
2 cups water
1 teaspoon salt
½ teaspoon pepper
8 bacon slices, cooked and crumbled
Shredded Cheddar cheese
Chopped green onions

Combine first 4 ingredients in a large Dutch oven; add water to cover. Bring to a boil; cover, reduce heat, and simmer 12 minutes or until potatoes are tender. Drain.

Beat cream cheese and butter in a medium bowl at medium speed with an electric mixer until creamy. Add cream of chicken soup, beating well. Gradually add milk, beating until smooth; add milk mixture to vegetable mixture. Stir in 2 cups water, salt, and pepper. Bring to a boil; reduce heat, and simmer, uncovered, 15 minutes, stirring occasionally.

To serve, ladle soup into individual bowls. Sprinkle each serving with crumbled bacon, Cheddar cheese, and green onions. Yield: 12½ cups.

Simple Pleasures: From Our Table to Yours
Arab Mothers' Club
Arab, Alabama

Cheese Soup

Pair this smooth cheese and wine soup with a loaf of hearty, earthy bread.

6 slices bacon	3 cups chicken broth
1 celery rib, chopped	3 tablespoons cornstarch
1 small onion, chopped	3 tablespoons cold water
⅛ teaspoon ground white pepper	3 cups (12 ounces) shredded sharp Cheddar cheese
⅛ teaspoon ground nutmeg	¼ cup dry white wine

Cook bacon in a small Dutch oven until crisp; remove bacon, and drain on paper towels, reserving 2 tablespoons drippings in pan. Crumble bacon, and set aside.

Sauté celery and onion in drippings 5 minutes or until tender. Stir in pepper and nutmeg; cook 30 seconds. Stir in chicken broth, and bring to a boil.

Combine cornstarch and water, stirring until smooth; stir into broth mixture. Bring to a boil, stirring constantly; boil, stirring constantly, 1 minute or until thickened.

Reduce heat to low; add cheese to soup, ½ cup at a time, stirring until cheese melts. Stir in wine.

To serve, ladle soup into individual bowls. Sprinkle each serving with bacon. Yield: 5 cups.   Marie Souza

Homemade with Love
Swanton-Missisquoi Valley Lions Club
Highgate Center, Vermont

Crème de Brie Soup

Fresh mushrooms and one of your favorite cheeses repackage French onion soup with a new twist. This soup's a showstopper for a special-occasion meal.

6 ounces Brie
¼ cup butter or margarine
1 pound onions, finely chopped
1 (8-ounce) package sliced fresh mushrooms
4 teaspoons minced garlic
1 cup dry white wine
¼ cup all-purpose flour
3½ cups chicken broth

1 bay leaf
2 cups heavy whipping cream
1 tablespoon chopped fresh thyme
1 tablespoon dry sherry
¼ teaspoon salt
¼ teaspoon pepper
12 slices French baguette, toasted
4 ounces Brie, cut into 12 slices

Remove and discard rind from 6 ounces of Brie. Cut cheese into cubes; set aside.

Melt butter in a Dutch oven over medium heat; add onion, mushrooms, and garlic, and sauté 5 minutes. Add wine, and cook 9 to 11 minutes or until wine has almost evaporated. Add flour, stirring until thoroughly blended. Add chicken broth and bay leaf. Bring to a boil, stirring constantly. Reduce heat, and simmer, uncovered, 5 to 6 minutes or until mixture thickens. Stir in whipping cream and thyme. Add 6 ounces Brie, and stir until cheese melts. Stir in sherry, salt, and pepper. Discard bay leaf.

Place 6 ovenproof soup bowls on a 15- x 10-inch jellyroll pan. Spoon about 1¼ cups soup into each bowl. Top each serving with 2 slices bread and 2 slices cheese. Broil 2 to 3 minutes or until cheese is melted and bubbly. Yield: 7½ cups.

Cooks of the Green Door
The League of Catholic Women
Minneapolis, Minnesota

Creamy Reuben Soup

Sauerkraut, cheese, corned beef, and caraway seeds make up the famed reuben sandwich and this soup, too. Serve it with a good rye bread.

2 cups milk
1 (10¾-ounce) can cream of
     celery soup, undiluted
1 (10-ounce) can Bavarian-style
     sauerkraut, drained
1 cup finely chopped deli
     corned beef (about ¼ pound)

¼ teaspoon caraway seeds
¼ teaspoon hot sauce
12 (¾-ounce) slices process
     American cheese, quartered

Combine first 6 ingredients in a large saucepan. Cook over medium heat, stirring constantly, 10 minutes or until mixture begins to simmer. Add cheese; cook, stirring constantly, 1 to 2 minutes or until cheese melts. Remove from heat. Serve immediately. Yield: 5 cups.

It's About Time: Recipes, Reflections, Realities
National Association Teachers of Family and Consumer Sciences
Bowling Green, Kentucky

Lentil and Sausage Soup

We doubt you'll have any leftovers of this soup, but if you do, you may want to add a bit of water when reheating to thin it a bit.

1 pound dried lentils
1 tablespoon butter or margarine
1 pound chorizo or smoked sausage, cut into ½-inch slices
⅔ cup thinly sliced carrot
½ cup finely chopped onion
½ cup finely chopped celery
2 (14½-ounce) cans chicken broth
1 garlic clove, minced
¼ teaspoon salt
½ teaspoon pepper
⅓ cup finely chopped fresh parsley
Hot cooked rice (optional)

Sort and rinse lentils; place in a Dutch oven. Cover with water 2 inches above lentils; soak 2 hours. Drain.

Melt butter in a Dutch oven over medium heat; add sausage, and sauté 3 to 5 minutes. Add carrot, onion, and celery; sauté 6 minutes or until tender. Stir in lentils, broth, and next 3 ingredients. Bring to a boil; cover, reduce heat, and simmer 45 minutes or until lentils are tender, stirring often.

Process 1¾ cups lentil mixture in a blender until smooth, stopping to scrape down sides. Return puree to soup. Sprinkle with parsley. Serve soup over rice, if desired. Yield: 8½ cups.   Helena Martinez

De Nuestra Mesa: Our Food, Wine, and Tradition
New Hope Charities, Inc.
West Palm Beach, Florida

Chicken Soup

Ladle up this comforting chicken soup right away for the best consistency. It may thicken if it sits awhile. If so, just add a little broth or half-and-half to the soup and slowly reheat.

1½ pounds chicken breast
    tenderloins
6 cups chicken broth
½ cup uncooked rice
3 medium carrots, thinly sliced
2 celery ribs, thinly sliced
½ cup thinly sliced green
    onions
2 small zucchini, diced
¼ cup chopped fresh parsley

6 tablespoons butter or
    margarine
6 tablespoons all-purpose flour
2 cups half-and-half
½ cup chopped fresh
    mushrooms
½ teaspoon salt
¼ teaspoon freshly ground
    pepper

Arrange chicken in a single layer in a lightly greased 15- x 10-inch jellyroll pan. Bake at 375° for 8 minutes; cool and coarsely chop. Set aside.

Bring chicken broth to a boil in a Dutch oven; add rice. Reduce heat; simmer, uncovered, 10 minutes. Add carrot, celery, and green onions; simmer 10 minutes. Add zucchini and parsley; simmer 2 minutes. Remove from heat; set aside.

Melt butter in a medium saucepan over medium-high heat. Whisk in flour until smooth. Cook 1 minute, whisking constantly. Gradually add half-and-half, and cook over medium heat, stirring constantly, 5 minutes or until thickened and bubbly. Stir in 1 cup soup, mushrooms, salt, and pepper.

Add half-and-half mixture and reserved chopped chicken to soup in Dutch oven; stir well. Bring to a boil; cook 2 minutes, stirring constantly. Serve immediately. Yield: 10½ cups. Jim White

Cooking with Class
Forest Hills Elementary School PTO
Lake Oswego, Oregon

Mark's Chicken Taco Soup

Lots of convenience products mean that this yummy soup is a little on the salty side. If salt is an issue in your diet, use no-salt-added products when possible.

4½ cups chopped cooked chicken
4 (10½-ounce) cans chicken broth
1 (15-ounce) can diced tomatoes, undrained
1 (15-ounce) can black beans, rinsed and drained
1 (15-ounce) can cream-style corn
1 (10-ounce) can diced tomatoes and green chiles, undrained
1 medium onion, chopped
1 small green bell pepper, chopped
1 teaspoon minced garlic
1 (1¼-ounce) envelope taco seasoning mix
1 (1.4-ounce) envelope Ranch-style dressing mix
½ teaspoon ground cumin
Garnishes: crumbled tortilla chips, sour cream, shredded lettuce

Combine all ingredients except garnishes in a large Dutch oven. Bring to a boil; reduce heat, and simmer, uncovered, 30 minutes. To serve, ladle soup into individual bowls. Garnish, if desired. Yield: 13 cups.

Mrs. Robert H. Hopkins

Tapestry: A Weaving of Food, Culture and Tradition
The Junior Welfare League of Rock Hill, South Carolina

Crab and Spinach Bisque

4 cups whipping cream
½ cup butter or margarine
2 cups chopped onion
½ cup chopped celery
½ cup chopped green bell pepper
¼ cup all-purpose flour
2 cups chicken broth
1 tablespoon Worcestershire sauce
1 bay leaf
¼ teaspoon dried basil
¼ teaspoon dried thyme
2 (10-ounce) packages frozen chopped spinach, thawed and drained
2 pounds fresh lump crabmeat
3 tablespoons chopped fresh parsley
1½ teaspoons salt
½ teaspoon pepper

Place whipping cream in a medium saucepan; cook over medium-low heat until thoroughly heated. Keep warm.

Melt butter in a Dutch oven over medium-high heat. Add onion, celery, and bell pepper; sauté 5 minutes or until tender. Add flour; stirring until blended. Cook 1 minute, stirring constantly. Gradually add warm whipping cream, broth, and next 4 ingredients; stir well. Bring just to a simmer; cook, uncovered, 10 minutes (do not boil). Add spinach and remaining ingredients; cook until thoroughly heated, stirring constantly. Discard bay leaf. Yield: 12 cups.

Settings on the Dock of the Bay
ASSISTANCE LEAGUE® of the Bay Area
Houston, Texas

Tomato-Dill Bisque

2 medium onions, finely
   chopped
1 garlic clove, minced
2 tablespoons olive oil
4 cups vegetable broth
8 medium tomatoes (about 3½
   pounds), peeled, seeded, and
   quartered
2¼ teaspoons fresh dill or
   1 teaspoon dried dillweed

¾ teaspoon salt
½ teaspoon freshly ground
   pepper
1 (8-ounce) container sour
   cream
Garnishes: fresh dill sprigs,
   sour cream

Sauté onion and garlic in hot oil in a Dutch oven over medium heat 5 to 7 minutes or until tender. Add broth and next 4 ingredients. Bring to a boil; cover, reduce heat, and simmer 10 minutes. Remove from heat, and cool 15 minutes.

Process half of tomato mixture in a blender until very smooth. Repeat procedure with remaining tomato mixture. Stir in sour cream until smooth. Cover and chill at least 8 hours.

To serve, ladle soup into individual bowls. Garnish, if desired. Yield: 10 cups.   Grace B. Borowitz

. . . And It Was Very Good
Temple Emeth
Teaneck, New Jersey

Shrimp-Scallop Chowder

Use cream of celery soup to form the base, then transform this soup's humble beginnings by adding fresh shrimp, scallops, and basil to the blend.

½ pound unpeeled, medium-size fresh shrimp
1 small onion, chopped
1 garlic clove, minced
1 tablespoon olive oil
1 (10¾-ounce) can condensed cream of celery soup, undiluted
1½ cups milk

2 tablespoons chopped fresh basil
¼ teaspoon salt
¼ teaspoon freshly ground pepper
½ pound fresh bay scallops
¼ cup dry white wine
Garnish: fresh basil sprigs

Peel shrimp, and devein, if desired. Set aside.

Sauté onion and garlic in hot oil in a medium saucepan over medium heat 5 minutes. Add soup and next 4 ingredients; bring to a boil. Add shrimp and scallops; bring to a simmer. Simmer 3 to 5 minutes or until shrimp turn pink and scallops are done. Stir in wine. To serve, ladle soup into individual bowls. Garnish, if desired. Yield: 5 cups.   Blanche Gorton

Over the Bridge
Corpus Christi Women's Guild
East Sandwich, Massachusetts

Seafood Gumbo

Stir the gumbo constantly to prevent scorching. If you get called away from the stirring and the unthinkable happens, save the mixture by immediately transferring it to a new pot without disturbing the burnt layer on the bottom of the pan.

2 pounds fresh okra
6 tablespoons vegetable oil, divided
2 tablespoons all-purpose flour
2 small onions, finely chopped
2 celery ribs, chopped
1 medium-size green bell pepper, finely chopped
1 cup finely chopped green onions
2 garlic cloves, minced
1 (6-ounce) can tomato paste
3 large bay leaves
1 tablespoon salt
1 tablespoon Worcestershire sauce

½ teaspoon freshly ground black pepper
¼ teaspoon ground red pepper
¼ teaspoon dried thyme
½ teaspoon hot sauce
1 (14½-ounce) can diced tomatoes, undrained
7 cups water
1 pound fresh crabmeat
2½ pounds unpeeled, large fresh shrimp, peeled and deveined
2 tablespoons chopped fresh parsley
4 cups hot cooked rice

Wash okra; trim stem ends, and cut okra into ½-inch slices. Sauté okra in ¼ cup hot oil in a Dutch oven over high heat 5 minutes. Reduce heat to medium-low, and cook 40 minutes, stirring often. Remove okra, and set aside.

Combine remaining 2 tablespoons oil and flour in Dutch oven; cook over medium-high heat 5 minutes, stirring constantly. Add onion and celery; cook 5 minutes. Add bell pepper, green onions, and garlic; cook 3 minutes. Add tomato paste and next 7 ingredients; stir well. Gradually stir in tomatoes, water, and reserved okra; bring to a boil. Cover, reduce heat, and simmer 30 minutes.

Meanwhile, drain and flake crabmeat, removing any bits of shell. Add crabmeat and shrimp; simmer 10 minutes or until shrimp turn pink. Stir in parsley. Discard bay leaves. Serve gumbo over rice. Yield: 15½ cups.

Secret Ingredients
The Junior League of Alexandria, Louisiana

Santa Fe Stew

This hearty southwestern stew is stocked with chicken, chiles, corn, and beans. Cornbread or tortilla chips on the side carry out the southwestern theme.

1 pound skinned and boned chicken breast halves, cut into ½-inch cubes
1 tablespoon vegetable oil
1 large onion, chopped
½ teaspoon garlic powder with parsley
3 (14½-ounce) cans diced tomatoes, undrained
1 (16-ounce) can pinto beans, rinsed and drained
1 (15¼-ounce) can whole kernel corn, drained
2 (4.5-ounce) cans chopped green chiles, undrained
½ cup chicken broth
1 (1-ounce) package taco spices and seasoning mix (we tested with Lawry's)

Cook chicken in hot oil in a large Dutch oven over medium-high heat until browned. Add onion and garlic powder; cook 5 minutes, stirring mixture constantly. Stir in tomatoes and remaining ingredients. Bring to a boil; cover, reduce heat, and simmer 30 minutes. Yield: 10½ cups.   Patsy Klingstedt

Menus & Memories
The University of Oklahoma Women's Association
Norman, Oklahoma

Vegetables

Sautéed Green Beans with Mushrooms, page 311

Spinach-Stuffed Artichoke Hearts

The delicate essence of newly picked artichokes is unbeatable, yet we know it takes a little time and effort to prepare fresh artichokes. Feel free to use canned artichoke hearts to conserve time. If you do, you'll need 8 hearts, two per serving since the canned ones will be smaller.

4 large artichokes
1 (10-ounce) package fresh spinach
5 tablespoons grated Parmesan cheese, divided
½ cup Italian-seasoned breadcrumbs (store-bought)
¼ cup butter or margarine, melted

1 tablespoon finely chopped onion
½ teaspoon dried thyme
½ teaspoon dried basil
¼ teaspoon pepper
¼ teaspoon hot pepper sauce
1 tablespoon butter or margarine, softened

Wash artichokes by plunging up and down in cold water. Cut off stem ends, and trim about ½ inch from top of each artichoke. Remove any loose bottom leaves. With scissors, trim one-fourth off top of each outer leaf.

Place artichokes in a Dutch oven; cover with water. Bring to a boil; cover, reduce heat, and simmer 35 minutes or until lower leaves pull out easily. Drain artichokes. Cool completely. Remove artichoke leaves, and spoon out thistle. Place artichoke hearts (bottom, tender part) in a greased 8-inch square baking dish. Set aside.

Cook spinach according to package directions. Drain spinach in a colander, pressing with paper towels to remove excess moisture; coarsely chop. Combine spinach, 4 tablespoons Parmesan cheese, and next 7 ingredients in a large bowl.

Divide spinach mixture evenly among artichoke hearts. Dot with butter; sprinkle with remaining 1 tablespoon cheese. Bake at 350° for 15 to 20 minutes. Yield: 4 servings.

Sidney Pauly

Breakfast in Cairo, Dinner in Rome
International School of Minnesota Foundation
Eden Prairie, Minnesota

Marinated Grilled Asparagus

¾ cup olive oil
¼ cup dark sesame oil
¼ cup rice wine vinegar
¼ cup soy sauce
¼ cup orange juice
2 tablespoons dried mint
1½ tablespoons ground cumin
1 tablespoon minced garlic

1 tablespoon minced fresh
  ginger
1 tablespoon garlic-chile sauce
2 teaspoons dried thyme
2 teaspoons pepper
2½ pounds fresh asparagus
Coulis

Combine first 12 ingredients in a food processor or blender. Pulse until smooth.

Snap off tough ends of asparagus. Pour marinade over asparagus; cover and let stand at room temperature 20 minutes. Remove asparagus, discarding marinade.

Grill, covered with grill lid, over medium-high heat (350° to 400°) about 4 minutes on each side or until crisp-tender. Top with Coulis, and serve immediately. Yield: 8 servings.

Coulis

2 large red bell peppers,
  halved and seeded
¼ medium onion
2 garlic cloves

1 tablespoon rice wine vinegar
½ teaspoon salt
¼ teaspoon pepper

Broil bell peppers, onion, and garlic on an aluminum foil-lined baking sheet 5½ inches from heat about 5 minutes on each side or until peppers look blistered. Place peppers in a heavy-duty zip-top plastic bag; seal and let stand 10 minutes to loosen skins. Peel peppers. Remove skins from garlic. Combine peppers, onion, and garlic in a food processor. Add vinegar, salt, and pepper. Pulse until smooth. Yield: 1½ cups. Nancy Shepherd

Look Who's Cooking in Louisville
Pitt Academy
Louisville, Kentucky

Black Bean Torta

2 (15-ounce) cans black beans, drained
¼ cup chicken broth
1 large purple onion, finely chopped
2 red bell peppers, cut into julienne strips
2 small zucchini, halved lengthwise and thinly sliced
2 garlic cloves, minced
1 tablespoon vegetable oil
1 cup frozen whole kernel corn, thawed
¾ teaspoon ground cumin
½ teaspoon salt
¼ teaspoon ground red pepper
5 (8-inch) flour tortillas
Salsa Fresca
2 cups (8 ounces) shredded Monterey Jack cheese

Process beans and chicken broth in a food processor until smooth. Set aside.

Sauté onion and next 3 ingredients in hot oil in a large skillet over medium-high heat 7 minutes or until tender. Add corn and next 3 ingredients, and sauté 3 more minutes.

Place 1 tortilla in a lightly greased 8- x 3-inch springform pan. Spread ½ cup bean mixture over tortilla; top with 1 cup sautéed vegetables. Spoon ¼ cup Salsa Fresca over vegetables, and sprinkle with ⅓ cup cheese. Repeat layering procedure 3 times; top with remaining tortilla, and sprinkle with remaining ⅔ cup cheese.

Bake, uncovered, at 375° for 45 minutes; let stand 5 minutes. Cut into wedges; serve with remaining Salsa Fresca. Yield: 8 servings.

Salsa Fresca

3 medium tomatoes, seeded and finely chopped
½ cup finely chopped purple onion
1 to 3 serrano chiles, seeded and minced
1 Anaheim chile, seeded and finely chopped
2 tablespoons minced fresh cilantro
1 tablespoon fresh lime juice
1 teaspoon sugar
½ teaspoon salt
¼ teaspoon freshly ground pepper

Combine all ingredients; cover and chill 1 hour. Yield: 3½ cups.

Savoring the Southwest Again
Roswell Symphony Guild
Roswell, New Mexico

Sautéed Green Beans with Mushrooms

Looking for a supper club side dish that's simple? This recipe delivers. It serves a crowd but can easily be cut in half to accommodate cozier gatherings.

3 pounds fresh green beans, trimmed
1 cup butter or margarine
2 (8-ounce) packages sliced fresh mushrooms

½ cup chopped onion
½ teaspoon salt
¼ teaspoon ground white pepper

Cook beans in boiling salted water to cover 6 to 8 minutes or until crisp-tender; drain well. Transfer to a serving bowl; keep warm.

Melt butter in a large skillet over medium heat; add mushrooms and onion, and sauté until tender. Pour onion mixture over green beans; sprinkle with salt and pepper, and toss to coat. Serve immediately. Yield: 10 to 12 servings.

Bara Lamon

Beyond Cotton Country
The Junior League of Morgan County
Decatur, Alabama

Basque Beans

Serve this spicy, earthy bean dish in bowls to capture its naturally scrumptious broth and with lots of rustic bread fit for sopping.

1 pound dried pinto beans
8 cups water, divided
½ pound bacon slices, cut into
  1-inch pieces
1 large green bell pepper,
  chopped
1 large onion, chopped
5 garlic cloves, finely chopped
½ pound chorizo sausage,
  thinly sliced

2 bay leaves
1 tablespoon chopped fresh
  parsley
1 teaspoon dried thyme
1 teaspoon chili powder
2 teaspoons Worcestershire
  sauce
½ teaspoon dried rosemary
1½ teaspoons salt

Sort and rinse beans. Place beans in a Dutch oven; add water 2 inches above beans. Bring to a boil. Boil 1 minute; cover, remove from heat, and let stand 1 hour. Drain. Bring beans and 4 cups water to a boil; reduce heat, and simmer, uncovered, 30 minutes.

Meanwhile, cook bacon in a large skillet until crisp; remove bacon, and drain on paper towels. Drain skillet. Add bell pepper, onion, and garlic to skillet; cook over medium-high heat, stirring constantly, 4 to 5 minutes or until tender. Stir in sausage and next 6 ingredients; add to beans. Bring to a boil; cover, reduce heat, and simmer 1½ hours or until beans are tender, stirring often. Discard bay leaves. Stir in salt. Yield: 9 servings.

Nancy Massin

Alaska's Best
Alaska Telephone Pioneers
Anchorage, Alaska

Warm Broccoli and Cauliflower Toss with Blue Cheese Cream

4 cups cauliflower florets
4 cups broccoli florets
¼ cup half-and-half
1 (4-ounce) package crumbled
  blue cheese

½ cup mayonnaise
½ cup chopped green onions
¼ cup chopped pecans, toasted

Arrange cauliflower in a steamer basket over boiling water. Cover and steam 3 minutes or until crisp-tender. Repeat procedure with broccoli florets.

Pour half-and-half into a small saucepan; cook over medium heat until warm (do not boil). Add cheese; cook, stirring constantly, until cheese melts. Remove from heat. Whisk in mayonnaise.

Combine cauliflower and broccoli in a large bowl. Add cheese mixture, and toss to coat. Sprinkle with green onions and pecans. Serve with a slotted spoon. Yield: 8 servings.   Marge Lathrop

Exclusively Broccoli Cookbook
Coventry Historical Society, Inc.
Coventry, Connecticut

Herbed Corn

Bits of parsley, thyme, and chives infuse fresh ears of corn with their aromatic goodness. Ground red pepper adds zip to the herb butter blend.

8 ears fresh corn	1 tablespoon chopped fresh
½ cup butter or margarine,	thyme
softened	½ teaspoon salt
2 tablespoons minced fresh	¼ teaspoon ground red pepper
parsley	
2 tablespoons chopped fresh	
chives	

Remove husks and silks from corn.

Combine butter and remaining 5 ingredients in a small bowl. Spread 1 tablespoon butter mixture over each ear of corn. Wrap each in heavy-duty aluminum foil. Grill, covered with grill lid, over medium heat (300° to 350°) 10 minutes or until corn is done, turning once. Yield: 8 servings.   Kathy VonKorff

Sharing Our Best
Hackensack American Legion Auxiliary Unit 202
Hackensack, Minnesota

Eggplant Enchiladas

These enchiladas break the traditional mold by wrapping a zesty mix of eggplant and mushrooms in flour tortillas. Add an enchilada sauce of your choosing as a topper, if you'd like.

1 small onion, chopped
1½ teaspoons vegetable oil
2 garlic cloves, minced
6 cups cubed, peeled eggplant
   (1 large)
1 green bell pepper, chopped
1 cup sliced fresh mushrooms
2 cups (8 ounces) shredded
   Monterey Jack cheese,
   divided
2 tablespoons chopped
   almonds, toasted

1 tablespoon minced fresh
   parsley
1 teaspoon freshly ground
   black pepper
½ teaspoon salt
1 teaspoon Worcestershire
   sauce
1 cup chicken broth
12 (6¾-inch) flour tortillas

Sauté onion in hot oil in a large skillet over medium-high heat 4 minutes or until tender. Add garlic; cook 1 minute, stirring constantly. Add eggplant, bell pepper, and mushrooms; cook 10 minutes, stirring occasionally. Remove from heat. Stir in ¾ cup cheese and next 5 ingredients. Set aside.

Bring broth to a boil in a small skillet over medium-high heat; remove from heat. Working with 1 at a time, quickly dip tortilla in hot broth to soften. Spoon ¼ cup filling down center of tortilla. Roll up tortilla; place seam side down in a lightly greased 13-x 9-inch baking dish. Repeat procedure with remaining tortillas. Sprinkle with remaining 1¼ cups cheese. Bake, covered, at 350° for 20 minutes. Yield: 6 servings.

I'll Cook When Pigs Fly
The Junior League of Cincinnati, Ohio

Wild Mushroom Stuffing

We used a crusty French bread for this distinctive mushroom stuffing. It's designed as an accompaniment with turkey rather than as a stuffing to be baked inside the bird.

¾ pound fresh shiitake
  mushrooms
1 cup butter or margarine
1 cup finely chopped shallots
1 cup finely chopped celery
2 (16-ounce) day-old French
  bread loaves, torn into small
  pieces (about 16 cups)

¾ cup minced fresh parsley
2 teaspoons ground sage
2 teaspoons dried thyme
1 teaspoon dried savory
¾ teaspoon freshly ground
  pepper
2 large eggs, beaten
4 cups chicken broth

Remove and discard stems from mushrooms. Finely chop mushrooms; set aside.

Melt butter in a large skillet over medium heat. Add shallots and celery, and sauté 5 minutes or just until tender. Add chopped mushrooms, and cook 5 minutes, stirring often. Set aside.

Place bread in a very large bowl; add mushroom mixture, parsley, and next 4 ingredients, and toss well. Add eggs and broth, stirring well. (Mixture will be very moist.) Transfer mixture to a greased 15- x 10-inch baking dish. Bake, covered, at 350° for 1 hour. Yield: 10 to 14 servings.

Perennial Palette
Southborough Gardeners
Southborough, Massachusetts

Stuffed Walla Walla Sweets

A sassy breadcrumb mix of pork sausage and Cheddar cheese stuffs hollowed sweet onions to perfection. A touch of cinnamon adds a surprising flavor note.

4 medium-size sweet onions
11 ounces ground pork sausage
¾ cup soft breadcrumbs
    (homemade)
⅓ cup (1.3 ounces) shredded
    Cheddar cheese
1 large egg, lightly beaten
3 tablespoons milk
2 tablespoons chopped fresh
    Italian parsley

½ teaspoon sugar
¼ teaspoon salt
¼ teaspoon freshly ground
    pepper
¼ teaspoon ground cinnamon
1 bacon slice, cooked and
    crumbled (optional)

Peel onions, and cut a ½-inch-thick slice from top of each. Cook onions in boiling water to cover 12 minutes or until tender but not mushy. Drain and cool. Remove centers of onions, leaving shells intact; chop onion centers, and reserve 2 cups.

Cook sausage in a large skillet, stirring until it crumbles and is no longer pink; drain well. Stir together reserved chopped onion, sausage, breadcrumbs, and next 8 ingredients. Fill onion shells with sausage mixture, and, if desired, sprinkle with bacon. Place in a greased 9-inch square pan. Bake, uncovered, at 350° for 30 minutes. Yield: 4 servings.

A Taste of Washington State
Washington Bed & Breakfast Guild
Seattle, Washington

Greek Potatoes

⅓ cup olive oil, divided
5 medium baking potatoes,
    peeled and cubed
3 medium onions, thickly
    sliced
1 jalapeño pepper, seeded and
    minced

1 (14½-ounce) can diced
    tomatoes, undrained
½ cup salad olives or pitted
    ripe olives, coarsely chopped
3 ounces feta cheese, crumbled

Heat a large cast-iron skillet over high heat until hot; add 3½ tablespoons oil. Add potato, and cook over medium-high heat 10 minutes or just until lightly browned, stirring occasionally. Bake, uncovered, at 350° for 15 minutes.

Meanwhile, heat a large skillet over medium-high heat until hot; add remaining 1 tablespoon plus 2½ teaspoons oil. Add onion and jalapeño pepper, and cook over medium-high heat 15 minutes or until onion is lightly browned, stirring often.

Spoon onion mixture over potato. Place tomatoes over onion mixture; sprinkle with olives and cheese. Bake, uncovered, at 350° for 20 minutes. Yield: 10 servings.   Sarah Fritschner

Look Who's Cooking in Louisville
Pitt Academy
Louisville, Kentucky

Tzimmes

A kiss of honey and ground cinnamon helps to seal the fruity flavors of this casserole-style dish traditionally served on Rosh Hashanah.

2 **pounds sweet potatoes, peeled and cut into 2-inch pieces**
1 **pound carrots, cut into 2-inch pieces**
1 **cup pitted prunes**
1 **cup dried apricots**
1 **tablespoon grated orange rind**
½ **cup fresh orange juice**
¼ **cup honey**
2 **tablespoons fresh lemon juice**
1 **teaspoon ground cinnamon**
¼ **teaspoon salt**

Cook sweet potato and carrot in boiling water to cover 18 minutes or until tender; drain.

Combine sweet potato, carrot, prunes, and remaining ingredients in a large bowl; stir well. Spoon mixture into a lightly greased 9-inch square baking dish. Bake, covered, at 350° for 30 minutes. Yield: 8 to 10 servings.   Susan Odessa Froehlich

A Taste of Tradition
Temple Emanu-El
Providence, Rhode Island

Baked Zucchini with Muenster

2 pounds zucchini, peeled and
  cut into ¼-inch-thick slices
1 medium onion, chopped
1 cup shredded carrot
1 (10¾-ounce) can cream of
  chicken soup, undiluted
1 (8-ounce) container sour
  cream

¼ teaspoon salt
¼ teaspoon pepper
½ cup butter or margarine,
  melted
½ (16-ounce) package
  herb-seasoned stuffing mix
1 cup (4 ounces) shredded
  Muenster cheese

Cook zucchini and onion in a large nonstick skillet over medium-high heat, stirring constantly, 5 minutes or until crisp-tender. Combine carrot and next 4 ingredients in a large bowl; stir well. Add zucchini mixture to carrot mixture; stir well.

Pour butter into an 11- x 7-inch baking dish; top with half of stuffing mix, and stir mixture well. Spoon carrot mixture over stuffing mixture, and sprinkle with cheese. Sprinkle with remaining half of stuffing mix. Bake, uncovered, at 350° for 35 minutes. Yield: 8 to 10 servings.

Norma Dipaoli

Classic Italian Cooking
Italian American Society of San Marco Island
Marco Island, Florida

Broiled Tomatoes with Olives and Garlic

2 medium tomatoes
3 kalamata olives, pitted and
  chopped
1 garlic clove, minced

1 tablespoon olive oil
¼ teaspoon salt
¼ teaspoon freshly ground
  pepper

Cut tomatoes into ½-inch-thick slices. Arrange slices in a single layer in a lightly greased 13- x 9-inch baking dish. Combine olives and remaining 4 ingredients; spoon over slices. Broil 3 inches from heat 7 minutes or until bubbly. Yield: 4 servings.

Bea Westin

. . . And It Was Very Good
Temple Emeth
Teaneck, New Jersey

Roasted Root Vegetables

Carrots, turnips, and parsnips roast alongside garlic, onions, leeks, potatoes, sweet potatoes, and acorn squash for a merry mix of flavors.

1 leek
¼ cup olive oil, divided
3 garlic cloves, unpeeled
3 medium carrots, cut into
   2-inch pieces
2 medium onions, peeled and
   cut into 2-inch pieces
1 medium turnip, peeled and
   cut into 2-inch pieces
1 medium parsnip, peeled and
   cut into 2-inch pieces

1 medium-size sweet potato,
   unpeeled and cut into 2-inch
   pieces
1 medium-size red potato,
   unpeeled and cut into 2-inch
   pieces
1 small acorn squash, unpeeled
   and cut into 2-inch pieces
2 teaspoons kosher salt

Remove root, tough outer leaves, and tops from leek, leaving 4 inches of dark leaves. Wash leek thoroughly. Cut leek lengthwise into quarters.

Coat a large roasting pan with 2 tablespoons oil. Place leek in pan. Toss garlic and next 7 ingredients with remaining 2 tablespoons oil and salt. Place vegetables in pan. Bake, uncovered, at 450° for 1 hour or until vegetables are tender, stirring occasionally. Yield: 6 to 8 servings.

The Kosher Palette
Joseph Kushner Hebrew Academy
Livingston, New Jersey

Acknowledgments

Each of the community cookbooks listed is represented by recipes appearing in *America's Best Recipes*. The copyright is held by the sponsoring organization whose mailing address is included.

202's Totally Tempting Treasures, American Legion Auxiliary Green-Pierce Unit 202, 1101 E. Scott St., Wichita Falls, TX 76301

Alaska's Best, Alaska Telephone Pioneers, 600 Telephone Ave., MS 10, Anchorage, AK 99503

Always in Season, Junior League of Salt Lake City, Inc., 526 E. 300 S., Salt Lake City, UT 84102

America Celebrates Columbus, Junior League of Columbus, Inc., 583 Franklin Ave., Columbus, OH 43215-4715

. . . And It Was Very Good, Temple Emeth, 1666 Windsor Rd., Teaneck, NJ 07666

Angels in the Kitchen, Grace Episcopal Church, 711 S. McDuffie St., Anderson, SC 29624

Angels in the Kitchen Cookbook, Community Presbyterian Church, P.O. Box 470053, Celebration, FL 34747

Art Fare: A Commemorative Celebration of Art & Food, Toledo Museum of Art Aides, P.O. Box 1013, Toledo, OH 43697

Atchafalaya Legacy, Melville Woman's Club, 255 Church St., P.O. Box 66, Melville, LA 71353

The Avery Family's Favorite Recipes, compiled by the Avery family to generate contributions for Pittsfield Community Church, 45967 Cemetery Rd., #2, Wellington, OH 44090

Bay Tables, Junior League of Mobile, 57 N. Sage Ave., Mobile, AL 36608

Beyond Cotton Country, Junior League of Morgan County, 109 2nd Ave. NE, Decatur, AL 35601

Black Tie & Boots Optional, Colleyville Woman's Club, P.O. Box 181, Colleyville, TX 76034

Blended Blessings, First Presbyterian Church, 308 W. Fisher St., Salisbury, NC 28144

Blest Recipes, Our Redeemer Lutheran Church, P.O. Box 670150, Chugiak, AK 99567

Bravo! Recipes, Legends & Lore, University Musical Society, 881 N. University Ave., Ann Arbor, MI 48109-1011

Breakfast in Cairo, Dinner in Rome, International School of Minnesota Foundation, P.O. Box 46060, Eden Prairie, MN 55344

Business is Cookin' with FBLA, Lakeview Future Business Leaders of America, 3744 83rd St., Columbus, NE 68601

Café Weller . . . Tastes to Remember, Apple Corps of the Weller Health Education Center, 325 Northampton St., Easton, PA 18042

A Century of Serving, Junior Board of Christiana Care, Inc., P.O. Box 1668, Wilmington, DE 19899

Chautauqua Celebrations, Wythe Arts Council, Ltd., P.O. Box 911, Wytheville, VA 24382

Christian Women's Fellowship, Oak Grove Christian Church, 6101 32nd Ave., Shellsburg, IA 52332

Classic Italian Cooking, Italian American Society of San Marco Island, 366 Wales Ct., Marco Island, FL 34145

The Cookbook Tour, Good Shepherd Lutheran Church, P.O. Box 355 Hwy. 42, Plainview, MN 55964

Cooking Up Memories, Tazewell County Genealogical and Historical Society, 719 N. 11th, Pekin, IL 61555-0312

Cooking with Class, Forest Hills Elementary School PTO, 1133 Andrews Rd., Lake Oswego, OR 97034

Cooking with Class, Timber Lake Booster Club, P.O. Box 62, Timber Lake, SD 57656

Cooking with Music: Celebrating the Tastes and Traditions of the Boston Symphony Orchestra, Boston Symphony Association of Volunteers, Symphony Hall, 301 Massachusetts Ave., Boston, MA 02115

Cookin' with Friends, National Presbyterian School Class of 2000, 4121 Nebraska Ave. NW, Washington, DC 20016

Cookin' with Pride, 4th Infantry Division, Ironhorse Gift Shop, P.O. Box 5009, Ft. Hood, TX 76544

Cooks of the Green Door, League of Catholic Women, 207 S. 9th St., Minneapolis, MN 55402

Creating a Stir, Fayette County Medical Auxiliary, 2628 Wilhite Dr., Ste. 201, Lexington, KY 40503-3304

A Dab of This and a Dab of That, Bethlehem Baptist Church Senior Missionary, 303 E. Main St., Ninety Six, SC 29666

Deborah Heart and Lung Center 75th Anniversary National Cookbook, Deborah Hospital Foundation, Cymrot Center, 212 Trenton Rd., Browns Mills, NJ 08015

De Nuestra Mesa: Our Food, Wine, and Tradition, New Hope Charities, Inc., 626 N. Dixie Hwy., West Palm Beach, FL 33401

Diamond Delights, Diamond Hill Elementary School, 104 Lake Secession Rd., Abbeville, SC 29620

Dining by Design: Stylish Recipes, Savory Settings, Junior League of Pasadena, 149 S. Madison Ave., Pasadena, CA 91101

The Dining Car, Service League of Denison, 418 W. Main, Denison, TX 75020

Divine Offerings: Recipes and Hints for the Kitchen, St. Charles Presbyterian Women, 131 Gamble St., St. Charles, MO 63301

Dixon Fixins, Dixon Ambulatory Care Center, 291 Stoner Ave., Westminster, MD 21157

Down Home Dining in Mississippi, Mississippi Homemaker Volunteers, Inc., 715 Markette St., Water Valley, MS 38965

Everything But the Entrée, Junior League of Parkersburg, Inc., 1301 Murdoch Ave., Parkersburg, WV 26101

Exclusively Broccoli Cookbook, Coventry Historical Society, Inc., P.O. Box 534, Coventry, CT 06238

Favorite Recipes, Friends of Memorial Hospital, 645 E. 5th, Weiser, ID 83672

Favorite Recipes Taste of Tradition, B.A. Ritter Senior Citizen Center, 914 Boston, Nederland, TX 77627

Feeding the Flock, St. Philips Episcopal Church, 3860 SE California, Topeka, KS 66609

Fine Food from the Friends, Friends of the Superior Public Library, Inc., 1530 Tower Ave., Superior, WI 54880

Flavor It Greek! A Celebration of Food, Faith and Family, Philoptochos Society of Holy Trinity Greek Orthodox Church, 3131 NE Glisan St., Portland, OR 97232

Flavors of Hawaii, Child and Family Service Guild, 200 N. Vineyard Blvd., Building B, Honolulu, HI 96817

Flavors of the Gardens, Callaway Gardens, P.O. Box 2000, Pine Mountain, GA 31822-2000

Flavors of the Tenderloin, Sidewalk Clean-Up, Recycling & Urban Beautification (SCRUB), 1278 44th Ave., San Francisco, CA 94122-1108

From Black Tie to Blackeyed Peas: Savannah's Savory Secrets, St. Joseph's Foundation of Savannah, Inc., 11705 Mercy Blvd., Savannah, GA 31419

From Our Homes to Yours, Baptist Homes of Western Pennsylvania, 489 Castle Shannon Blvd., Pittsburgh, PA 15234

Gifts from Our Heart, Mercy Special Learning Center, 830 S. Woodward St., Allentown, PA 18103-3440

Glen Haven Community Cookbook 1999, Glen Haven Area Volunteer Fire Department,
P.O. Box 88, Glen Haven, CO 80532

Good Food, Served Right, Traditional Arts in Upstate New York, 2 W. Main St., Canton,
NY 13617

Gracious Gator Cooks, Junior League of Gainesville, 430-A N. Main St., Gainesville,
FL 32605

The Guild Collection: Recipes from Art Lovers, The Guild, Museum of Fine Arts,
1001 Bissonnet, Houston, TX 77005

The Heart of Pittsburgh, Sacred Heart Elementary School PTG, 325 Emerson St.,
Pittsburgh, PA 15206

Heaven's Bounty, Long Beach Catholic School Parents' Club, Long Beach Catholic
School, 735 W. Broadway, Long Beach, NY 11561

Historically Heavenly Home Cooking, Corry Area Historical Society, P.O. Box 107, Corry,
PA 16407

Homemade with Love, Swanton-Missisquoi Valley Lions Club, P.O. Box 376,
Highgate Center, VT 05459

I'll Cook When Pigs Fly, Junior League of Cincinnati, 3500 Columbia Pkwy., Cincinnati,
OH 45226

Inman Pioneer Day Cookbook, Inman Community Improvement Council, 295 Main St.,
Inman, NE 68742

It's About Time: Recipes, Reflections, Realities, National Association Teachers of Family and
Consumer Sciences, 2604 Kiwanis Dr., Bowling Green, KY 42104-4229

It's a Snap!, Haven of Grace, 1133 Benton St., St. Louis, MO 63106

Jubilee 2000 Recipe Collection, St. Alphonsus Liguori Parish—Hospitality Committee,
411 N. Wheeling Rd., Prospect Heights, IL 60070

Keittokirja: Kaleva Centennial Cookbook, Project Kaleva/Kaleva Historical Society,
14551 Wuoksi Ave., Kaleva, MI 49645

The Kosher Palette, Joseph Kushner Hebrew Academy, 110 S. Orange Ave., Livingston,
NJ 07039

Lake Waccamaw United Methodist Church Cookbook, Lake Waccamaw United Methodist
Church, 506 Lake Shore Dr., Lake Waccamaw, NC 28450

Lighthouse Secrets: A Collection of Recipes from the Nation's Oldest City, Junior Service
League of St. Augustine, Inc., P.O. Box 374, St. Augustine, FL 32085

A Little DAPS of This . . . A Little DAPS of That, Dallas Area Parkinsonism Society
(DAPS), 3003 LBJ Freeway, Ste. 125E, Dallas, TX 75234-7755

Look What's Cooking . . . , Temple Sinai Sisterhood, 30 Hagen Ave., Cranston,
RI 02920

Look Who Came to Dinner, Junior Auxiliary of Amory, Inc., 1603 Woodview Cir., Amory,
MS 38821

Look Who's Cooking in Louisville, Pitt Academy, 4605 Poplar Level Rd., Louisville,
KY 40213

Made in the Shade, Junior League of Greater Fort Lauderdale, 704 SE 1st St.,
Fort Lauderdale, FL 33301

McInnis Bobcat Favorites, McInnis Elementary PTA, 5175 N. U.S. Hwy. 17,
DeLeon Springs, FL 32130

Meet Us in the Kitchen, Junior League of St. Louis, 10435 Clayton Rd., St. Louis,
MO 63131

Menus & Memories, University of Oklahoma Women's Association, 100 Timberdell Rd.,
OU Foundation, Norman, OK 73072

More Enchanted Eating from the West Shore, Friends of the Symphony, P.O. Box 1603,
Muskegon, MI 49443

North Country Cooking, 51st National Square Dance Convention, 7125 River Shore Ln.,
Champlin, MN 55316-2134

"NOT" Just Desserts, St. Isidore Parish—Administration Commission, 427 W. Army Trail
Rd., Bloomingdale, IL 60108

NPT's Community Cookbook, Neighborhood Pride Team, 7455 SE 52nd Ave., Portland,
OR 97206

Of Books and Cooks, Woman's Book Club, 202 Magnolia, Harrison, AR 72601

Ofukuro No Aji: Favorite Recipes from Mama's Kitchen, Hōkūlani Cultural Exchange
Committee (Hōkūlani Elementary School), 2940 Kamakini St., Honolulu, HI 96816

Oh My Stars! Recipes That Shine, Junior League of Roanoke Valley, Inc., 541 Luck Ave.,
Ste. 317, Roanoke, VA 24016

Olivet Heritage Cookbook, Olivet Presbyterian Church, 2575 Garth Rd., Charlottesville,
VA 22901

On Course, Women Associates of the Buffalo Power Squadron, P.O. Box 45, Lancaster,
NY 14086-0045

Our Favorite Recipes, Lutheran Church of the Good Shepherd, 1108 24th St. W.,
Billings, MT 59102

Over the Bridge, Corpus Christi Women's Guild, 324 Quaker Meetinghouse Rd.,
East Sandwich, MA 02537-2170

Panthers' Pantry, Children's Educational Foundation, 16436 Paula Rd., Madera,
CA 93638

Past and Present Meatless Treasures, Kaneohe Seventh-day Adventist Church,
45-566 Mahinui Rd., Kaneohe, HI 96744

A Peach Flavored Past, Altrusa International, Inc., of Palisade, P.O. Box 424, Palisade,
CO 81526

Perennial Palette, Southborough Gardeners, P.O. Box 184, Southborough,
MA 01772

Picnics, Potlucks & Prizewinners, Indiana 4-H Foundation, Inc., 225 S. East St., Ste. 760,
Indianapolis, IN 46202

Pot Luck O' the Irish, Maud Gonne Division #32-LAOH, 2321 Manor Ave., Pittsburgh,
PA 15218-2238

Rave Reviews, Ogunquit Playhouse, Route One North, Ogunquit, ME 03907

Recipes and Recollections, Hitchcock Heritage Society, 9306 Woodacres, Hitchcock,
TX 77563

Recipes from the Heart, Littleton Regional Hospital Helping Hands, 600 St. Johnsbury
Rd., Littleton, NH 03561

Recipes from the Heart of Maine, Friends of the Millinocket Memorial Library, 5 Maine
Ave., Millinocket, ME 04462

Recipes from the Kitchens of Family & Friends, Gresham Women of Elks, P.O. Box 42,
Gresham, OR 97030

Savoring the Seasons: Riverside, Craven Regional Medical Center Foundation,
P.O. Box 1576, New Bern, NC 28562

Savoring the Southwest Again, Roswell Symphony Guild, P.O. Box 3078, Roswell,
NM 88202

Savor the Flavor: Delightfully Vegetarian, Portland Adventist Community Services,
11020 NE Halsey St., Portland, OR 97220

Savory Secrets, P.E.O. Chapter LR, ℅ Jean Szoko, 22 Lake Forest Dr., St. Charles,
MO 63301

Seasons of Santa Fe, Kitchen Angels, 1222 Siler Rd., Santa Fe, NM 87505

Secret Ingredients, Junior League of Alexandria, Inc., 1082 Alexandria Mall,
3437 Masonic Dr., Alexandria, LA 71301

Sesquicentennially Delicious, Western Pennsylvania Hospital, 4800 Friendship Ave.,
   Pittsburgh, PA 15224

Settings on the Dock of the Bay, ASSISTANCE LEAGUE® of the Bay Area,
   P.O. Box 590153, Houston, TX 77259-0153

Sharing Our Best, Bull Run Parent Teacher Club, 41515 SE Thomas Rd., Sandy,
   OR 97055

Sharing Our Best, Hackensack American Legion Auxiliary Unit 202, 202 1st St.,
   P.O. Box 414, Hackensack, MN 56452

Sharing Our Best, Poyen Assembly of God Youth Ministry, P.O. Box 189, Poyen,
   AR 72128

Sharing Our Best, The Arrangement Hair Salon, 2982 E. Broad St., Columbus,
   OH 43209

Sharing Recipes from Green Road Baptist Church, Green Road Baptist Church, HC 83,
   Box 210, Green Road, KY 40946

Simple Pleasures: From Our Table to Yours, Arab Mothers' Club, P.O. Box 884, Arab,
   AL 35016

Simply Divine, Second-Ponce de Leon Baptist Church, 2715 Peachtree Rd., Atlanta,
   GA 30327

Sounds Delicious: The Flavor of Atlanta in Food & Music, Atlanta Symphony Orchestra,
   1293 Peachtree St., Ste. 300, Atlanta, GA 30309-3552

Southern Elegance: A Second Course, Junior League of Gaston County, Inc., 2950 S. Union
   Rd., Ste. A, Gastonia, NC 28054

Specialties of the Haus, TCM International, Inc., 6337 Hollister Dr., Indianapolis,
   IN 46224

Spice It Up!, Baton Rouge Branch of American Association of University Women,
   10345 Barbara St., Baton Rouge, LA 70815

Splendor in the Bluegrass, Junior League of Louisville, Inc., 501 S. Second St., Louisville,
   KY 40202

St. Andrew's Cooks Again, Presbyterian Women of St. Andrew, 1350 N. 23rd St.,
   Beaumont, TX 77706

A Sunsational Encore, Junior League of Greater Orlando, 125 N. Lucerne Cir. E,
   Orlando, FL 32801

Tapestry: A Weaving of Food, Culture and Tradition, Junior Welfare League of Rock Hill,
   958 W. Main St., Rock Hill, SC 29730

Taste Buds–A Collection of Treasured Recipes, Alliance of the Illinois State Dental Society,
   101C S. Second St., Springfield, IL 62704

A Taste of Tradition, Temple Emanu-El, 99 Taft Ave., Providence, RI 02906

A Taste of Washington State, Washington Bed & Breakfast Guild, 2442 NW Market St.,
   Seattle, WA 98107

A Taste Tour, Gingko Twig of Muhlenberg Hospital, Plainfield, New Jersey, 809 Village
   Green, Westfield, NJ 07090

A Thyme to Remember, Dallas County Medical Society Alliance, 5500 Swiss Ave., Dallas,
   TX 75214

Tried and True from Riverview, Riverview Hospital Auxiliary, 410 Dewey St., Wisconsin
   Rapids, WI 54494

Tucson Treasures: Recipes & Reflections, Tucson Medical Center Auxiliary, 5301 E. Grant
   Rd., Tucson, AZ 85712

Twice Treasured Recipes, The Bargain Box, Inc., 546 William Hilton Pkwy., Hilton Head
   Island, SC 29928

Vintage Virginia: A History of Good Taste, Virginia Dietetic Association, P.O. Box 439,
   Centreville, VA 20122

Walking with Christ, First Baptist Church, ℅ Shirley W. Brinkley, 342 Pineview Dr., Mount Airy, NC 27030

We're Cooking Up Something New: 50 Years of Music, History, and Food, Wichita Falls Symphony League, 4500 Seymour Hwy., Wichita Falls, TX 76309

The Western New York Federal Court Centennial Cookbook, U.S. District Court, Western District of New York, 68 Court St., Room 304, Buffalo, NY 14202

What Can I Bring?, Junior League of Northern Virginia, Inc., 7921 Jones Branch Dr., Ste. 320, McLean, VA 20165

Wildcat Valley: Recipes & Remembrances, Keats Lions Club, 4970 Anderson Ave., Manhattan, KS 66503

Yuletide on Hilton Head: A Heritage of Island Flavors, United Way of Beaufort County, P.O. Box 22961, Hilton Head Island, SC 29925

Index

Almonds
Biscotti, Chocolate-Almond, 124
Butter, Almond-Peach, 286
Cheesecake, Luscious Almond, 112
Couscous Amandine, 52
Appetizers
Antipasto Kabobs, 8
Bacon Appetizers, 36
Cheese
Balls with Sun-Dried Tomatoes, Cheese, 11
Pie, Chutney, 58
Puffs, Hot Cheese, 63
Crab Tarts, Cheesy, 66
Crostini with Wild Mushroom Ragoût, 62
Dips
Brown Sugar Dip for Fruit, Buttery, 58
Caramel Dip for Apples, 282
Crab, Brie, and Artichoke Dip, Baked, 59
Granola, Tropical Crunch, 69
Mango and Prosciutto, 36
Pâté, Chicken, 12
Pecans, Spiced Holiday, 37
Portobello Appetizer, Roasted, 60
Profiteroles with Smoked Salmon, 65
Quesadillas, Crab, 66
Sausage and Cheese Tartlets, 64
Shrimp and Artichoke Hearts, Marinated, 12
Shrimp with Feta Cheese, 68
Shrimp Wrapped in Pea Pods, Marinated, 67
Spanakopita Rolls, 8
Spreads
Cheese, Palmetto, 10
Cheese Spread with Spinach, Two-, 10
Pesto, Tony Caputo's Red, 60
Tortilla Cakes, Corn and Black Bean, 61
Apples
Baked Apples, Honey-Wine, 138
Cheesecake, Caramel Apple, 113
Coffee Cake, Apple, 81
Dip for Apples, Caramel, 282
Enchiladas, Apple, 138
Glaze, Apple-Cinnamon, 237
Pie, Crunchy Caramel Apple, 228
Salad, Apple, Chicken, and Wild Rice, 22
Salad, Apple-Potato, 278
Sauté with Calvados, Apple, 55
Snowballs, Apple Orchard, 242
Tart, Apple Custard, 237
Applesauce Spice Muffins, 78
Apricots
Bread, Marbled Apricot, 83

Chicken, Apricot and Currant, 244
Pound Cake, Apricot-Pecan, 108
Artichokes
Bread, Garlic and Artichoke, 84
Dip, Baked Crab, Brie, and Artichoke, 59
Focaccia, Tomato and Artichoke, 168
Frittata, Baked Artichoke and Onion, 155
Marinated Shrimp and Artichoke Hearts, 12
Salad, Artichoke and Mandarin Orange, 266
Salad, Uptown Bluegrass, 272
Shrimp with Artichokes, 43
Soup, Cream of Artichoke, 292
Strata, Goat Cheese, Ham, and Artichoke, 165
Stuffed Artichoke Hearts, Spinach-, 308
Asparagus
Congealed Asparagus, Tangy, 264
Marinated Grilled Asparagus, 309
Oven-Roasted Asparagus with Thyme, 52
Salad, White Bean-Asparagus, 267
Vinaigrette, Asparagus, 19
Avocado Salad, Orange and, 265

Bacon
Appetizers, Bacon, 36
Eggs Bel-Mar, 160
Salad, Uptown Bluegrass, 272
Venison Rollemachen, 210
Banana Pancakes, Easy, 39
Barbecued Chicken, Bruce's Bluegrass, 244
Barbecued Shrimp, 181
Beans
Basque Beans, 312
Black Bean Cassoulet, 208
Black Bean Enchiladas, Chicken
and, 255
Black Bean Torta, 310
Black Bean Tortilla Cakes, Corn and, 61
Chili, 10-Minute Spicy Black Bean, 49
Green Beans with Mushrooms, Sautéed, 311
Salads
Black Bean and Orzo Salad, 274
Black Bean Salad, Mexican, 18
Green Bean-Mozzarella Salad, 19
Pasta Salad, Greek, 276
White Bean-Asparagus Salad, 267
Soup, Tortellini Bean, 293
Beef. See also Beef, Ground.
Brisket, Sweet-and-Sour, 193
Reuben Pie, 200
Reuben Soup, Creamy, 299
Roast, Royal Rib-Eye, 192

Steaks
    Double-D Ranch Steaks with Jalapeño
        Pepper Sauce, 196
    Filet Mignon Bundles, 197
    Filets Mignons with Brandy, Roquefort, 46
    Flank Steak, Blue Cheese, 194
    Thai Beef Grill, 195
Beef, Ground
  Casserole, Meatball Sub, 198
  Casserole, Million Dollar Spaghetti, 221
  Chili, 10-Minute Spicy Black Bean, 49
  Meatballs, Italian, 47
  Sauce, Chili Dog, 283
  Sloppy Josés, 199
Beets
  Pickles, Beet, 288
  Salad, Two Shades of Red, 268
Beverages
  Alcoholic
    Cappuccinos, Frozen, 70
    Margaritas, Watermelon, 72
    Punch, Mocha Cappuccino, 74
    Punch, Special Party, 73
    Refresher, Barbara's Summer, 15
    Snowballs, Whiskey, 16
  Cappuccino, 69
  Chocolate Mix, Camper's, 16
  Frosty, Peach, 38
  Juice, Zahna, 71
  Punch, Cranberry, 73
  Punch, Spiced Cider, 38
  Smoothie, Tropical, 70
  Tea, Rarin'-to-Go, 37
  Tea, Summer Iced, 71
Biscuits, Sour Cream 'n' Chive, 76
Blackberry Grunt, 139
Blueberries
  Cake, Blueberry-Lemon, 101
  Cobbler, Best-Ever Blueberry, 240
  Coffee Cake, Blueberry Bundt, 82
  Sauce, Blueberry, 282
Breads. *See also* specific types.
  Apricot Bread, Marbled, 83
  Bread Machine
    Italian Herb Bread, Rapid, 89
  Crostini with Wild Mushroom
    Ragoût, 62
  Focaccia, Tomato and Artichoke, 168
  French Bread with Pesto and Sun-Dried
    Tomatoes, 39
  French Honey Bread, 84
  Garlic and Artichoke Bread, 84
  Hawaiian Loaf, 26
  Pudding, Bon Ton Bread, 142
  Yeast
    Carrot Bread, 85
    Figassa, Authentic Italian, 90

King Cake, 86
Norwegian Christmas Bread, 88
Pretzels, Ballpark Soft, 94
Broccoli and Cauliflower Toss with Blue Cheese
  Cream, Warm, 312
Broccoli-Rice Casserole, 53
Bulghur Salad, 275
Butter
  Almond-Peach Butter, 286
  Chive Butter, 287
  Cilantro Butter, Grilled Swordfish
    with, 174
  Cinnamon-Maple Butter, 286
  Dill Butter, 287
  Fines Herbes Butter, 287
  Flavored Butters, 286
  Honey-Orange Butter, 286
  Strawberry Butter, 286

Cakes
Blueberry-Lemon Cake, 101
Butterscotch-Pumpkin Cake, 106
Cheesecakes
  Almond Cheesecake, Luscious, 112
  Café au Lait Cheesecake, 114
  Caramel Apple Cheesecake, 113
  Chocolate Malt Cheesecake, 115
  Peanut Butter Cheesecake, 116
Chocolate
  Blake's Chocolate Cake, 96
  Carrot Cake, Chocolate, 103
  Fudge Cake, Chocolate, 105
  Marble Cake, The Best, 104
  Roll, Chocolate-Zucchini, 117
  Truffle Cake, Souffléed, 100
Cinnamon Cake, Quick, 97
Coffee Cake, Apple, 81
Coffee Cake, Blueberry Bundt, 82
Crumb Cake, Aunt Lillian's, 96
Cupcakes, Orange, 118
Harvey Wallbanger Cake, 107
King Cake, 86
Lemon Cake, Double, 99
Lemon Platinum Cake, 102
Pound
  Apricot-Pecan Pound Cake, 108
  Caramel-Nut Pound Cake, 109
  Lemon Pound Cake, 110
  Mocha Pound Cake Freeze, 32
Pumpkin Pie Cake, 98
Shortcake, Grandma's Strawberry-Brown
  Sugar, 120
Shortcakes, Peach Melba, 119
Sponge Cake, Hot Milk, 111
Torte, Frozen Lime, 34
Candies
  Chocolate Caramel Candy, 132

Candies *(continued)*

Fudge, White Chocolate-Eggnog, 134
Pralines, Chocolate, 133
Truffles, Ebony and Ivory Chocolate, 135
Carrots
Bread, Carrot, 85
Cake, Chocolate Carrot, 103
Cookies, Frosted Carrot, 122
Supreme, Golden Carrots, 54
Casseroles. *See also* Lasagna.
Blend of the Bayou, 186
Breakfast, Midnight, 41
Crab Shells, Maryland, 215
Egg Bake, Breakfast Blue Cheese, 161
Egg Casserole, Greek, 162
Eggs Bel-Mar, 160
Macaroni and Cheese, Baked, 218
Meat
Meatball Sub Casserole, 198
Spaghetti Casserole, Million
Dollar, 221
Strata, Country Ham, Shiitake, and
Leek, 164
Strata, Goat Cheese, Artichoke, and
Smoked Ham, 165
Strata, Spinach and Ham, 166
Veau, Codellets de, 202
Noodle Bake, Night Nurse, 219
Poultry
Chicken and Black Bean Enchiladas, 255
Turkey Enchiladas, Green, 14
Turkey Tetrazzini, 260
Vegetable
Broccoli-Rice Casserole, 53
Mushrooms, Horseradish, 192
Potatoes, Greek, 316
Tzimmes, 317
Zucchini with Muenster,
Baked, 318
Cauliflower Toss with Blue Cheese Cream,
Warm Broccoli and, 312
Cheese. *See also* Appetizers/Cheese.
Breads
Crescent Cheese Twists, 41
Muffins, Tex-Mex, 79
Rolls, Herb Cheddar, 93
Casseroles
Breakfast, Midnight, 41
Egg Bake, Breakfast Blue Cheese, 161
Macaroni and Cheese, Baked, 218
Meatball Sub Casserole, 198
Strata, Goat Cheese, Artichoke, and
Smoked Ham, 165
Turkey Tetrazzini, 260
Zucchini with Muenster, Baked, 318
Chicken, Creamy Gorgonzola, 251

Chicken Stuffed with Spinach and Feta
Cheese, 250
Cream, Berry Tart with Mascarpone, 238
Cream, Warm Broccoli and Cauliflower Toss
with Blue Cheese, 312
Filets Mignons with Brandy, Roquefort, 46
Flank Steak, Blue Cheese, 194
French Velvet, 143
Frosting, Citrus Cream Cheese, 101
Grits, Cheese, 184
Pie, Reuben, 200
Rarebit, Shrimp, 163
Risotto with Feta Cheese, Onion, 223
Salad, Green Bean-Mozzarella, 19
Salad, Walnut-Gorgonzola, 271
Salad with Blue Cheese, Chili-Toasted Pecans,
and Pears, Romaine, 270
Sauce, Brie, 201
Seafood Thermidor, 190
Soufflé, Pepper Jack Cheese and Herb, 158
Soup, Cheese, 297
Soup, Crème de Brie, 298
Spread, Orange-Cream Cheese, 289
Timbales, Roquefort, 159
Torta Rustica, 167
Turkey Burgers, Cheese-Stuffed, 261
Cheesecake. *See* Cakes/Cheesecakes.
Cherries
Cookies, White Chocolate-Cherry, 124
Sauce, Duck with Cherry, 262
Thing, Cherry, 29
Chicken
Apricot and Currant Chicken, 244
Baked Chicken, Crispy Onion, 44
Barbecued Chicken, Bruce's Bluegrass, 244
Chutney, Chicken with, 248
Enchiladas, Chicken and Black Bean, 255
Fettuccine with Chicken and Vegetables,
Pesto, 214
Fried Chicken, Crispy Lemon, 245
Fried Chicken, Indonesian, 247
Gorgonzola Chicken, Creamy, 251
Green Chile Chicken, 252
Grilled Pesto-Prosciutto Chicken with Basil
Cream, 253
Jerk Chicken, Jack and Lin's Jamaican, 246
Oriental Nectar Chicken, 46
Paella, 188
Pasta, Mexican Chicken, 213
Pâté, Chicken, 12
Pecan Chicken, Alexander's, 44
Phyllo, Chicken Breasts in, 249
Pizza, Marinated Chicken, 256
Pot Pie with Cornbread Crust, Chicken, 257
Ramen Chicken, Amen, 45
Salads
Apple, Chicken, and Wild Rice Salad, 22

Island Chicken Salad, 276
Wild Rice and Chicken Salad, 277
Soup, Chicken, 301
Soup, Mark's Chicken Taco, 302
Stew, Santa Fe, 306
Stir-Fry, Cashew Chicken, 254
Strips, Cajun Chicken, 254
Stuffed with Spinach and Feta Cheese,
    Chicken, 250
Chili, 10-Minute Spicy Black Bean, 49
Chocolate
  Bars and Cookies
    Biscotti, Chocolate-Almond, 124
    Bonbons, Fudgy, 131
    Brownie Bites, Mocha Fudge, 128
    Brownies, Bourbon, 27
    Macadamia Bars, 128
    Peanut Butter Fingers, 130
    Peanut Butter Squares, 56
    10-Cup Cookies, 123
    Turtle Bars, 129
    White Chocolate-Cherry Cookies, 124
  Cakes and Tortes
    Blake's Chocolate Cake, 96
    Carrot Cake, Chocolate, 103
    Cheesecake, Café au Lait, 114
    Cheesecake, Chocolate Malt, 115
    Cheesecake, Peanut Butter, 116
    Fudge Cake, Chocolate, 105
    Marble Cake, The Best, 104
    Mocha Torte, Frozen, 151
    Roll, Chocolate-Zucchini, 117
    Truffle Cake, Souffléed, 100
  Candies
    Caramel Candy, Chocolate, 132
    Fudge, White Chocolate-Eggnog, 134
    Pralines, Chocolate, 133
    Truffles, Ebony and Ivory Chocolate, 135
  Cookies and Cream Freeze, 31
  French Velvet, 143
  Ice Cream Balls, Chocolate, 148
  Ice Cream, Unbelievable Chocolate, 147
  Mix, Camper's Chocolate, 16
  Pies and Tarts
    Fat Pie, Rich's, 234
    Frozen Pie, Grasshopper Delight, 235
    Key Lime Pie with Chocolate Crust, 33
    Turtle Tart, Chocolate, 236
    White Chocolate Magnolia Pecan
        Pie, 232
  Punch, Mocha Cappuccino, 74
  Roscoe's Special, 56
  Soufflés, Chocolate, 146
  Truffle in Custard Sauce, Chocolate-
      Hazelnut, 30
Chowder, Shrimp-Scallop, 304
Chutney Pie, 58

Cookies
  Autumn Elegance, 126
  Bars and Squares
    Brownie Bites, Mocha Fudge, 128
    Brownies, Bourbon, 27
    Macadamia Bars, 128
    Orange Delight, 127
    Peanut Butter Fingers, 130
    Peanut Butter Squares, 56
    Turtle Bars, 129
  Biscotti, Chocolate-Almond, 124
  Bonbons, Fudgy, 131
  Drop
    Carrot Cookies, Frosted, 122
    Peanut Butter Burst Cookies, 122
    10-Cup Cookies, 123
  Shortbread Cookies, Pecan, 125
  White Chocolate-Cherry Cookies, 124
Corn
  Creamed Corn, 54
  Herbed Corn, 313
  Muffins, Chez Betty's Housemade Corn, 40
  Tortilla Cakes, Corn and Black Bean, 61
Cornbread Crust, Chicken Pot Pie with, 257
Cornish Hens with Curried Rice, Glazed, 258
Couscous Amandine, 52
Crab
  Bisque, Crab and Spinach, 302
  Cakes with Cool Lime Sauce, Crab, 176
  Deviled Crab, 177
  Dip, Baked Crab, Brie, and Artichoke, 59
  Étouffée, Crawfish and Crab, 178
  Quesadillas, Crab, 66
  Shells, Maryland Crab, 215
  Tarts, Cheesy Crab, 66
Cranberry Punch, 73
Cranberry Streusel Pie, 228
Custard. See also Mousse, Puddings.
  Flan, 141
  Sauce, Custard, 30

Desserts. See also Cakes, Candies, Cookies,
    Custard, Frostings, Ice Cream, Mousse,
    Pies and Pastries, Puddings.
  Apples, Honey-Wine Baked, 138
  Cherry Thing, 29
  Enchiladas, Apple, 138
  French Velvet, 143
  Frozen
    Cookies and Cream Freeze, 31
    Mocha Pound Cake Freeze, 32
    Pie, Crème de Menthe Ice
        Cream, 32
    Torte, Frozen Lime, 34
    Torte, Frozen Mocha, 151
    Torte with Strawberry-Raspberry Sauce,
        Lemon Ice, 152

Desserts, Frozen *(continued)*

Truffle in Custard Sauce, Chocolate-
Hazelnut, 30
Grunt, Blackberry, 139
Pizza, Peach, 28
Pizza, Strawberry, 240
Roscoe's Special, 56
Sauces
Blueberry Sauce, 282
Caramel Sauce, Warm, 236
Custard Sauce, 30
Strawberry-Raspberry Sauce, 152
Whiskey Sauce, 142
Soufflés, Chocolate, 146
Torte, Butterscotch, 149
Donut Holes, Baked, 76
Duck with Cherry Sauce, 262
Dumplings, Pear, 241

Eggplant Enchiladas, 314
Eggs
Bake, Breakfast Blue Cheese Egg, 161
Bel-Mar, Eggs, 160
Breakfast, Midnight, 41
Casserole, Greek Egg, 162
Frittata, Baked Artichoke and Onion, 155
Omelet, Fluffy Harvest, 157
Omelet with Garlic-Onion Potatoes and Bacon,
Killer, 156
Spaghetti, "Eggstra" Special, 50
Strata, Country Ham, Shiitake, and
Leek, 164
Strata, Goat Cheese, Artichoke, and Smoked
Ham, 165
Strata, Spinach and Ham, 166
Enchiladas
Apple Enchiladas, 138
Chicken and Black Bean Enchiladas, 255
Eggplant Enchiladas, 314
Turkey Enchiladas, Green, 14

Fettuccine with Chicken and Vegetables,
Pesto, 214
Fish. *See also* Crab, Lobster, Mussels, Salmon,
Scallops, Seafood, Shrimp, Tuna.
Catfish, All King's Day, 170
Crawfish and Crab Étouffée, 178
Grouper, Grilled, 170
Halibut, Oven-Fried, 42
(Red Snapper Fingers), Pargo Perle, 172
Red Snapper Puttanesca, 173
Sea Bass Provençal, Roasted, 174
Swordfish with Cilantro Butter, Grilled, 174
French Toast, Peach, 154
Fritters, African Butternut Squash, 77
Fritters with Red Sauce, Shrimp, 182

Frostings and Toppings
Apple-Cinnamon Glaze, 237
Basil Cream, 253
Butterscotch Icing, 108
Coulis, 309
Cream Cheese Frosting, Citrus, 101
Lemon Frosting, 99
Sugars, Colored, 87
Fruit. *See also* specific types.
Dip for Fruit, Buttery Brown Sugar, 58
Juice, Zahna, 71
Salad, Tantalizing Fruit, 265
Salsa, Fresh Fruit, 285
Salsa, Island, 23
Smoothie, Tropical, 70
Soup, Wild Berry, 25
Tart with Mascarpone Cream, Berry, 238

Garlic
Beans, Basque, 312
Bread, Garlic and Artichoke, 84
Brisket, Sweet-and-Sour, 193
Chicken, Green Chile, 252
Dip, Baked Crab, Brie, and Artichoke, 59
Meatballs, Italian, 47
Paella, 188
Pork Chops with Curried Apple and Onion
Sauce, 206
Pork, Cuban Roast, 204
Sauce, Chili Dog, 283
Shrimp, Garlic, 183
Turkey, Ginger-Glazed Garlic, 260
Turkey, Lemon-Rosemary, 259
Granola, Tropical Crunch, 69
Grapes
Muscadine Pie, 230
Gravy, Fried Venison with Pan, 209
Grilled. *See also* Barbecue.
Beef Grill, Thai, 195
Fish and Shellfish
Grouper, Grilled, 170
Lobster Tails, Grilled, 179
Scallops, Melon and Prosciutto Salad with
Grilled, 279
Shrimp, Barbecued, 181
Swordfish with Cilantro Butter, Grilled, 174
Tuna Steaks with Feta Cheese, Grilled, 175
Flank Steak, Blue Cheese, 194
Ham Steak, Orange-Glazed, 49
Lamb Burgers with Yogurt-Dill Sauce, 203
Pork Tenderloin with Fresh Rosemary Salsa, 205
Poultry
Chicken, Bruce's Bluegrass Barbecued, 244
Chicken, Jack and Lin's Jamaican Jerk, 246
Chicken with Basil Cream, Grilled Pesto-
Prosciutto, 253
Turkey Burgers, Cheese-Stuffed, 261

Vegetables
    Asparagus, Marinated Grilled, 309
    Corn, Herbed, 313
    Salad with Greens, Grilled Vegetable, 269
Grits
    Cheese Grits, 184
    Shrimp 'n' Grits, 184
    Soufflé with Caramelized Onions, Grits, 226
Gumbo, Seafood 305

Ham. *See also* Pork.
    Apple Cider Ham with Mustard, 207
    Country Ham, Shiitake, and Leek Strata, 164
    Prosciutto Chicken with Basil Cream, Grilled
        Pesto-, 253
    Prosciutto, Mango and, 36
    Prosciutto Salad with Grilled Scallops, Melon
        and, 279
    Steak, Orange-Glazed Ham, 49
    Strata, Goat Cheese, Artichoke, and Smoked
        Ham, 165
    Strata, Spinach and Ham, 166

Ice Cream
    Balls, Chocolate Ice Cream, 148
    Chocolate Ice Cream, Unbelievable, 147
    Peach Sorbet, Simple, 147
    Pie, Crème de Menthe Ice Cream, 32
    Pie, Grasshopper Delight Frozen, 235
    Pie, Rich's Fat, 234

Jam, Easy Rhubarb, 289

Kabobs, Antipasto, 8

Lamb
    Burgers with Yogurt-Dill Sauce,
        Lamb, 203
    Marinade, Sweet Asian Lamb, 284
    Rack of Lamb with Honey-Hazelnut
        Crust, 202
Lasagna, Easy, 216
Lasagna, Fresh Vegetable, 217
Lemon
    Chicken, Crispy Lemon Fried, 245
    Desserts
        Cake, Blueberry-Lemon, 101
        Cake, Double Lemon, 99
        Cake, Lemon Platinum, 102
        Cake, Lemon Pound, 110
        Frosting, Lemon, 99
        Mousse, Lemon Curd, 145
        Pie, Amish Lemon, 229
        Pie, Heavenly, 233
        Torte with Strawberry-Raspberry Sauce,
            Lemon Ice, 152
    Dressing, Lemon-Basil, 21
    Sauce, Orzo with Dilled Lemon, 220

    Soup, Lemon-Mango, 24
    Tea, Rarin'-to-Go, 37
    Turkey, Lemon-Rosemary, 259
    Vinaigrette, Lemon-Herb, 175
Lentil and Sausage Soup, 300
Lime
    Pie with Chocolate Crust, Key Lime, 33
    Sauce, Crab Cakes with Cool Lime, 176
    Torte, Frozen Lime, 34
Linguine with Pepper Breadcrumbs, 50
Linguine with Sherry Cream Sauce, Shrimp
    and 218
Lobster Tails, Grilled, 179

Macadamia Bars, 128
Macadamia Yams, 55
Macaroni and Cheese, Baked, 218
Mangoes
    Prosciutto, Mango and, 36
    Salad, Strawberry-Mango Mesclun, 266
    Soup, Lemon-Mango, 24
    Tarts, Mango, 239
Marmalade, Peach, 290
Melons
    Chilled Cantaloupe Soup, 292
    Salad with Grilled Scallops, Melon and
        Prosciutto, 279
    Watermelon Margaritas, 72
Microwave
    Corn, Creamed, 54
    Desserts
        Bonbons, Fudgy, 131
        Brownies, Bourbon, 27
        Cake, Butterscotch-Pumpkin, 106
        Fritters, African Butternut Squash, 77
        Tarts, Cheesy Crab, 66
Mousse. *See also* Custard, Puddings.
    Lemon Curd Mousse, 145
Muffins
    Applesauce Spice Muffins, 78
    Corn Muffins, Chez Betty's Housemade, 40
    Donut Holes, Baked, 76
    Tex-Mex Muffins, 79
Mushrooms
    Filet Mignon Bundles, 197
    Green Beans with Mushrooms, Sautéed, 311
    Horseradish Mushrooms, 192
    Portobello Appetizer, Roasted, 60
    Portobellos, Ziti and, 222
    Shiitake, and Leek Strata, Country
        Ham, 164
    Wild Mushroom Ragoût, Crostini with, 62
    Wild Mushroom Stuffing, 315
    Wild Rice, Mushrooms, and Asparagus, 225
Mussels Steamed in White Wine, 180

Noodle Bake, Night Nurse, 219

Olives
  Fusilli Tricolor with Olives, Basil, and Brie, 212
  Relish, Italian, 288
  Salad with Olives, Minted Fennel, 20
  Tomatoes with Olives and Garlic, Broiled, 318
Onions
  Brisket, Sweet-and-Sour, 193
  Caramelized Onions, 226
  Chicken, Crispy Onion Baked, 44
  Frittata, Baked Artichoke and Onion, 155
  Noodle Bake, Night Nurse, 219
  Risotto with Feta Cheese, Onion, 223
  Sauce, Chili Dog, 283
  Sauce, Pork Chops with Curried Apple and
      Onion, 206
  Sloppy Josés, 199
  Stuffed Walla Walla Sweets, 316
Oranges
  Butter, Honey-Orange, 286
  Desserts
      Cupcakes, Orange, 118
      Delight, Orange, 127
      Frosting, Citrus Cream Cheese, 101
      Walnuts, Orange-Sugared, 136
  Ham Steak, Orange-Glazed, 49
  Salads
      Artichoke and Mandarin Orange
          Salad, 266
      Avocado Salad, Orange and, 265
      Frozen Orange-Pecan Salad, 17
  Sauce, Orange-Ginger, 25
  Spread, Orange-Cream Cheese, 289
Orzo Salad, Black Bean and, 274
Orzo with Dilled Lemon Sauce, 220

Pancakes, Easy Banana, 39
Pancakes with Smoked Salmon and Caviar,
      Mustard-Dill, 64
Parsnip Soup, 295
Pastas. See also Couscous, Fettuccine, Lasagna,
      Linguine, Macaroni, Noodles, Orzo,
      Spaghetti.
  Capellini with Fresh Tomato and Basil
      Sauce, 212
  Chicken Pasta, Mexican, 213
  Fusilli Tricolor with Olives, Basil, and
      Brie, 212
  Rigatoni, Vodka, 220
  Salad, Greek Pasta, 276
  Sauce, Florida Style, Pasta, 188
  Seafood Wonder, 13
  Shells, Maryland Crab, 215
  Tortellini Bean Soup, 293
  Tortellini Salad, 51
  Tortellini with Feta Cheese, Tomato, and
      Basil, 222
  Ziti and Portobellos, 222

Peaches
  Autumn Elegance, 126
  Butter, Almond-Peach, 286
  French Toast, Peach, 154
  Frosty, Peach, 38
  Marmalade, Peach, 290
  Pie, Peach-Raspberry, 231
  Pizza, Peach, 28
  Shortcakes, Peach Melba, 119
  Sorbet, Simple Peach, 147
Peanut Butter
  Cheesecake, Peanut Butter, 116
  Cookies, Peanut Butter Burst, 122
  Cookies, 10-Cup, 123
  Fingers, Peanut Butter, 130
  Squares, Peanut Butter, 56
Pea Pods, Marinated Shrimp Wrapped
      in, 67
Pear Dumplings, 241
Pear Slaw, Napa Cabbage and, 273
Pecans
  Bars, Turtle, 129
  Bread, Norwegian Christmas, 88
  Cake, Apricot-Pecan Pound, 108
  Cherry Thing, 29
  Chicken, Alexander's Pecan, 44
  Cookies, Pecan Shortbread, 125
  Cookies, 10-Cup, 123
  French Velvet, 143
  Pie, White Chocolate Magnolia Pecan, 232
  Pilaf, Pecan, 224
  Pralines, Chocolate, 133
  Salad, Frozen Orange-Pecan, 17
  Spiced Holiday Pecans, 37
  Toasted Pecans, Chili-, 270
  Veal Pecan with Brie Sauce, 201
Peppers
  Chile Chicken, Green, 252
  Chile Dressing, Creamy, 265
  Coulis, 309
  Enchiladas, Green Turkey, 14
  Jalapeño Tartar Sauce, 187
  Muffins, Tex-Mex, 79
  Salsa Fresca, 310
Pesto, Tony Caputo's Red, 60
Pickles, Beet, 288
Pies and Pastries
  Apple Pie, Crunchy Caramel, 228
  Chutney Pie, 58
  Cobbler, Best-Ever Blueberry, 240
  Cranberry Streusel Pie, 228
  Fat Pie, Rich's, 234
  Grasshopper Delight Frozen Pie, 235
  Heavenly Pie, 233
  Ice Cream Pie, Crème de Menthe, 32
  Key Lime Pie with Chocolate Crust, 33
  Lemon Pie, Amish, 229

Main Dish
    Chicken Breasts in Phyllo, 249
    Chicken Pot Pie with Cornbread Crust, 257
    Filet Mignon Bundles, 197
    Reuben Pie, 200
Muscadine Pie, 230
Pastries and Crusts
    Apple Orchard Snowballs, 242
    Cheese Puffs, Hot, 63
    Dumplings, Pear, 241
    Éclair Torte, 150
    Pineapple Crisp, 140
    Profiteroles with Smoked Salmon, 65
    Rolls, Spanakopita, 8
    Sweet Pastry Dough, 238
    Torta Rustica, 167
Peach-Raspberry Pie, 231
Pumpkin Praline No-Bake Pie, 234
Raisin-Nut Pie, 232
Tarts
    Apple Custard Tart, 237
    Berry Tart with Mascarpone Cream, 238
    Chocolate Turtle Tart, 236
    Crab Tarts, Cheesy, 66
    Mango Tarts, 239
    Sausage and Cheese Tartlets, 64
    White Chocolate Magnolia Pecan Pie, 232
Pineapple Crisp, 140
Pineapple Salad, Frozen, 18
Pizza
    Chicken Pizza, Marinated, 256
    Peach Pizza, 28
    Strawberry Pizza, 240
Pork
    Chops with Curried Apple and Onion Sauce,
        Pork, 206
    Meatballs, Italian, 47
    Roast Pork, Cuban, 204
    Spareribs, Potluck, 206
    Tenderloin Diane, Pork, 48
    Tenderloin with Fresh Rosemary Salsa,
        Pork, 205
Potatoes. See also Sweet Potatoes.
    Buns, Spicy Hot Cross, 92
    Greek Potatoes, 316
    Omelet with Garlic-Onion Potatoes and Bacon,
        Killer, 156
    Salad, Apple-Potato, 278
    Salad with Goat Cheese and Roasted Red
        Peppers, Potato, 274
    Soup, Golden Cream, 294
    Soup, Potato, 296
    Tzimmes, 317
Pretzels, Ballpark Soft, 94
Puddings. See also Custard, Mousse.
    Bread Pudding, Bon Ton, 142
    Cinnamon Pudding, 144

Pumpkin
    Cake, Butterscotch-Pumpkin, 106
    Cake, Pumpkin Pie, 98
    Pie, Pumpkin Praline No-Bake, 234

Quesadillas, Crab, 66

Raspberries
    Pie, Peach-Raspberry, 231
    Sauce, Strawberry-Raspberry, 152
    Shortcakes, Peach Melba, 119
    Vinaigrette, Quick and Easy Raspberry, 24
Relish, Italian, 288
Rhubarb Jam, Easy, 289
Rice
    Brown Basmati Rice, Malaysian, 224
    Casserole, Broccoli-Rice, 53
    Curried Rice, Glazed Cornish Hens with, 258
    Pilaf, Pecan, 224
    Risotto with Feta Cheese, Onion, 223
    Wild Rice
        Mushrooms, and Asparagus, Wild
            Rice, 225
        Salad, Apple, Chicken, and Wild Rice, 22
        Salad, Wild Rice and Chicken, 277
Rolls and Buns
    Cinnamon Twists, 91
    Crescent Cheese Twists, 41
    Dinner Rolls, Simple, 40
    Herb Cheddar Rolls, 93
    Hot Cross Buns, Spicy, 92

Salad Dressings
    Basil Dressing, Creamy, 280
    Chile Dressing, Creamy, 265
    Honey-Bourbon Salad Dressing, 280
    Honey-Herb Salad Dressing, 51
    Lemon-Basil Dressing, 21
    Mustard Dressing, Spicy, 272
    Vinaigrette, Lemon-Herb, 175
    Vinaigrette, Quick and Easy Raspberry, 24
Salads
    Apple-Potato Salad, 278
    Artichoke and Mandarin Orange Salad, 266
    Asparagus Vinaigrette, 19
    Bean
        Black Bean and Orzo Salad, 274
        Black Bean Salad, Mexican, 18
        Green Bean-Mozzarella Salad, 19
        White Bean-Asparagus Salad, 267
    Bulghur Salad, 275
    Chicken
        Apple, Chicken, and Wild Rice Salad, 22
        Island Chicken Salad, 276
        Wild Rice and Chicken Salad, 277
    Congealed Asparagus, Tangy, 264
    Fennel Salad with Olives, Minted, 20

Salads *(continued)*

Fruit Salad, Tantalizing, 265
Melon and Prosciutto Salad with Grilled
        Scallops, 279
Orange and Avocado Salad, 265
Orange-Pecan Salad, Frozen, 17
Pasta Salad, Greek, 276
Pineapple Salad, Frozen, 18
Potato Salad with Goat Cheese and Roasted Red
        Peppers, 274
Red Salad, Two Shades of, 268
Romaine Salad with Blue Cheese, Chili-Toasted
        Pecans, and Pears, 270
Slaws
        Napa Cabbage and Pear Slaw, 273
        Piquant Coleslaw, 273
        Rodeo Coleslaw, 22
Strawberry-Mango Mesclun Salad, 266
Tabbouleh Salad, 21
Tomato Treats, Zesty, 53
Tortellini Salad, 51
Uptown Bluegrass Salad, 272
Vegetable Salad with Greens,
        Grilled, 269
Walnut-Gorgonzola Salad, 271
Wild Rice and Chicken Salad, 277
Salmon
Fillets, Pepper-Crusted Salmon, 172
Glazed Salmon, Asian-, 171
Sauce, Salmon with Oriental Mahogany, 42
Smoked Salmon and Caviar, Mustard-Dill
        Pancakes with, 64
Smoked Salmon, Profiteroles with, 65
Sauces. *See also* Desserts/Sauces; Pesto.
Blueberry Sauce, 282
Brie Sauce, 201
Cherry Sauce, Duck with, 262
Chili Dog Sauce, 283
Curried Apple and Onion Sauce, Pork Chops
        with, 206
Dilled Lemon Sauce, Orzo with, 220
Dipping Sauce, 247
Green Peppercorn Cream Sauce, 283
Jalapeño Pepper Sauce, Double-D Ranch
        Steaks with, 196
Jalapeño Tartar Sauce, 187
Lime Sauce, Crab Cakes with Cool, 176
Marinade, Sweet Asian Lamb, 284
Orange-Ginger Sauce, 25
Oriental Mahogany Sauce, Salmon
        with, 42
Pasta Sauce, Florida Style, 188
Red Sauce, 182
Salsa Fresca, 310
Salsa, Fresh Fruit, 285
Salsa, Fresh Rosemary, 205

Salsa, Island, 23
Sherry Cream Sauce, Shrimp and Linguine
        with, 218
Tomato and Basil Sauce, Capellini with
        Fresh, 212
Yogurt-Dill Sauce, 203
Sausage
Breakfast, Midnight, 41
Casserole, Million Dollar Spaghetti, 221
Cassoulet, Black Bean, 208
Soup, Lentil and Sausage, 300
Tartlets, Sausage and Cheese, 64
Walla Walla Sweets, Stuffed, 316
Scallop Chowder, Shrimp-, 304
Scallops, Melon and Prosciutto Salad with
        Grilled, 279
Seafood. *See also* Crab, Fish, Lobster, Mussels,
        Salmon, Scallops, Shrimp.
Blend of the Bayou, 186
Cakes with Jalapeño Tartar Sauce, Miami
        Seafood, 187
Gumbo, Seafood, 305
Paella, 188
Sauce, Florida Style, Pasta, 188
Thermidor, Seafood, 190
Wonder, Seafood, 13
Seasoning Mix, Taco, 284
Shrimp
Artichokes, Shrimp with, 43
Barbecued Shrimp, 181
Chowder, Shrimp-Scallop, 304
Feta Cheese, Shrimp with, 68
Fritters with Red Sauce, Shrimp, 182
Garlic Shrimp, 183
Grits, Shrimp 'n', 184
Linguine with Sherry Cream Sauce, Shrimp
        and, 218
Marinated Shrimp and Artichoke Hearts, 12
Marinated Shrimp Wrapped in Pea Pods, 67
Provençal, Shrimp, 185
Rarebit, Shrimp, 163
Slow Cooker
Venison Roast, Crock-Pot™, 208
Soufflés
Cheese and Herb Soufflé, Pepper Jack, 158
Chocolate Soufflés, 146
Grits Soufflé with Caramelized Onions, 226
Soups. *See also* Chili, Chowder, Gumbo,
        Stews.
Artichoke Soup, Cream of, 292
Berry Soup, Wild, 25
Bisque, Crab and Spinach, 302
Bisque, Tomato-Dill, 303
Butternut Squash Soup, 294
Cantaloupe Soup, Chilled, 292
Cheese Soup, 297
Chicken Soup, 301

Chicken Taco Soup, Mark's, 302
Cream Soup, Golden, 294
Crème de Brie Soup, 298
Lemon-Mango Soup, 24
Lentil and Sausage Soup, 300
Parsnip Soup, 295
Potato Soup, 296
Reuben Soup, Creamy, 299
Tortellini Bean Soup, 293
Spaghetti Casserole, Million Dollar, 221
Spaghetti, "Eggstra" Special, 50
Spinach
    Artichoke Hearts, Spinach-Stuffed, 308
    Bisque, Crab and Spinach, 302
    Chicken Stuffed with Spinach and Feta
        Cheese, 250
    Spanakopita Rolls, 8
    Strata, Spinach and Ham, 166
    Torta Rustica, 167
Spread. See also Appetizers/Spreads.
    Orange-Cream Cheese Spread, 289
Squash. See also Zucchini.
    Butternut Squash Fritters, African, 77
    Butternut Squash Soup, 294
Stews
    Étouffée, Crawfish and Crab, 178
    Ragoût, Crostini with Wild Mushroom, 62
    Santa Fe Stew, 306
Strawberries
    Butter, Strawberry, 286
    Pizza, Strawberry, 240
    Salad, Strawberry-Mango Mesclun, 266
    Sauce, Strawberry-Raspberry, 152
    Shortcake, Grandma's Strawberry-Brown
        Sugar, 120
Stuffing, Wild Mushroom, 315
Sweet Potatoes
    Yams, Macadamia, 55

Tabbouleh Salad, 21
Taco Seasoning Mix, 284
Taco Soup, Mark's Chicken, 302
Timbales, Roquefort, 159
Tomatoes
    Bisque, Tomato-Dill, 303
    Broiled Tomatoes with Olives and
        Garlic, 318
    Cream, Basil, 253
    Focaccia, Tomato and Artichoke, 168
    Pesto, Tony Caputo's Red, 60
    Red Snapper Puttanesca, 173
    Salad, Two Shades of Red, 268
    Salsa Fresca, 310
    Salsa, Fresh Rosemary, 205
    Sauce, Capellini with Fresh Tomato and
        Basil, 212
    Sun-Dried Tomatoes, Cheese Balls
        with, 11

Sun-Dried Tomatoes, French Bread with Pesto
    and, 39
Treats, Zesty Tomato, 53
Tortillas
    Cakes, Corn and Black Bean Tortilla, 61
    Quesadillas, Crab, 66
    Torta, Black Bean, 310
Tuna Steaks with Feta Cheese, Grilled, 175
Turkey
    Burgers, Cheese-Stuffed Turkey, 261
    Enchiladas, Green Turkey, 14
    Garlic Turkey, Ginger-Glazed, 260
    Lasagna, Easy, 216
    Lemon-Rosemary Turkey, 259
    Tetrazzini, Turkey, 260

Veal
    Codellets de Veau, 202
    Pecan with Brie Sauce, Veal, 201
Vegetables. See also specific types.
    Antipasto Kabobs, 8
    Fettuccine with Chicken and Vegetables,
        Pesto, 214
    Gumbo, Seafood, 305
    Lasagna, Fresh Vegetable, 217
    Omelet, Fluffy Harvest, 157
    Roasted Root Vegetables, 319
    Salads
        Bulghur Salad, 275
        Coleslaw, Rodeo, 22
        Grilled Vegetable Salad with Greens, 269
        Tabbouleh Salad, 21
        Tortellini Salad, 51
    Salsa, Island, 23
    Seafood Wonder, 13
    Shrimp Provençal, 185
    Stew, Santa Fe, 306
Venison
    Fried Venison with Pan Gravy, 209
    Roast, Crock-Pot™ Venison, 208
    Rollemachen, Venison, 210

Waffles, Tex-Mex, 80
Walnuts
    Cake, Aunt Lillian's Crumb, 96
    Cake, Caramel-Nut Pound, 109
    Orange-Sugared Walnuts, 136
    Pie, Raisin-Nut, 232
    Salad, Walnut-Gorgonzola, 271

Zucchini Roll, Chocolate-, 117
Zucchini with Muenster, Baked, 318

Your Community Cookbook Could Win an Award

Each fall enthusiasm fills the air on Avery Island, Louisiana, as the McIlhenny family homestead and company sponsors the Tabasco® Community Cookbook Awards Competition for nationwide service organizations. All community cookbooks published within the last two years are eligible for this annual event that celebrates the history and preservation of local culinary traditions.

The editors of America's Best Recipes congratulate the winners of the 2001 Tabasco® Community Cookbook Awards competition and are proud to feature many of their recipes in this volume. The McIlhenny Company awarded prize money to the winning entries of the 2001 competition. The first place winner received $2,500, followed by $1000 for second place, and $750 for third. Each regional winner was awarded $500. The sponsoring organization of the winning cookbooks, in turn, donated the prize money to charities of their choice.

The 2001 Tabasco® Community Cookbook Awards winners were:

- **First Place Winner:** *California Fresh Harvest: A Seasonal Journey through Northern California,* Junior League of Oakland-East Bay, Inc., Lafayette, CA
- **Second Place Winner:** *Entirely Entertaining: In the Bonnet House Style,* Bonnet House and Gardens, Fort Lauderdale, FL
- **Third Place Winner:** *Art Fare: A Commemorative Celebration of Art & Food,* Toledo Museum of Art Aides, Toledo, OH
- **New England:** No winner
- **Mid-Atlantic:** *The Bounty of Chester County,* Chester County Agricultural Development Council, West Chester, PA
- **South:** *Meet Me at the Garden Gate: An Invitation to Seasonal Traditions and Southern Hospitality,* Junior League of Spartanburg, Inc., Spartanburg, SC
- **Midwest:** *Cross Village: A Selection of Tastes, Art, and Memories,* Cross Village Community Services, Cross Village, MI
- **Southwest:** *Cooking with the Original Search Engine: Libraries Have it All,* Fort Worth Public Library, Fort Worth, TX
- **West:** No Winner
- **Special Merit:** *Forget Me Not: Recipes and Stories to Remember,* Hospice and Palliative Care of Greensboro, NC
- **Walter S. McIlhenny Hall of Fame 2001:** *We Make You Kindly Welcome,* Shaker Community at Pleasant Hill, Harrodsburg, KY
- **Walter S. McIlhenny Hall of Fame 2001:** *Necessities and Temptations,* Junior League of Austin Publications, Austin, TX

For information on the Tabasco® Community Cookbook Awards or for an awards entry form, send a self-addressed stamped #10 (legal size) envelope to
Tabasco Community Cookbook Awards
% Hunter Public Relations
41 Madison Ave.
New York, NY 10010-2202

For a free booklet about producing a community cookbook, send a self-addressed stamped #10 (legal size) envelope to
Compiling Culinary History
% Hunter Public Relations
41 Madison Ave.
New York, NY 10010-2202